THE GREAT WINES
OF GERMANY

Plate 1 (*overleaf*). André L. Simon and S. F. Hallgarten.

THE GREAT WINES
OF GERMANY

and its famed vineyards

ANDRÉ L. SIMON
AND
S. F. HALLGARTEN

with color photographs by Percy Hennell
and maps by Sheila Waters

McGRAW-HILL BOOK COMPANY, INC.
NEW YORK TORONTO LONDON

Designed and produced for McGraw-Hill Book Company, Inc., 330 West 42nd Street, New York 36,
by George Rainbird Ltd, 2 Hyde Park Place, London W2.
The photographs for the color plates and for the
endpapers and jacket were taken by Percy Hennell.
The text was printed by Drukkerij Holland N.V., Amsterdam, Holland.
The color plates were made by Austin Miles Ltd, London,
and printed by Henry Stone and Son (Printers) Ltd, Banbury, England.
The maps, endpapers and jacket were printed by L. Van Leer and Company N.V., Amsterdam.
The book was bound by Van Rijmenam N.V., The Hague, Holland.

First published 1963

PRINTED IN THE NETHERLANDS

CONTENTS

CONTENTS

COLOR PLATES

MAPS

at the end of the book

FOREWORD

by André L. Simon

When I first visited the vineyards of the Rhineland, in the summer of 1911—and what a wonderful summer it was!—I fell in love with the Rhine and the Moselle. How could I, or anybody else with eyes to see, fail to do so? The only two rivers that I knew at all well at the time were the Seine of my native Paris and the Marne from Tours-sur-Marne to Epernay, both famous in French history but not comparable in beauty with the Rhine and the Middle Moselle.

It was certainly no youthful infatuation, and on the far too few occasions when I have revisited the Rhineland, the fact that I have seen by now the Dordogne and the Douro, the Hudson and the Victoria Falls, has made no difference at all to my first love. The Rhine and the Moselle, the Nahe, the Ruwer and the Saar, seem as they were when I first knew them over fifty years ago, their terraced vineyards as beautiful and their quaint villages as charming as ever. Social and economic conditions are very different, though, while science has brought improved varieties of grapes, mechanical means of cultivation, and wine-making techniques entirely new to octogenarians like me—and not only new, but almost beyond our ken.

This is why I have had much pleasure in paying one more visit, perhaps my last, to the vineyards of the Rhineland: a visit of the imagination, in this book, in the company of a younger and far better informed man than myself. Born in the Rhineland, Fritz Hallgarten is now at the head of a famous firm of German wine importers, and his knowledge of the vineyards and wines of Germany is unsurpassed.

Chapter One

A SHORT HISTORY OF
GERMAN WINE

There has been wine in the Rhineland for nearly two thousand years; that is, ever since the Romans settled there and had it sent to them from Italy. It was not long, however, before they taught the natives how to grow grapes and make wine. Long before Romulus and Remus were born there had been vines growing wild and un-attended not only in the Rhineland but in many parts of Germany, their wayward tendrils clinging where they climbed from bush to tree. But the first wine to be drunk on the banks of the Rhine and Moselle must have been Italian commissariat wine that came with the Roman legions. The planting of new vineyards in Gaul, Spain and North Africa was not encouraged, and on several occasions it was prohibited altogether by Rome, because there was wine in plenty in Italy but often a grievous shortage of corn and other cereals. It must have been obvious from the first, however, that the steep wooded hills of the Rhine and Moselle could never be cornlands, whereas those of their slopes which faced south, south-east and south-west offered excellent sites for vineyards; all that was needed was muscle and sweat—of which there was no shortage, we can well imagine, where Rome ruled.

Trier or Trèves, on the Moselle, claims to be the oldest city in western Europe, built by a Prince Trebets who is believed to have come all the way from India many years before Rome was founded. It is by no means certain that it was so, but we do know that Augusta Trevisorum, as the Romans called this city of the Trevii, their capital beyond the Alps, was second only to Rome for the number and beauty of its temples, palaces and baths. Roman emperors often resided there, and there must have been a great deal of social activity and many festive occasions, resulting in a large wine consumption. It is quite possible that better wines were imported from Italy or Gaul, by or for patricians and officials, but it is certain that in all parts of the land under Roman rule not only the army, but also the civilian population who had adopted the Roman way of life, must have been drinking home-grown wine in plenty.

Remains of Roman drinking cups and vessels have been found in great quantities in many parts of the Rhineland, proving beyond doubt that wine was in common use during the first century of the Christian era. This could not have happened had there not been vineyards at hand.

The best possible evidence that vineyards flourished on the hills of the Moselle at the beginning of the fourth century is to be found in the writings of Ausonius, a Roman proconsul who was born near Bordeaux and held an important post at Trier for some years. The hillside vineyards of the Moselle immediately bring back to his mind those of the Côte Pavie as seen from the terrace of Château Ausone, and he exclaims: "O patria, insignem Bacho..." (Oh, my native land, dedicated to Bacchus...) There follows a heroic poem in praise of the wine-bearing hills of the Moselle, the echo of which may still be heard today along the banks of the same river, but in another tongue: "O Mosella! Du hast ja so viel Wein!"

There are numerous records of early vineyards in many parts of the Rhineland. Such was the vineyard which the monks of Haslach, near Strasbourg, planted in A.D. 613. Others were being cultivated in A.D. 628 and A.D. 638 in the Ladenburg district and the lower Neckar Valley, at the time when, in A.D. 634, Dagobert confirmed the then Archbishop of Trier in all grants of vineyards in the valleys of the Rhine, Moselle and Loire. In A.D. 644, the Monastery of Wissemburg owned vineyards at Lautenbach, Grunnesbrunnen and fifteen other places.

At the beginning of the ninth century, we find in the household regulations of Charlemagne many instructions and remarks concerning wine and vineyards in Germany. It is during this century that appear the earliest records of such renowned vineyards as those of Rüdesheim, Geisenheim, Kreuznach, Eisenach, and a great many more, whilst Nierstein wines are mentioned at the close of the tenth century.

Although we may give the Romans credit for being the first to bring to the Rhineland the right type of wine-making vines, and to teach the natives how to make wine, we also have ample evidence that Germany, and not only the Rhineland, owes a far greater debt of gratitude to the church. The early missionaries who brought Christianity to the heathen populations of Central Europe were not merely preachers of the Gospel but priests of a church for which the Eucharist was then, as it is today, the all-important sacrifice of atonement. Without both bread and wine there could be no Mass. Hence the records of vineyards planted in Saxony and as far north as the Baltic, as soon as those missionaries were able to build a church or monastery.

Strange as it seems to us, there were German wines from northern vineyards which enjoyed a very fair reputation for a long time.

Plate 2. Riesling grapes.

In the Rhineland, where climatic conditions and the nature of the soil were much more favourable, viticulture became at an early date one of the more important branches of agriculture, one which has retained not only its economic interest but its human appeal to this day, in spite of adverse conditions from time to time. Charlemagne was so generous in his gifts of land, including some vineyards which are among the most famous to this day, that he laid the foundation of the extraordinary power, temporal as well as spiritual, which a wealthy church enjoyed in Germany from the tenth to the sixteenth century. The archbishops of Mainz, Trier, Cologne, Augsburg and other cities became very powerful sovereign princes, as did also the abbots of Fulda, Gall and other famous abbeys. The Archbishop of Mainz already owned the whole of the Rheingau, including Hochheim, when in A.D. 983, the emperor gave him Bingen as well.

A number of emperors of the Holy Roman Empire and some German princes followed the example set by Charlemagne, and gave land to the church, or built abbeys and churches which they endowed by the gift of vineyards. It was also a common practice during the Middle Ages for gifts of money and land to be bequeathed to the church of one's parish or to the bishop of one's diocese. As ecclesiastical property was never sold or confiscated in those days, the church in Germany became the owner of a very considerable proportion of the Rhineland vineyards.

The medieval archbishops owned so many vineyards and so much land that they could well afford to be generous. Thus, in the eleventh century one of them gave to the Benedictines of the St Alban's Priory the Mons Episcopi, the Bishop's Hill, above Winkel, where they planted a vineyard and renamed the hill St John's Hill or Johannisberg; they must have made good wine until the sixteenth century when the hill was taken back from them by the Archbishop of Mainz; later, in 1716, it became the property of the Prince Abbot of Fulda. Not far away, the Cistercian monks of Eberbach cleared the forest of Steinberg in the twelfth century, and planted a vineyard which they surrounded by a wall, just as at Clos Vougeot; they went on making good wine there for some seven hundred years, until Napoleon turned them out.

In the Moselle Valley, it was very much the same story. The Benedictines of St Maximin Abbey of Trier owned vineyards at a very early date at Detzem, Leiwen and Longuich, so much so that in A.D. 783—evidently a good vintage year—they cellared 900 Fuder or 3,000 double aums of wine. Another Benedictine Abbey, St Eucharius, owned vineyards in the eleventh century at Bernkastel/Cues, on the Moselle, and Trittenheim in the Saar valley. In 1136, Archbishop Albero of Trier presented the Cistercians with land at Himmerode, near Wittlich, and they later acquired many vineyards in the valley of the Moselle, the famous Tiergarten at Trier, as well as at Casel and Eitelsbach on the Ruwer, where the Karthäuserhofberg still bears witness to their earlier ownership.

There are many other such names today which provide ample evidence of the great influence which ecclesiastical communities and religious orders enjoyed throughout the

Rhineland vinelands in former times. We shall refer to them when we take our journey through the wine districts.

It is likely that the wine made from grapes grown in the better vineyards belonging to church, abbey or college, and under the direct supervision of their owners, was of much better quality than the wines made by tenants who, besides rent and various "dues", had to pay a tenth, or *dîme* or *Zehnt*, to the church. This *Zehnt*, which had passed from the Old Testament to the New, was the ordained share of the poor; it was paid to the church, not for church needs but to be given to the poor. The church was at that time solely responsible for the care of the poor, the sick and the aged, and for the safety of students, pilgrims and others who journeyed from university to university or from shrine to shrine. Wayfarers in those times carried no money, a wise precaution when travelling through lands infested by highwaymen and marauding barons: they knew that they could always be sure of a free meal and a roof over their heads at any of the numerous monasteries on their route.

If further proof were needed of the prosperity of viticulture in the Rhineland at an early date, it would be found in the importance of the sales of German wines in northern lands, the cities of the Baltic, Flanders and particularly England. There are recorded sales of wine in England, for instance, during the reign of Otto the Great in Germany (936–973) and that of Ethelred (978–1016) in England.

William of Malmesbury, the Benedictine historian who wrote in the twelfth century, remarks that "the noble city of London, rich in wealth of its citizens, is filled with the goods of merchants from every land, and especially from Germany". German merchants were clearly given special trading privileges in England and the right to have a *Hanse* or guildhall of their own, not only in London but in Boston, Lynn and other cities at a very early date, for these privileges were not first granted but only confirmed by William the Conqueror and by the Plantagenets after him. In London, the German traders' headquarters, known as the Steelyard, was an important house even before 1260, when it was enlarged by the purchase of the adjoining house and garden.

Henry II of England, a Frenchman by birth and parentage, owned far more vineyards from Angers to Bordeaux than his cousin, the king of France, but he was none the less anxious not to let this fact interfere with the commercial relations between England and Germany. In 1157 he wrote to the Emperor Frederick: "Let there be between ourselves and our subjects an indivisible unity of friendship and peace, and safe trade of merchandise." Henry followed this declaration by extensive privileges granted particularly to the merchants of Cologne. They were to be safeguarded as his own men; their merchandise, their possessions and their house in London were to be protected, and no one could impose new exactions on them. Later, they obtained a further concession allowing them to sell their wines on the same terms as French wines. Again, when King Richard I returned from captivity he passed through Cologne and was most lavish in his grants to the traders there; they were to pay two shillings yearly for their guildhall in London, to be free of all tolls and customs in the City, and to be at liberty to buy and sell at fairs throughout the land. This charter was subsequently confirmed by King John and Henry III.

Henry II also regularly purchased Ruwer and Moselle wines for his household, and so did his two Bordeaux-born sons when they became King Richard and King John. In 1174 Henry II purchased some Moselle wines at 2d per gallon plus cost of transport. In 1213 some 358 casks of wine were bought for King John; most of it came from Bordeaux and other French districts, but there were three casks "de Saxonia", the only mention in royal accounts of any Saxon wine. In 1243 twenty-two tuns of St John and Moselle wines were bought for the King in London at the rate of 1½d per gallon; a further quantity was purchased at Sandwich in 1246 for 1¾d per gallon.

When in 1453 Henry VI lost the last of the great Plantagenet vineyards in France, the wines of Bordeaux and La Rochelle lost their English citizenship and became taxable on a par with other "aliens" like Rhenish. Their higher cost in England was responsible for an increased demand for the wines of the Rhine and Moselle. Unfortunately, politics interfered with economics then as they have done on many occasions since. In 1493 Henry VII, being angry at the protection given by the Dowager Duchess of Burgundy to Perkin Warbeck, banished all Flemings out of England and prohibited all trade with the Netherlands. This brought to an end all imports of Rhenish wine until 1495, when matters were mended by the *Intercursus Magnus* or Great Treaty which gave rise to prolonged public rejoicings.

In 1520 the merchants of the Steelyard, having been asked to pay for a licence if they were to sell Rhenish wine in London, protested that Edward IV had renewed their ancient privileges and that the Royal Grant had been confirmed by an Act of Parliament.

In 1547 Parliament granted Edward VI an additional Tonnage due of 12d per aum of Rhenish wine.

In December 1550 Lord Rutland, riding from Eagle, his Lincolnshire Manor, to London, stayed overnight at an inn at Stamford. The account which was presented to him the next morning included "4 pottells and 1 quart of *Raynsche wyne*" for which he was charged 4s 6d, as well as "2 pottells and one pint of Claret", costing 1s 6d, apples and oranges 6d, "fire in the Chamber where the gentlemen supped 3s 4d", and—hottest of all—"fyer in the kechen 2s". This account is of particular interest as evidence that Rhenish was being sold in the country at inns and was not imported solely for members of the royal household and nobility.

Most, if not all, of the wines which reached England from the Rhineland during the Middle Ages were bought either in London or in east coast ports and cities such as King's Lynn, Canterbury, Orwell, Durham and Deal where they were brought by merchants from Lübeck, Bremen, Dordrecht, Bruges and Antwerp. A tavern close by the Steelyard was known as the Rhenish or the German tavern, where none but German wines were sold.

Ever since 1369 the sale of German wines had been prohibited in taverns where Gascon or Bordeaux wine was sold. The Vintners' Company, one of the twelve

great livery companies of the City, still flourishing today, was then called the Merchant
Vintners of Gascony, and had the right of "search" within the boundaries of the City
of London. This meant that their officials could, and did, visit all London taverns
where Gascony wine was sold—and roughly 80 per cent of the wine then coming to
England came from Bordeaux—and had the right to condemn and destroy any wine
which they considered faked or unsound. It was therefore much safer, even if the sale
of it had been legal, for Rhenish wine not to be found in the same cellar as Gascon wine
by the Vintners' searchers.

Every year the maximum prices at which bread and wine were allowed to be sold
were published by the newly elected Lord Mayor, either in November or early December. This was known as the Assize of Bread and the Assize of Wine. The first time
the retail price of Rhenish wine was fixed by the Assize of Wine was in 1420: 4d per
gallon was then its maximum price in London. There is every reason to believe, however, that the price of German wines in London during the Middle Ages was what
they would fetch in the market.

In 1515, 1517 and 1530, three years when supplies of Rhenish wine must have been
adequate, its selling price was recorded in the Assize of those years as 10d per gallon.
In 1539 it was raised to 1s per gallon. Records of prices paid for Rhenish wine in
different parts of the country show remarkably few changes in the course of a hundred
years, from the mid-fifteenth century to the mid-sixteenth, but there was a sharp rise
during the second half of the sixteenth century.

In two of the Guildhall Letter Books we are given the figures of stocks of wine in
some of the London taverns on the same day in five consecutive years. They show that
there was not much Rhenish wine in stock but that the taverns were never without it:

	Sweet wines	Gascon and French	Rhenish
1578	816 tuns	337 tuns	9½ tuns
1579	621 tuns	281 tuns	196 tuns
1580	724 tuns	496 tuns	7 fattes
1581	543 tuns	405 tuns	32 fattes
1582	480 tuns	618 tuns	17 fattes

There is a good deal of evidence to show that during the fifteenth century a great
deal of attention was paid in the Rhineland to all matters pertaining to viticulture and
the art of making better wines. To sell wine, more particularly to sell the wine made
from one's own grapes, was regarded in an entirely different light from any branch of
commerce, and membership of the various Wine Guilds was a privilege which many
members of the Rhineland aristocracy eagerly sought.

During the sixteenth century, according to Andrea Bacci, the reputation which the
wines of the Rhineland enjoyed in many markets, and more especially in England and
Scotland, was much greater than it had ever been before. Bacci gives a list of names,

some of them impossible to identify today, of German wines which were popular in 1596. Stuttgart, Heidelberg and Cologne appear to have been three of the more important centres of the German wine trade, and Bacci praises the wine of Franconia, from the Main valley, and those of the hillsides in Württemberg and Baden.

It is surprising to find Bavaria, which we associate with beer, praised solely for its wines, and it comes as a shock to find that, in November 1543, John Grousby "gentleman", and William Wurden, merchant of the Steelyard, were granted a special licence to export 800 tuns of English beer on condition that they imported 800 tuns of Rhenish wine. Three other conditions were stipulated in the licence granted to them:

1. The wine must be of the finest quality, "such as the Emperor and the Duke of Cleves and other persons of high rank did drink";
2. The price must not be above 30s per gallon;
3. 400 aums of 36 gallons each must be imported for the King's use before Christmas 1543; more of the same wine to bring the total to 400 tuns must be imported before Easter 1544; the balance of 400 tuns must be imported by midsummer 1544.

Such a large quantity as 800 tuns of Rhenish wine would have been unusual at any time, but it was exceptional at a time when religious feuds in Germany between Catholics and Protestants greatly added to difficulties of wine supply and transport. What is of particular interest in this contract is the stipulation that the wine must be of the "finest quality" and such as "persons of high rank did drink". This is a reminder that then, as now, there was a good deal of sharp, acid wine made from grapes of indifferent summers which had found it difficult to ripen, whilst there never was enough of the really fine wine of good vintages.

It was ever thus, and it cannot be otherwise, for the vineyards of the Rhineland happen to be at the northern limit beyond which grapes cannot reach full maturity except in years with particularly fine summers. At a much later date it was not exceptional for the owner of a cask of fine wine to refuse to sell it unless the buyer agreed to buy a like quantity of a cheaper and poorer wine. The gap between the wines of good and of bad vintages still exists, but it is not quite so great today, thanks to Gall and Chaptal, who taught us that sugar added to the reluctantly fermenting juice of imperfectly ripe grapes will mend matters to a certain—alcoholic—extent. We can well imagine how difficult it must have been in those days to buy wines of the highest quality and such as persons of "high rank" were privileged to enjoy. It is not much easier to do so to-day.

It is very likely that the majority of German wines sold in England were the wines which William Turner, who was at the time one of the doctors of Queen Elizabeth, had in mind when he wrote about the "small and subtil" Rhenish. In his little book, the first book on wine written and published in English, William Turner defended Rhenish wines against those in the medical profession who claimed that such wines were not safe for people suffering from bladder or kidney troubles; a claim which we know, as

William Turner also knew four hundred years ago, to be utterly baseless. Here is the whole title of his book: "A new Boke of the natures and properties of all wines that are commonly used here in England, with a confutation of an error of some men, that holds that Rhenish and other small white wines ought not to be drunken of them that either have, or are in danger of the Stone, the reume, and divers other diseases, made by William Turner, Doctor of Phisicke" (*London, Seres, 1568*).

A hundred years later another English medical authority, William Salmon, also shared Dr Turner's faith in Rhenish wine, only more so. He wrote in his *Compleat English Physician* (1693 edition, p. 926): "It [Rhenish] is a good nephritic and vehemently diuretick, opening all obstructions of urinary parts, and bringing away stones, sands and gravel, and other tartarous matter from the reins, uretera and bladder; it strengthens the stomack admirably, causes a good appetite and a good digestion, and opens obstructions of the lungs."

All German wines, whether they came from the Rhine, the Palatinate, the Neckar or the Main, were uniformly known in England as Rhenish wine. This is clear from all the references to the wines of Germany in contemporary records and documents of the sixteenth century and of the greater part of the seventeenth century. Shakespeare, for instance, invariably uses "Rhenish" for German wine.

Although records of sales of Rhenish wine in England during the seventeenth century are comparatively few, they suffice to show that there was a demand for this wine at all times, and that it was obtainable in some if not all the London taverns. Rhenish wine was served not only at Charles II's royal table but also at Cromwell's more frugal board. If the quantities of Rhenish wine that reached England appear very modest, and they certainly do, we must not suppose that the wine was in short supply: it was not. It is on record, for instance, that in 1631, when the troops of Gustavus Adolphus of Sweden occupied the Rheingau, they demanded an "indemnity" of 46,000 Thaler, a very large amount of money at the time; merchants of Frankfurt found the cash which saved the land from the scorched earth treatment, but the real saviours of the homeland were the wine growers of the Rheingau who promised to give to the Frankfurt bankers 1,650 Fuder of wine—a very large quantity (360,000 gallons U.K. or 470,000 gallons U.S.A.)— before March 1634; and they duly delivered the wine on time.

It was only during the second half of the seventeenth century that two Rhineland place-names replaced the popular generic name of Rhenish: they were Bacharach and Hochheim. The second was soon anglicized into "hock", the name which has generally been used for all Rhine wine to this day, wherever English is spoken. There were, of course, vineyards in those days, as there are now, both at Bacharach and Hochheim, but there is no reason to believe that the quality of the wines they produced was responsible for their greater popularity overseas. The truth is that all the wines of Franconia sent down the Main to Frankfurt were shipped from Hochheim down the Rhine to Antwerp and other ports, and thence to London, Ipswich, Lynn and other east coast ports. Bacharach—named after Bacchus—was the last port of call for the fairly large

Plate 3. Marienburg Castle and the *Leisten* vineyard, at Würzburg, in Franconia.

Plate 4. Weibertreu vineyard, near Heilbronn, in Württemberg.

boats which were unable to negotiate the Bingen "Hole". There were no other means of sending any of the wines of the Pfalz or Palatinate and those of Rheinhessen to Bonn, Cologne and the North Sea except from Bacharach by the Rhine.

It was therefore not so much the excellence of what little wine was made from the vineyards of Bacharach that was responsible for the great reputation the name acquired during the seventeenth and eighteenth centuries, as Bacharach's privileged position as a port on the Rhine. In the fourteenth century Nuremberg had to send the king every year a fee of a Fuder of wine, and it had to be Bacharach wine. In the fifteenth century Pope Pius II also claimed a Fuder of Bacharach wine every year, and he declared that in his opinion it was the best German wine. There were many people in England who agreed with the Pope, on this count at least, even after the Reformation. In 1634, Howell wrote: "The prime wines of Germany grow about the Rhine, specially in the Pfalz and Lower Palatinate, about Bacharach".

In a very old German song Bacharach is given first place among the best wines of Rhine and Main:

> Zu Bacharach am Rhein,
> Zu Klingenberg am Main,
> Zu Würzburg am Stein,
> Sind die besten Wein.

Shirley, in his comedy *The Lady of Pleasure* (Act v, sc. 1) alludes to the German Wine House by the Steelyard where what he calls "Deal wine", German wine landed at Deal from Holland, and Bacharach wine were sold.

On September 8, 1681, Charles Bertie wrote from London to his niece, the Duchess of Rutland: "I am glad your hogshead of Bacharach is arrived. Very little pure Rhenish is drunk in England. I will try to help you to another hogshead of Moselle or Pincair. I have written for a foudre of Hochheim."

In Oldham's *Paraphrases from Horace*, published in 1681, wealthy merchants count among their more costly wines "Their Aums of Hock, of Bachrag and Moselle". In this instance, "Hock" stood for Hochheim, but from that time to our own "Hock" has been used in England as a generic term for all Rhine wines in place of "Rhenish".

At a time when wines were mostly drunk young, Hock appears to have stood the test of time better than other wines, and "old hock" was practically the only old wine to be offered by merchants or sung by poets. Thus in Gay's poem *Wine* (1708) the waiter asks some guests as they enter the tavern, what they will be pleased to order:

> Name, Sirs, the wine that most invites your
> taste, Champagne or Burgundy or Glorence pure,
> or Hock antique, or Lisbon new or old,
> Bordeaux, or neat French wine, or Alicant.

Bickerstaffe, in *Lionel and Clarissa*, also refers to old hock:

COLONEL OLDBOY: Well, but, zounds! Jenkins, you must not go till you drink something. Let you and I have a bottle of hock.

JENKINS: Not for the world, Colonel! I never touch anything strong in the morning.

COLONEL OLDBOY: Never touch anything strong! Why, one bottle won't hurt you, man, this is old and as mild as milk.

The appeal of old hock must have been handed from one generation to another since we find it, as young as ever, in Meredith's *The Egoist* (Chapter 20) when Dr Middleton, the wine-loving divine, delivers the following judgment upon an "aged and a great wine" in Sir Willoughby Patterne's cellar:

> Hocks, too, have compassed age. I have tasted senior Hocks. Their flavour is a brook of many voices; they have depth also.

In 1831, at the Vauxhall Royal Gardens in London, both Moselle and old hock were listed, the first at 6s per bottle, which was also the price charged for a bottle of Port, Sherry, Lisbon, or Bacellas, and old hock, which cost 12s per bottle, the same as a bottle of Hermitage, Champagne, Burgundy or Arrack.

In 1878 Sir Walter Trevelyan, Bt, died, and the cellar of wine which he had inherited from his father in 1846, at Wallington, was sold. Among the contents of this famous cellar there were four magnums of hock, which the cellarbook faithfully recorded as having been there since before 1777! Old hock, indeed! Old, of course, but far, far older hock was uncorked on July 7, 1961, in London, in the offices of Messrs Ehrmanns, the Grafton Street wine merchants. The two oldest wines were not only pre-*Phylloxera* but pre-Shakespeare—Steinwein of 1540—the two youngest were two 1857 Rüdesheimer, and there was also a Johannisberger of 1822. All these venerable bottles came from the royal cellars of Ludwig II, the "mad" king of Bavaria, and they had been purchased by Ferdinand Bazuch Ehrmann in 1887, when the contents of the royal Bavarian cellars were sold by public auction, a year after the king's death.

The 1857 and 1822 were opened first. They were dead; not vinegar, but just dumb wet rags. Not so the 1540! Of course it was old, and very old, but not dead: there was a vinous quality reminiscent of some antique Madeira, and the wine was clear up to the last fifth of the bottles. It certainly bore out the centuries-old tradition that there never was in Germany a wine comparable to the wine that was made in 1540, a year quite unique in the annals of German viticulture. The warm weather started on February 22 and the flowering of the grapes began on April 5. By August, the grapes were more like raisins: then came the rain, and the swollen grapes, which were picked in October, gave a wine of outstanding excellence which appeared to defy decay for centuries.

Rhenish, then Hochheim and Bacharach, hock and old hock were for a very long time the only names by which the wines of the Rhineland were known in England. The names of grape and vineyard responsible for the wine in the bottle were not recorded on label or invoice before the nineteenth century. The names of important wine-producing villages, more particularly of the Rheingau and Palatinate, frequently appear on eighteenth-century German bottles, but, curiously, their wines were exported anonymously. Strange as it may seem, it was the French Revolution which brought about a change so complete that it may rightly be called revolutionary in the viticulture and the wine trade of the Rhineland. The French Revolution was responsible for the situation in which Napoleon came to power, and Napoleon was responsible for the Treaty of Lunéville of 1803 which secularized all religious orders, causing some of the largest and best vineyards of the Rhineland to be split up among a very large number of small holders; these could hope to make a living only if they could sell at a fairly high price the limited quantities of wine they were able to make whenever the sun smiled upon them and their grapes. They not only took far greater care to make better wine than their fathers, who had farmed the same vineyards for some noble lord, some archbishop or abbot, but they gave to their vineyards individual names by which their individual wines were to be known and to become famous, as so many of them have remained to this day.

However, the practice of giving to all quality wines the name of their native village, with the name of their individual site added, did not really become general in the Rhineland before 1830. It was in that year that the provincial authorities decreed that the names of all vineyards, together with the names of their owners, of the nearest village or township, and of their own site should be recorded in an official land register. Mention was also to be made in this register of the nature of the soil of each vineyard, and of the species of the vines planted therein; the standard of quality of the wine and its chief characteristics were also to be recorded. This land register led to some kind of unofficial classification of the chief growths of the Rhineland, but its original purpose had been to provide a guide for the collector of taxes: the better the soil, the better the wine and the better its selling value: so, the better also the land tax it was to pay.

The first immediate result of the land register was to increase the demand for the better "registered" wines and to render very much more difficult the sale of the commoner types of wine, the price of which, in Germany, fell from 250 to 10 or 20 thaler per hectolitre or 22 gallons; many winegrowers failed to sell their wines at any price. Conditions became so desperate in some of the vinelands that for a few pfennigs a toper would be given the key of the cellar and allowed to drink as much wine as he could carry, and land might be sold at one to two pfennigs per square yard. It was then that quite a number of Rhineland families left Germany for Australia, the Argentine, Brazil and North America.

In 1834 came the German Customs Union, which did away with all the fiscal barriers between the different German states. It was immediately responsible for a considerably greater demand, in all parts of Germany, for the better wines of the Rhineland—Riesling wines from named vineyards—whilst the commoner, anonymous wines made from any kind of grape, anywhere and anyhow, were not wanted. It proved to be a lesson which led all the growers who could raise credit to replant their vineyards with Rieslings and give greater care to the making of the wines. They were particularly fortunate in having an unprecedented run of fine vintages in 1857, 1858 and 1859; for when in 1860 Mr Gladstone reduced the duty on all table wines to one shilling per gallon, they were in a position to take advantage of the opportunity to sell a far greater quantity of hocks and Moselles in England than ever before. Good German wines could then be bought in England at such low prices that they were for the first time within the reach of practically everybody in the land, except the really poor.

As was to be expected, the demand for hocks and Moselles now grew year by year, much faster than the supply. And it was in 1871 that Bismarck robbed France of Alsace and parts of Lorraine; the vineyards of Alsace produced a great deal of wine which the shippers of German wines found most useful.

Ever since the first big drive to export hocks and Moselles in the 1860's, most German wines, the great names excepted, were sold at exceptionally low prices in overseas markets by shippers who paid the growers famine prices. Then, in 1874, the *Phylloxera vastatrix* was first reported in the Palatinate, and although its progress was not as rapid and catastrophic as in the Médoc, it steadily spread and destroyed vineyard after vineyard. The *Phylloxera* was the worst scourge of all because this accursed vine louse cannot be seen: it sticks to the roots of the vines and sucks their life sap.

Other enemies of the vine attacked it above ground and cost the unfortunate *vignerons* a considerable amount of extra work and expenditure merely to save at least some proportion of the year's grapes. The *oidium, mildew* and *black rot* are cryptogamic diseases which attacked the leaves and the fruit of the vine, whilst a number of insect pests—the *Cochylis* the worst of all—did their best to rob the *vignerons* of any hope of a bumper crop of fine grapes, even in the all too few years when there had been no late spring frosts and when the sun had done its best during the summer and autumn!

To make matters worse, it was at this time that the German banks decided that it was in their own and in the country's best interests to give all possible financial backing to industry and no longer to viticulture.

Much as one may—and must—regret it, one cannot be greatly surprised that quite a number of those unfortunate *vignerons* resorted to means, not illegal at the time, of producing more and cheaper wine. The commonest offence was over-chaptalization, the adding of some water and a great deal of sugar to the grapes that were being pressed, in order to raise both the quantity and eventual alcoholic strength of the wine.

It was to put an end to such malpractices that the German Wine Law of 1909 was enacted and strictly enforced. It was the beginning of a long struggle, which has lasted fifty years and is still going on, to protect the public from misrepresentation and to protect honest growers and merchants from unfair competition.

During the last decade of the nineteenth century and the first fourteen years of the twentieth, the wine trade of Germany enjoyed its highest measure of prosperity. Hocks and Moselles were exported to all civilized lands throughout the world, and they were awarded many honours at a number of international exhibitions. On the wine lists of the luxury hotels and restaurants of Europe and America there were more German wines listed—dearer as well as cheaper—than white wines from all other vinelands.

Then came the First World War, which all but halted the export trade of hocks and Moselles for nearly five years. When resumption became possible in 1919 German wine shippers could no longer get cheap wines from Alsace, and the world economic crisis, which the appalling cost in lives and treasure of the war had rendered inevitable, meant that the demand for the better and highly priced wines of the Rhineland was non-existent in countries like Russia and much smaller in countries like the United Kingdom and the United States.

Nature did its best to come to the help of the Rhineland *vignerons* and the German wine trade by giving them two very fine vintages in 1920 and 1921, when wines of quite exceptional quality were made in fairly large quantity. There was a satisfactory quantity of wine made in the Rhineland during the twenty years of truce between the two wars, and the German wine trade regained a large share of its pre-1914 prosperity. But the Second World War not only halted their export trade once again, but impoverished the whole world to such an extent that new methods had to be found to reduce the cost of production.

Science has by now made such progress in all departments of viticulture and oenology that vines are now grown which give more grapes than ever before, and—*mirabile dictu* —vines also that beat the frost! As to wine, it can now be made to look, smell and taste well every year, sun or no sun,—though the better wines, of course, still depend on the sun shining as it should. Science has also beaten present economic difficulties by making it possible to enjoy really good wine when it is months old instead of years old.

As we shall see when we review the Rhineland vintages later on, there has been a great deal of good quality wine made in the Rhineland since the end of the Second World War, some wines of superlative excellence which command superlative prices, and many more which are quite reasonable in price and of very fair quality.

In 1958, for the first time since 1913, the exports of German wine reached the two million gallons figure, the United Kingdom and United States of America being responsible for over 50% of the total, as the following figures show:

	U.K.	U.S.A.	Others	Total
1954	373,648	331,782	803,230	1,508,660
1955	439,252	369,358	822,054	1,630,464
1956	472,494	472,648	954,250	1,899,392
1957	497,992	514,580	899,416	1,911,888
1958	565,004	543,488	1,104,576	2,125,200
1959	673,068	797,740	1,104,576	2,485,334
1960	953,062	717,112	1,195,238	2,865,412

Chapter Two

FROM VINE TO BOTTLE

The most picturesque process in the manufacture of wine is the gathering of the grapes. Many a traveller has been attracted to a particular locality in the hope of watching activities during the harvest season in the vineyards. Few, however, suspect how much the quantity and the quality of any vintage depend on the proper selection of the date on which the fruit is to be gathered. Yet this date is vitally important, a fact that has been recognised by wine growers from time immemorial. In feudal times it was the seigneurs who set the date and kept a strict eye on the peasant to see that no one entered the vineyard without special permission, particularly when the grapes were nearly ripe. This was not only to guard against pilfering, but in order to ensure delivery of a flawless harvest of fruit and grape-juice (must), for no berry was allowed to be severed from the vine before it was fully ripe. Even when the grape harvest was in full swing, the vineyard might be entered only at specified times, the object of this precaution being to prevent a neighbouring grower from trespassing and taking one's fruit.

The same ancient rules are still in force, though for different reasons. Harvesting dates are now set by the Commissions which exist in every grape-growing community and are composed of the leading growers. Their main object is to secure the best possible vintage in every respect, by choosing the most favourable date. The riper and juicier the grapes, the richer the wine, not only in sugar content, but also in the etheric substances on which its bouquet and flavour depend. Even when the grape-gathering has officially started the growers are not allowed to harvest their fruit when they please. Wine must never be watery, so that grapes must not be gathered if they are wet with dew or raindrops: the Commission makes daily observations and then orders the ringing of local church bells to denote the beginning and ending of picking time. At the sound of this early bell, whole families—men, women and children—stream forth to the vineyards, vine-cutters in their hands. There is work for all and plenty to spare.

The picking of the grapes is of necessity preceded by considerable preliminary preparation in the pressing houses and cellars. The cellar-master and vineyard owner have to work in close co-operation to see that no mistakes occur which might impair the good quality of the future wine. The necessary tools must be clean; the scissors handed to the pickers have to be sharp to ensure a clean separation of each bunch from the vine and so that no grapes fall to the ground. The casks, too, have to be prepared for the reception of the must; and so on. Undoubtedly there is a great deal of work to be done.

In ancient days there were progressive methods of picking the grapes. The Greeks, and later the Romans, held the same views on the picking and selection of the grapes. They knew that different kinds of grape ripened at different times; they knew also how to get the best out of the grapes by letting them remain on the vine until they were over-ripe and then making special collections of dry berries. Strangely enough, in Germany this technique was not used until the eighteenth century. The revival, according to legend, was due to chance. The Bishop of Fulda, owner of vineyards in the Rheingau, is said to have delayed sending his permission to begin grape-harvesting until too late; in other words, until the fruit had become over-ripe. To everybody's amazement, the resulting vintage was superb.

From the moment the must reaches the cellar, the vintner has but one aim—to give it the finest treatment so that the wine comes to the drinker in the best possible condition.

We must not forget that tastes have changed. Whereas fifty years ago Rhine and Moselle wines were served in tinted cut glasses, today the glasses are colourless. The wine drinker wants to enjoy the beautiful colour of the wine and to be able to judge its age from the development of that colour. From the moment the wine goes into bottle ready to be sent out to the consumer, therefore, it must be star-bright. And, as the wine grower says, it must have the capacity to withstand a journey either to the North Pole or to the Equator.

Furthermore, it must be sound, it must be digestible and, above all, it must be enjoyable. To attain this goal the grower has to observe the wine in all its stages, and if he finds any fault he has to try to eradicate it exactly as one eradicates a fault in a naughty child. After long years of experiments, scientists have put at the disposal of the wine grower many means of reaching this aim. The grower moreover knows full well that prevention is better than cure, and does his utmost to clear the must of any impurities before fermentation ever begins. Growers who can afford it accomplish this by means of centrifuging the must, but the same result can also be reached by cheaper means. If the grapes taken off the vines contain many rotten or diseased berries, or are very dirty, it is necessary first to remove the sludge from the must. The freshly pressed must is allowed to stand for some time—perhaps twenty-four hours. This enables all solid and flocculent sediments, stemming either from the actual flesh of the grapes or from foreign bodies such as fungi or ordinary dirt, to settle and leave a completely clean liquid above, entirely free from flocculence.

The grape-must delivered by the wine press is treated to such an extent that the incidence of fermentation is delayed by several days. The must is then left to itself in as cool a room as possible, and all bad and wild ferments which effect a quick fermentation—and a quick fermentation is likely to impair the quality of the future wine—are killed. After a day or two, the clarified must is separated from the flocculence by draining it off (racking). It is then transferred to a warmer fermentation cellar where it is left to ferment, sometimes with the addition of biologically pure yeast, which is normally taken from the lees of some high-class wine. There is no doubt that this treatment of the must effects a slow fermentation, and, even more important, a fermentation which can be controlled. The fermentation can be controlled more easily if it takes place in hermetically sealed vats, or in the pressure tanks which abound in the Rhineland today.

Now that we have seen the must supply deposited in its vat, there to await fermentation and gradual transformation into a wine fit for the bottle, it is time to consider more closely some particular aspects of wine-making.

What, for example, is this "must" we have been discussing? Clear must is an aqueous solution of various substances, the most important quantitatively being sugar and acids. The average content of sugar is from 14 to 22 per cent. An unseasonal crop of unripe berries can bring this down to 6 or 7 per cent, while a crop of "sleepy" grapes will yield a sugar content of 35 per cent or more. Selected 1921 and 1959 vintages show as much as 52 per cent, and those of 1949 43 per cent.

The sugar content is not uniform, but is composed on the one hand of grape-sugar (dextrose, glucose) and on the other, of fruit-sugar (levulose, fructose). Fully matured grapes contain about equal quantities of the two kinds of sugar; unripe grapes have a preponderance of grape-sugar, while over-ripe and "sleepy" grapes have more fructose.

The more noteworthy acids found in must are tartaric acid, malic acid, and tannic acid. Tartaric acid, absent in almost all other fruits, is characteristic of the grape. Its quantity increases until the fruit begins to ripen and then remains practically static until full maturity is reached.

It is, however, malic acid, a frequent phenomenon in all fruits, that fills the leading role of all wine acids. It is almost always present and increases rapidly in quantity up to the moment when the fruit begins to ripen; then it decreases, but even in the ripe grape does not entirely disappear.

The amount of tannic acid in must depends on the way the mash is treated. The longer the mash is allowed to stand, the more tannic acid is present in the must and, eventually, in the wine itself. If the mash is put through the wine presses immediately, the resulting wine is poor in tannic acid; whereas if the mash is allowed to stand and ferment (as with red wines) the tannic acid content is high.

Plate 5. Cellars of the State Domain (*Hofkellerei*),
at Würzburg, in Franconia.

Besides sugars and acids, grape-juice contains traces of numerous other substances all of which have their part to play in determining the development and the quality of the wine. Among these are the nitrogenous compounds—albumen, peptones, amides, ammonium salts, and nitrates—which provide the ferment with its nitrogen, and the mineral components from which the ferment derives the bases needed for its development, namely, potassium, phosphoric acid, and calcium.

Of inestimable value to the wine are the substances which give it its "bouquet", or peculiar aromatic odour. In the must the only recognisable aroma is that of the primitive grape-bouquet, the chemical origin of which is still unknown. Its nature is decisive for the value of the wine, and in certain kinds of grapes, such as Muscats, Gewürztraminer (spicy Traminer), and Riesling, the primitive bouquet has a particularly strong influence on the wine's final character.

Finally, the must contains colouring matter. Both white and red must will invariably absorb decomposition particles from the chlorophyll in the grape-skin and stalks, and it is these latter which give hock its characteristic colour.

When grape juice is transformed into wine by fermentation, the most noteworthy chemical development is the change of the sugar content into roughly equal quantities of alcohol and carbon dioxide. The alcohol content of any wine is somewhat less than half the sugar content of the must.

The flesh of red grapes is white and if red grapes are pressed immediately and treated like white grapes, the resulting wine is white, or perhaps a wine with just a slight tinge of rose colour. It is the skin of the red grape which contains the colouring particles. In order to extract the colour from the grape skins, fermentation must take place before the grapes are pressed.

During the last few years great progress has been made in methods of fermenting red grapes. For centuries the process took place in upright, open casks. When the mash was put into these casks, fermentation started at once; the ensuing escape of carbonic acid would lift the grape-skin above the level of the liquid, with the result that the "hat" was in the open, not being covered by the wine, or must, and it was the task of the wine grower to be ready at any moment to push the "hat" back into the liquid. If the "hat" were left in the open, there would be a risk of acetic acid bacteria infection, which produces acetic acid by oxydation of the alcohol that was produced during the fermentation. Furthermore, if the "hat" were outside the liquid, the wine would not acquire its characteristic colour and, even worse, such colour as had already been produced might well be destroyed. All in all, it was extremely important to prevent the "hat" from leaving the liquid, and many were the devices invented for the purpose.

Today, the fermentation of red wine often takes place in hermetically sealed enamel or glass-lined pressure tanks. These tanks are kept at a constant temperature of approximately 22° centigrade and fermentation is terminated within three to four days. It is no longer necessary to stand by and watch the "hat" emerging from the must; the carbonic acid resulting from the fermentation is collected at the top of the pressure tank and the formation of a "hat" is avoided by the simple manipulation of a switch. The mash is put on the press, and further vinification and treatment of the red wine takes place in wooden casks. This results in milder, rounder and perhaps more velvety wines.

Unfavourable climatic conditions in many German wine-growing districts often prevent a (varying) proportion of the grapes from reaching full maturity. In most years, therefore, many German wine growers are unfortunately compelled to take steps to improve a large part of their crop. This improvement is effected by adding sugar or sugar solution to the deficient must. Unripe grapes produce a wine which not only keeps badly, falling an easy prey to acidification and other diseases, but also one which is unpalatable, since, when alcohol and acid are blended in the wrong proportions, a lack of "body" is the inevitable outcome. Yet the effect of the climate in these districts is by no means entirely a bad one, since it is the climate that is largely responsible for the variety in type, the flavour and other individual characteristics of the resulting wines.

The German Wine Law lays down that sugar or sugar dissolved in pure water may be added to grape-must or wines derived from home-grown grapes, provided that this is done for the sole purpose of supplementing the natural sugar or counteracting natural excess acidity—and only enough to reproduce the same sugar content as that of a wine made in a good year from exactly similar grapes. Moreover, this proceeding is legal only if the defects are due to natural causes. It is not permissible in cases where the premature gathering of the grape is deliberate and unjustifiable. It is therefore wrong to suspect all German wines of being doctored simply because in certain specified cases it is permissible to add extraneous sugar. It is not only in Germany that such measures are allowed. Other countries too, even those with more favourable climatic conditions than Germany, make similar concessions to their growers. French growers, for example, are permitted to add sugar or sugar-water to their wines, though if they do add sugar-water they lose the right to market their products with the title *appellation controlée*. Tarragona wines are usually sweetened with grape juice, while the sweet taste of port wine is preserved only by interrupting fermentation by means of the addition of brandy.

Wine control in Germany is efficiently organized. Trading is supervised from the moment the wine reaches the presses until it is sold for consumption. Wine Controllers with expert knowledge are appointed for each of the German regions. They have wide powers and can, at their own discretion, visit growers and merchants, check their books, correspondence, price lists, etc. (there are detailed provisions for obligatory book-keeping), and taste the wine in storage. Should the Controller find anything amiss, or become suspicious of any of the products, he can impound samples for chemical analysis. If the analysis shows grounds for objection, the owner will then be prosecuted and the wines may be confiscated, or their sale permitted for the manufacture of vinegar only.

Soon after the must has been deposited in the vats, the vital process of fermentation starts. Yeasts act on the fermentable sugars and generate not only alcohol and carbon dioxide, but also glycerine, succinic acid, volatile acids, higher alcohols and various esters (bouquet compounds).

Fermentation is a gradual process. By the time it ceases, the sugar has been broken down, and the expiring yeast precipitated to the bottom of the cask. Not very long ago people liked to see the fermentation finished in a very short time, and spoke of a very "stormy" fermentation—*Stürmische Gärung*. The aim of the grower was to have the fermentation concluded as quickly as possible, and in a fermentation-cellar one always found a coke-oven for increasing the temperature of the cellar in order to speed up fermentation. Today the coke-ovens have disappeared and the young must is laid down in very cold, or at least cool, cellars, so that fermentation goes forward very slowly. This has the great advantage that the fermentation may come to a standstill and leave some unfermented sugar in the wine. If the grower succeeds in balancing this remaining sugar content against the acid content, he will produce a very harmonious wine which is both mild and round—in any case not harsh and hard. These wines, bottled later through a sterilising filter, keep this remnant of sugar and produce a sweeter type of German wine than was known forty or fifty years ago.

The so-called cold fermentation has great advantages. Most important of all, the alcohol content of the wines is increased; in a stormy fermentation the aroma material and the carbonic acid—the natural contents—of the wine are torn out of the cask.

During January the young wine can generally be separated from the sediment by racking, i.e. draining off into another cask. This racking is repeated two or three times (second racking approximately six weeks, third racking approximately four months, after the first racking) and is usually supplemented by a mechanical clearing of the young wine by "fining", or filtering in an asbestos filter which retains all the sediments and impurities. Success or failure of the resulting wine may depend on the proper and well-timed application of these measures and on the selection of the right moment for bottling.

Another important factor in determining the quality of the wine is the manner in which it is stored. For many centuries, both theory and practice followed the principle of allowing wines to ferment in wooden vats and of storing them in the same way, the idea being that wines must "breathe" and that only porous wood would allow them to do so. These techniques have undergone a great deal of modification in recent years. Immense progress has been made and experiments are still continuing. For example, it has been found that the carbon dioxide that develops in the hermetically sealed tank is the best medium for regulating fermentation. If it can then be preserved in the wine itself, the result is a mild and pleasant drink which is just perceptibly sweet. Wines which are bottled with a relatively high natural carbon dioxide content are less likely to suffer from a slight sediment of sugar particles than others which are poor in carbon dioxide content. Their flavour is also more aromatic. Another advance of knowledge was made when it was found that, in the case of "little" wines, not more than a residual sweetness can be achieved by controlled fermentation. It was further observed that in small vintages no more aroma and bouquet can be obtained by tank fermentation than by fermentation in the cask. Lovely as the transient stronger fermentation bouquets may be, they remain a characteristic of young, unfinished wines. If small, ordinary wines with residual sugar are fermented by prolonged, controlled fermentation methods, the final result is only slightly better than that obtained by fermenting in a normal wooden cask. In the case of medium vintages, tank fermentation automatically produces an improvement. In the case of good class wines, i.e. with musts above 90 and 95 Öchsle, controlled fermentation in the tank may well produce very much better results than those obtainable by cask methods.

The great economic advantage of the tank is that it has an inert surface, is always ready for use, and can be charged in turn with all kinds of wine, whereas the wooden cask needs a lot of attention and may occasionally have an adverse influence on the wine. A tank has the further advantage that finished wines can be stored in it for years and still retain their freshness without appreciably ageing, whereas wines can be stored in wooden casks for a short time only, and in consequence are often subject to premature bottling.

All this does not mean, however, that in future growers will dispense with their wooden casks. There is no doubt that good wines do acquire an individual regional character through being stored in the wood after fermentation in tanks, and it is unlikely that the old methods will ever be entirely superseded.

In the tank the wine undergoes some degree of chemical change. Tank wine has invariably 2–3 gr./litre alcohol more than cask wine, the must weight being equal. On the other hand, the contents of extract and glycerine are sometimes lower. Tank wines require more sulphur than cask wines and take a longer time seasoning. Where it is possible also to control fermentation in the cask by clarifying the must and keeping the temperature in the cellar low, the same advantages in respect of taste can be obtained as with the tank. The great expectations the trade had in connection with tank fermentation a few years ago have, in part, been realised, but in other cases, more especially in the case of small vintages, not to the extent hoped for. Most suitable for tank fermentation are good, harmonious vintages.

When fermentation is over and the wine has been drawn off from the lees—first racking—growers and wine merchants start its treatment for bottling. In former days this process was left to nature; that is, the wine was left in cask until it became impervious to air and had lost every vestige of cloudiness. This usually entailed a succession of rackings and often operated to the detriment of the consumer, the wine having lost its freshness by the time it was finally bottled.

Old wine in our sense has become known only since the middle of the eighteenth century. Until that time no means had been discovered of preserving wine from deterioration. For a long time wine was drunk very young as must, in all stages of fermentation (*Federweisser*, see page 43)—but only for one year after the harvest. Longer than that it would not keep, and its quality suffered from many apparently incurable diseases. It was

Plate 6. Spätburgunder grapes.

not until the use of sulphur was introduced into vinification that it became possible to bring wine to the stage where it could be stored or bottled without turning acid or being affected by other diseases.

Sulphurization as a method of treating wine has long been known, but opinion of its suitability and usefulness has differed through the centuries. In 1465 a councillor in the town of Cologne was deprived both of his position and of his licence as a wine trader on the grounds that he had used sulphur in vinification; and at the end of the last century some eminent authorities declared that a high content of sulphur would be dangerous to health.

Today the sulphurization of wines is regulated by law, a very necessary precaution in the interests both of viticulture and of the ultimate consumer. The wine law does not define exactly how much sulphur may be used, but just as (it will be recalled) the addition of sugar is permitted only within certain natural limits, so the use of sulphur is confined to the absolute necessities of good cellarage. Sulphurization is needed to keep the wines sound and prevent the formation of organisms which might cause decomposition. The quantity which is absolutely necessary depends upon the type of wine: rich wines need more sulphur to mature than do ordinary wines. But German food chemists have agreed that it is essential for the quality of the wine that a maximum should be set for the use of sulphur. With regard to ordinary wines the limit should stand at 200 milligrammes per litre, to include no more than 50 milligrammes of the free (sulphurous) acid.

It may be interesting to show the limits of sulphurization fixed by various countries (in milligrammes per litre): Germany, 200; Spain, 450; France, 450; Portugal, 350; Italy, 200; S. Africa, 200 for dry wine, 357 for sweet wine; England, 450.

The last stage of development concerns the storage of the finished wine. Here the cellarman's main purpose is to keep the wine both fresh and young and also, if possible, to improve its quality.

The wine drinker of today asks for wines which are star-bright. The first aim of the wine grower is, therefore, to stabilize the wine. In order to do this, he may utilize refrigeration, heat, separation by centrifuge, filtration or sterilization.

Fifty years ago it would have been considered a crime to filter wine when bottling. Racking and fining were the only means used to make the wine ready for bottling. Growers had plenty of time and money, and the chemical and physical proceedings during the maturation of the wine were not well-known as they are today. When the first filter appeared on the market, everybody said the filtration would "dem Wein den Rock ausziehen"—in other words, would take the cream from the milk (literally, "tear the coat off the wine").

"Airing" of the wine was, in olden times, the most important means of stabilization. All German wines, with the possible exception of Moselles, were exposed to air as much as possible during the first racking, because the cellarmaster knew that wines which had been aired would become ready for bottling more quickly. But the immediate result of the airing was that the wine became cloudy when the albumen and other materials contained in the wine were deposited. The disadvantages of airing were indeed manifold. A wine treated in this way was likely to lose its freshness, age quickly and take on a murky-brown colour; from a chemical viewpoint, the sulphurous acid—previously a free compound in the wine—would become oxidized into fixed sulphur and the eventual formation of sulphuric acid would render the wine dull and old. Today, airing of wine takes place only in exceptional cases (if the wine is faulty, if it has a taste of mould, etc.) since scientists have at last evolved a method of fining which avoids these hazards.

The modern methods of fining are founded on important and thorough scientific experiments, so that it is now possible to stabilize wine accurately and achieve the exact state required. No damage is done to the wine—on the contrary, those particles which are taken away during the fining and stabilization are those which tend to undermine the fine and noble bouquet and aroma material which are so important in the judgment of a good wine. By quick work it is possible to save all the fine parts of a wine.

Today, with the help of scientists, the treatment of wine is carried out in such a way that bottling of the small, average wines is effected before the summer. Such wines will thus not be left in cask during the summer when the cellar is likely to be warmer. They are put into bottle young and fresh so that they can have all the development in bottle which they previously had in cask. Formerly, the influence of the air made them lose both bouquet and aroma, whereas when they are lying in bottle this influence cannot have any effect.

We know that bacteria may be eliminated by filtering. Obviously the filter used for this purpose cannot be one of the ordinary asbestos filters used for clearing the wine of impurities, but must be specially constructed. Sterilization filters are made on the model of the cellar-presses which were formerly in common use in wine cellars. The minute pores of the filter sheets will not allow even the smallest microscopic particles to penetrate, which means that they are capable of excluding not only dirt, but also bacteria and fermenting fungi. This method makes it possible to sterilize liquids without heating them—i.e. by a "cold" process. The replacement of pasteurizing apparatus (until recently still employed for sterilizing wines) by these filters represents an immense improvement. The pasteurization of wine meant heating it to 167° Fahrenheit, the temperature at which all undesirable bacteria and fermenting fungi may be considered to be rendered harmless; the filter achieves the same object at normal cellar temperature, thus removing the risk of change in the character of the wine which is inevitable whenever heat is applied. Sterilization filters may also be used for the bottling of wines which, though perfectly healthy and fully matured, still contain a quantity of unfermented sugar. The use of the filter eliminates the risk that such wines will later become clouded with lees or turn acid.

The development of the wine will not be hampered by the use of sterilization filters. It is true that they destroy any ferments which have been left in the wine, but, after all, no ferment should remain in the wine once it has finally been bottled. In the making of port, the growers use brandy to stop the fermentation and kill any remaining ferments; for table wines, sterilization filters serve the same purpose.

It was actually the sterilization filter which made it possible for the German grower to keep his wines sweet—very often too sweet in comparison with the alcohol content.

In 1958 a new law introduced yet another innovation. For many years opinions had differed regarding the treatment of German wines and many complaints had been made to the effect that the new vinification would kill the character of German wines. This was a reference to the so-called *süssgehaltene* wines—those wines in which fermentation had been interrupted artificially by sterilization, filtration, or refrigeration, and where a high percentage of sugar was left unfermented. Under the new law this treatment must not result in a wine which contains more than twenty per cent of the original sugar in an unfermented state at the time when the wine is being marketed, i.e. either offered *en carafe* or bottled for sale. The law, of course, recognises that in some vintages certain wines, especially of the Auslese, Beerenauslese and Trockenbeerenauslese classes, may contain so much original sugar that it is impossible to gain a full fermentation. Such wines always have a great amount of unfermented sugar.

Bottling through a sterilizing filter prevents a secondary fermentation in bottle, but before the bottler can take this step he must know that the wine is stable in other ways and that no turbidity is to be feared. Chemical processes are going on in the wine all the time, processes which create turbidity. If he can get rid of the causes, the bottler can bottle the wine young and fresh. One of the causes is the presence of metals—such as iron, copper and zinc—or of albumen, tannic acid, and tartaric acid, which prevent the wine from remaining bright. Iron is the main cause of chemical turbidity.

Most of the copper is precipitated during fermentation, probably as cuprous sulphate or phosphate, or possibly through combination with yeast-gum. The copper traces that remain can be eliminated by what is known as "blue-fining". So, incidentally, can any zinc particle (found in wine only when zinc-coated apparatus has been used), as well as the traces of iron always present in natural wines. In combination, as iron phosphates, iron traces frequently produce a whitish-grey turbidity in the wine which shows an obstinate tendency to recur even when temporarily removed by filtration. A fining with potassium ferrocyanide, a non-poisonous compound, is the remedy. When it is added to the wine, the latter takes a dark blue colour: hence the term "blue-fining".

The use of potassium ferrocyanide was legalised as far back as 1923 because other clarifying media merely remove the solid substances which make the wine cloudy; to deal with the heavy metal salts dissolved in the wine, it is necessary first to turn them into solids. The action of potassium ferrocyanide on the metal salts does that, and the precipitated solids are then easily removable.

Experiments had been undertaken to precipitate the iron content of wine in the form of ferrous tannin by the addition of oxygen, but it turned out that wines thus treated with oxygen took on a very dark colour and were apt to age very quickly. This method was therefore abandoned in favour of blue-fining.

In all German establishments wine is bottled through asbestos filters. Wines which still contain a small proportion of unfermented sugar are, however, always bottled through sterilizing filters. The grower takes special precautions when bottling these classes of wine; not only the filter but also the corks and the bottles are sterilized.

After bottling, the wine is stored in special wine-cellars; it is now on the way to maturity. Whereas some wines take only a short time to mature, others need years, sometimes decades—especially the fine Riesling and Traminer wines, which obtain their full finesse only after years of storage.

Plate 7. Berncastel, with Landshut Castle, in the Moselle district.
Plate 8. Zell, in the Moselle district.

Chapter Three

NAMING THE WINES

Quality in wine cannot be won except at the expense of quantity. Small-bearing but noble species of grapes, be they Rieslings or Pinots, grown on poor soil, on Moselle slate or Champagne lime, will yield a poor crop in terms of gallons per acre. They will, however, be wines of quality, the kind of wines which possess body and bouquet and breeding in perfect harmony. This is true of all the vine-lands and wines of the world, but what is absolutely unique in the history of wine is the degree of individuality which, after a century of untiring efforts towards perfection, the better wines of Germany have managed to attain.

The wine made from the first pickings of grapes will eventually be offered for sale by the vintner, after vinification and bottling, with its birth certificate printed on a label which provides the following information:

1. The name of the village or town where it was grown—Zeltingen, Piesport, Geisenheim, Rüdesheim, Forst, Deidesheim, Nierstein, Oppenheim, etc.
2. The name of the particular vineyard within the administrative bounds of the said town or village—Schlossberg, Kirchenstück, etc.
3. The name of the grape from which the wine was made—Riesling, Sylvaner, Scheurebe, etc.
4. The date of the vintage when the wine was made.

A bottle bearing all such credentials indicates that it contains a good wine. But it is not necessarily the best; there are a number of rungs to climb before getting to the top.

The German wine grower has developed various special harvesting procedures to enhance the excellence of his wine. Words like Spätlese, Auslese, Beerenauslese and Trockenbeerenauslese on the labels imply such special procedures. What do they mean? First, according to the German Wine Law a wine with *any* of the above labels must be a wine to which no sugar has been added, a 100% natural wine.

SPÄTLESE

The grapes which are used for making a *Spätlese* must have been harvested only after the general picking of the grapes and must have been in a state of full ripeness. In other words, the Spätlese label shows that the wine is natural and the grapes have been gathered with special care. The small grower who depends upon the harvest for his livelihood for the next year will not wait longer than he has to for gathering his crop; and as soon as the Commission has given its licence he will pick his grapes regardless of their degree of maturity, for the Commission presumably knows that they contain sufficient sugar to produce wine. But a Spätlese must contain grapes in full-ripe condition only; the state of full ripeness is recognised by the highest possible content of sugar and the lowest possible content of acidity. When the grape starts the ripening process, i.e. when it goes soft and yellow and its skin becomes so thin that the inner part of the grape is visible, the sugar content and the content of acidity are approximately 21–31 promille; but with the progressive ripening of the grape the content of sugar increases and the content of acidity decreases.

Grapes also contain a proportion of malic acid. The riper the grape, the lower the content of malic acid. The characteristic acidity of the grape—tartaric acid—should outweigh the malic acidity when the grapes are fully ripe.

It is only during the ripening process that the aroma materials—the etheric oils—are formed in the grape. Only at this stage is the actual bouquet developed which will later play such a great part as the distinguishing mark of each individual wine (i.e. Riesling, Muscatel, Traminer, etc.).

When the grower leaves his wines until after the general picking of the grapes, and is harvesting only the grapes of one single vineyard, then we have a Spätlese wine.

AUSLESE

The *Auslese* constitutes another method of increasing the quality of the wine. Again the Auslese grapes must be fully ripe, but the procedure is somewhat different. There are in fact three alternative procedures which may be resorted to in order to produce an Auslese.

The most refined method is to gather all bad, sick, rotting or otherwise damaged grapes and leave the remainder hanging on the vines. The grower then has the choice either of gathering his good grapes immediately or of leaving them on the vines with the opportunity of ripening still further. The process can be repeated again, but this time it is not the damaged but the over-ripe grapes which are selected. This procedure may be repeated as often as the grower wishes until he is satisfied that all the grapes have been gathered. Clearly, this procedure is exceptionally expensive since it involves an enormous amount of labour; yet there is no doubt that it is by this method that the finest Auslese wines are produced.

A more usual procedure is as follows. Again, all the bad grapes are gathered at one special picking. The grape-picker is then provided with either a container divided into two or three compartments or one large container with two small sickle-shaped buckets attached. The picker will then separate the berries according to their degree of ripeness and place them in the correct container or compartment—Auslese, Beerenauslese and Trockenbeerenauslese.

The third method is for the picker to put all the grapes into a single container, leaving out only the diseased and damaged grapes. The real sorting process then takes place at a spot just outside the vineyard. The grapes are spread out on a large trestle table and the experts separate the berries into their various grades. This method has the advantage that the standards adopted are more or less uniform and not those of the individual picker.

BEERENAUSLESE AND TROCKENBEERENAUSLESE

The Beerenauslese is made by selecting for separate pressing only over-ripe or "sleepy" grapes. The *Trockenbeerenauslese* is much the same, only more so; as its name implies, it consists in the selection of "sleepy" berries which have been semi-dried by the sun to an almost raisin-like consistency.

"Sleepiness" in grapes is caused by the fungus known as *Botrytis cinerea*, which is apt to attack the fruit in a mild and sunny autumn. Its action is beneficial and greatly improves the quality of the grape. Depending for its existence on large quantities of acid, it destroys the grape-skin by means of its mycelial filaments, causing the water in the berry to evaporate in the dry, sunny, autumn air; the fruit pulp thus grows more concentrated, with a relatively high sugar content, until the berry is finally sun-dried into a natural raisin. The dehydration process may result in the evaporation of as much as three quarters of the water content, bringing the harvest down to a mere quarter of its normal amount.

When gathering the grapes, the harvesters collect these rarer, raisin-like berries in special sickle-shaped containers hung in the punnets into which they throw the rest of the fruit. A foreman in charge of every eight to ten women keeps careful watch to see that no ordinary grapes are mistaken for the genuine sleepy berries and wrongly placed in the special containers. By this process it takes anything up to twenty workers a full two weeks to gather enough fruit from a vineyard of three hectares (nearly seven and a half acres), and the net result may be no more than 300 litres of must.

The highly concentrated must from the over-ripe berries dried up on the vine is so rich in sugar that it may fairly be described as syrupy. This makes its fermentation and after-fermentation a difficult task which can be entrusted only to an expert with long experience and specialized knowledge. Once it has been accomplished, however, the result is a dream of perfection. The finesse, the delicate aroma, the rare bouquet and the noble quality are indescribable. Honey-sweet richness tempered by the clean, pure, finely acidulated flavour of the grapes make this wine the connoisseur's joy. Not easily obtainable, it is of course correspondingly high-priced. The greatest wines of this class are probably the highest-priced in the world.

The partial dehydration of over-ripe grapes which turns them into raisins is an ancient process. It is mentioned in the Old Testament, and Homer speaks both of allowing the grapes to hang on the vines till they are over-ripe and partially dried, and of the process by which they are dried (after picking) by being exposed to the sun on hurdles or beds of straw.

After the wines have been classified by degree there are further categories of selection which are to be found on the wine labels. Thus a wine may be described as *Kabinett*, or *Cabinet*.

KABINETT (CABINET)

What is a *Kabinett* wine? The German Wine Law gives no answer to this question. *Kabinett-Wein* is mentioned in only one byelaw, Article 5, where it is merely defined as a term which may be applied to natural wines only. The expression has yet to be given a judicial definition.

Without doubt, the name *Kabinett* originated in the Rheingau under the administration of the dukes of Nassau, who in Napoleon's time obtained control of many important vineyards. Ducal administrators stored a few casks of their best wines in small cellars (hence the name), and it is said that the top class wines of the Steinberg vineyard were the first wines to receive this additional designation. At that time the label of a *Kabinett* wine bore the signature of the cellarmaster or of two officials of the domain, and this can still be seen in facsimile. Later on, some estates, now confined to the Rheingau, named their best wines in this way, so that in time *Kabinett* became a special guarantee that the wine was natural.

The name *Kabinett*, wherever it is found, is the personal guarantee of the wine grower that he considers the wine under this label to be of specially high quality. One important point is that *Kabinett* wines need not be estate-bottled.

Whilst the *vigneron* who owns, say, a dozen or so acres of *Montrachet* will equalise his whole crop and therefore make only one single wine, his opposite number in the Rhineland, with the same acreage or less, may make five different wines, each of a different degree of sweetness and excellence. He is, indeed, a perfectionist! So much so, in fact, that he goes still one step further, or one rung higher: the wine of each grade or quality is not averaged down or blended, as at Château d'Yquem, but the wine of each cask is kept separate to be bottled and sold under its own number—Fass No., or Fuder No., clearly stated on the wine label.

No wonder the label on a bottle of German wine is of such importance! It gives the whole history of the wine within the bottle—its place and date of birth, its grape, whether it has been produced from specially selected or over-ripe grapes, whether it is an *Original-Abfüllung*, *Kellerabfüllung*, or *Schlossabzug*. All these last expressions mean that the wine has been *château-* or cellar-bottled by the grower. If the wine is not bottled by the grower the label carries the word *Creszenz*, *Gewächs* or *Wachstum* ("the growth of") followed by the name of the grower who, or the concern which, owns the vineyard. All the above expressions contain the guarantee according to German law that the wine is natural.

These, then, are the best wines of Germany. Many of them are indeed great wines and for that reason perhaps they are the exception rather than the rule, just as great men are the exception rather than the rule.

When the label simply bears the expression *natur* or *naturrein*, it means that the wine is natural, genuine, made from the fermented grape juice without any added sugar. But absence of these descriptions does not necessarily denote that the wine is sweetened. Sugar is a carbohydrate which will ferment and raise the alcoholic strength of the new wine. Sugar addition will not add anything to the bouquet or charm, but will provide a drinkable wine. Among this category of "improved" wines we must also mention the wines which are sold under popular names such as Moselblümchen or Liebfraumilch but which may be blends of different vineyards or different vintages; the names are invented names and do not exist geographically.

All this adds up to one important conclusion: the importance of the guarantee of quality which rests on the reputations of *vignerons* and merchants.

There are not many vineyards in the Rhineland and Moselle owned by one single proprietor: most of them are shared by two, three or more growers, all of whom have an equal right to sell their wine under the same vineyard name. Yet it is quite certain that while the names will be the same, the wines will be different. This is inevitable since it is unlikely that any two *vignerons* could be found with identical views on the use of fertilizers, the time of day to pick the grapes, the most effective methods of mashing, the handling of the fermentation, and finally the nurturing and storage of the newly-made wines. Even if their views were identical on such matters, they would be unlikely to have the same financial and natural facilities available; and it would prove impossible for them to produce exactly similar wines.

EISWEIN (ICE WINE)

An interesting phenomenon met only in German wines is the so-called ice wine. In a report dating from 1869 there is evidence that a grower in Traben–Trarbach had produced "ice wine" as early as 1842. Finding that his grapes had become frozen, he nevertheless continued with picking and pressing, more or less as a desperation measure, and was astonished and delighted to discover that he had produced a most beautiful wine which contained not the slightest taste of frost.

In the year 1890 the ripe berries on the vines of certain vineyards were frozen by an "ice rain", that is, by rain falling at a temperature below freezing point. Despite all prophecies to the contrary, the wine proved to be exquisite. The water in the berries had turned to ice, leaving the remaining grape-juice more concentrated and proportionately richer in sugar content. The wines made from this thick syrup were so sweet and fine as to be comparable with outstanding *Auslesen*.

It is, of course, essential that the grapes be gathered and pressed immediately, while the ice remains frozen within the body of the grape. The so-called grape-cake consists of a large lump of ice, and the resulting wine is really the extract of the grape. Moreover, the grapes should already be over-ripe when first affected by the frost. In a year when the grapes have not achieved the maximum degree of ripeness an extract may still be made by the ice-wine process, but the absence of the necessary aroma materials inevitably results in a lack of true finesse.

Ice wine has seldom been made. Over the last hundred years, it is known to have been produced in only ten vintages: 1875, 1880, 1890, 1902, 1908, 1912, 1949, 1950, 1961 and 1962. (Attempts to make ice wine in 1954 and 1956 met with little success.) Most of these vintages produced only small quantities—two casks in 1949, for instance, and one in 1950. Large quantities were made in 1961 for the first time in the history of German viticulture, and in 1962 production increased. In those two years, the cold weather came unusually early.

In order to make real ice wines, the weather during the late harvesting must be exceptionally dry, so that the grapes remain healthy before they are attacked by frost. When the frost comes, they must also be so ripe that the wine retains no disagreeable frosty taste—which is caused by the green stalks of unripe grapes.

The vinification of ice wines is discussed in Appendix 7.

ST NIKOLAUS WINE

A special Spätlese is the *St Nikolaus Wine*.

In Germany one celebrates St Nikolaus' Day on December 6. St Nikolaus is the German Father Christmas; on December 6, his name-day, he visits the children to ask if they have been good during the past year, and to hear their wishes for Christmas. In some vintages, if the weather is favourable, the grower waits to gather his grapes until St Nikolaus' Day; he may lose the whole harvest, but if he succeeds, the grapes may be more concentrated, and the wine may be a fuller, fruitier wine than the wines gathered earlier. In any case, St Nikolaus wines have some sentimental value. In 1961 this risk was taken by quite a number of wine growers in Rhinehessia and the Nahe. St Nikolaus wines do not attain the concentration of ice wines; the ice wines in the Moselle district, reached 146°, and those of the Nahe 115°, but the Nikolaus wine only between 95° and 100°. These wines, however, reflect the risk the grower has taken; he is proud of his venture, and wine lovers value it.

It seldom happens that the grapes remain in the vineyards until the beginning of

January, but it has happened that grapes were gathered on January 6, Twelfth night. These "Three Kings" wines are always a curiosity, available in very small quantities only, and actually considered museum-pieces. This shows what *can* be done in the moderate climate of the German wine-growing districts! Wine made from grapes gathered on New Year's Eve (St Sylvester's Day) is called Sylvester wine.

Incidentally, the Nahe in 1920 produced 12–14 Half-Stücks of St Nikolaus wines, which were considered the best wines of this century, and which kept better than the 1921 of the same district.

FEDERWEISSER

When the must is deposited in the fermentation cask and fermentation has proceeded for a short while, leaving behind a remnant of sugar, the must takes on a milky colour and contains plenty of carbonic acid. This "new" wine is called *Federweisser* and the local inhabitants—especially in the Palatinate district—like drinking the must in this state of fermentation. They drink it to the accompaniment of brown bread and the new season's walnuts or chestnuts. The wine remains in this condition, of course, for only a very short time, and it could never be exported, or even bottled, in this state. It has to be drawn from the cask and drunk on the spot.

MAIWEIN (MAY WINE)

May wine is actually one of the many *Bowle*, or hock cups. The mixing of cups, an old German custom, is the characteristic form of German conviviality. The name *Bowle* is taken from the vessel—the bowl—in which these drinks are mixed. The wines used are usually the most ordinary light table wines. Whereas most cups are based on fruits, such as strawberries, peaches, and pineapple, May wine is based on the fragrant woodruff (*Waldmeister*), the herbal plant growing wild in many German woods. The woodruff is put into a mixing vessel, and wine is added and sugared according to taste.

May wine is bottled commercially in small quantities, using woodruff essence, but May wine remains essentially the thirst-quenching drink for May or June.

JUNGFERWEIN (VIRGIN WINE)

Jungferwein is the first wine produced from a newly planted vineyard. After a vineyard has been left uncultivated for some years, the new wine—which is produced three or four years after re-planting the vineyard—is considered especially good and elegant as the vine has been able to get all the nourishment from ground which has been unproductive for so many years. Generally speaking, the *Jungferwein* has no staying power, but when drunk young it shows an especially fine bouquet and flavour.

Chapter Four

THE VINEYARDS OF GERMANY
AND THEIR GRAPES

Virtually all the vineyards of Germany have always been and still are in the south-west; roughly speaking, in the basin of the Rhine. All the best vineyards, that is to say the vineyards responsible for the best German wines, are those which grace both banks of the Rhine from Frankfurt, where the Main flows into the Rhine, to Bingen, at the junction of the Nahe; those of the Palatinate; those of the Moselle, Saar and Ruwer valleys from Trier to Koblenz; those of the Main valley from Hochheim to Würzburg and beyond; and those of the Nahe and other tributaries of the Rhine.

There are no longer any important vineyards in Silesia, Saxony or other northern and northeastern parts of Germany. Vines could still be coaxed to grow here, as they were in former times, but they would not pay, and never did pay, a worthwhile dividend.

During the last decade of the nineteenth century the total acreage of the German vineyards was about 300,000 acres. By the end of the Second World War, they hardly covered half that area. There were several reasons for this sensational reduction. First in importance was the return of Alsace to France in 1918, which removed at one stroke some 93,000 acres from the viticultural map of Germany. The *Phylloxera* pest may be given second place, since it destroyed many more vineyards than the growers could or would replant with the right grapes; for the law of the land henceforth prohibited the planting of hybrids, hardy and free-bearing grapes, the kind of grapes from which only the common wines could be made. Another adverse factor was the growing attraction of the industrial centres, which offered the younger generation higher wages and brighter social amenities than their native villages could provide. This was not a trend peculiar

Plate 9. Schloss Vollrads, in the Rheingau.

to Germany, but the German vineyards suffered more than most because of their steep gradients, on which it was impossible to replace manpower by tractors and other mechanical devices.

However, the higher prices paid for grapes and wines since 1949 have encouraged the replanting of many more vineyards. Unfortunately these have not always been in sites suitable for the production of quality wines—hence, in 1959, yet another new law, limiting the range of districts where new vineyards could be planted.

The progress made by the replanting of Rhineland vineyards since 1949 is borne out by the following figures (in acres):

1949	128,718	1954	145,355	1958	147,840
1951	131,362	1955	149,902	1959	152,488
1952	133,398	1956	149,238	1960	160,450
1953	136,215	1957	146,858		

The 1960 total acreage was divided as follows:

Palatinate	38,660	Rheingau	6,292
Rhinehessia	36,300	Franconia	5,900
Baden–Württemberg	32,205	Middle Rhine	4,042
Moselle, Saar, Ruwer	21,043	Ahr	1,283
Nahe	7,410	All others	7,315

Although the acreage of the German vineyards is appreciably less than it was in pre-war times, the production of German wines has not decreased in anything like the same proportion; far from it. Thanks to the use of more effective fertilizers and other scientific methods of cultivation, an acre of vines now produces nearly three times as much wine as it did fifty years ago under similar weather conditions. Progress in viticulture and the promotion of quality wines has, moreover, been effectively aided by viticultural associations like the Deutsche Weinbauverein. The viticultural colleges founded in all wine districts help in the education of the wine grower, who as a rule has had only an elementary education.

Since we are not so ambitious as to try to deal with all the wines of Germany, but only with the great ones, we do not propose to give more than a few courtesy lines to the vineyards of the Ahr, the Middle Rhine, the Bergstrasse and the Bodensee. We shall deal mostly, if not solely, with the vineyards responsible for the finest wines of Germany, many of which are the peers of the great white wines of the world—some of them the greatest of all. But first a word about the grapes which produce these wines.

THE GRAPES

Whatever the care and skill of the grower, it is the nature of the soil and the local climatic conditions that are responsible for the proportion of quality wine which may be made from any vineyard. The geological formation of the vineyard's soil must necessarily be accepted for what it is, although manure and fertilizers can certainly help a great deal. But there is nothing that can be done about the climate. Rain and sunshine come as and when they choose—not to mention late spring frosts, hail storms and other unpredictable freaks of the weather.

There is, however, one factor man is free to choose as he thinks best: the right kind of grape to grow, the grape that is most likely to flourish and yield the best wine. In Germany, as it happens, there is virtual unanimity as to the most suitable grape for quality wines: it is the *Riesling*. The Riesling is to the Sylvaner what the Pinot is to the Gamay. It is a truly noble grape, responsible for the outstanding excellence and inimitable distinctiveness of all the finer German wines.

The Riesling is practically the only grape grown in all the named sites of the Rheingau, Moselle, Saar and Ruwer vineyards. Other parts of the Rhineland grow a greater or lesser proportion of other grapes, mostly Sylvaner grapes but also some Elbling, Traminer and Gutedel for white wines and Portuguese and Pinot for red wines. But although the greatest of all fine German wines have always been made from Riesling grapes, it must not be forgotten that Rieslings must be given the soil, the aspect and the other conditions which happen to suit them best. They cannot be grown anywhere and everywhere. In the sandstone of the Mittelhaardt of the Palatinate, for instance, the *Traminer* (or *Gewürztraminer*)—also a noble grape—is more suitable than the Riesling. The Traminer is also grown in the better vineyards of Baden, where they usually know it by the name of Klevner.

The Riesling grape has, however, the grave faults of bearing fewer bunches and of being more susceptible to frost than other species. Hence the many attempts which have been made to cross the Riesling with the hardier Sylvaner. The *Sylvaner* grape is grown to a greater extent than any other species, including the Riesling. It enjoys this privileged position because it matures earlier than the Riesling and because its vines thrive in the richer soil of plains and plateaus, yielding a greater quantity of grapes from which a high grade of wine can be made. Such wine is made in some parts of Rhinehessia, the Palatinate, the Nahe valley, Franconia and Württemberg.

One of the most successful of the attempts to cross the Riesling with the Sylvaner resulted in the grape known as the *Müller Thurgau*, which not only bears more fruit than the Riesling but ripens two or three weeks earlier. From an economic point of view both Sylvaner and Müller Thurgau grapes commend themselves to wine growers and wine merchants. They produce many more grapes per acre than the Riesling and the Traminer, and their wines are ready to drink in a matter of months, sometimes weeks, rather than years. Sylvaner-made wines are fresh and pleasing, but of course they do not possess anything like the body or bouquet of Riesling-made wines, let alone their "breeding".

So far the most successful of the many attempts at crossing Sylvaner and Riesling with the object of producing a quality wine is Herr Scheu's *Scheurebe*, a grape utterly unlike the Müller Thurgau. Its good points are that it bears more fruit and ripens ten to fourteen days earlier than the Riesling; it also has a much greater volume of bouquet. It grows best in the Palatinate, although many sites in the Rheingau and Rhinehessia have been planted with the grape. The Scheurebe thrives on poor rather than rich soil.

Further new crossings are: the *Morio-Muscat*, a cross between Sylvaner and Pinot blanc; the *Siegerrebe*, a cross between Riesling and Traminer, also grown by Herr Scheu, producing mild wines with a fine Traminer flavour; the *Main-Riesling*, a crossing of Rhine-Riesling and Franconian Sylvaner which ripens a fortnight before the Riesling grape and, on good or even average sites, produces a really fine wine with all the characteristics of the original Riesling. The name Main-Riesling has been considered misleading, and a different name will be adopted in the near future.

There are quite a number of other grapes grown for the making of the commoner sorts of table wine. Such is the *Elbling*, also called *Räuschling* and *Kleinberger*; these are cultivated in various places but never in large quantities. Wine of indifferent quality is also made, in small quantities only, from the *Chasselas*, a table grape which is very sweet because of its lack of acidity; it is known in Germany as the *Gutedel*. The *Auxerrois* and *Ruländer* are white grapes from France grown in some vineyards of the Upper Moselle, the Saar, Baden and Franconia for the making of good white wines. Their chief asset is that the grapes ripen earlier than either Riesling or Sylvaner.

The latest and most remarkable species of grape introduced in Germany is the *Würzburg Perle* which can stand an unheard-of degree of cold—minus 35 degrees centigrade during the winter and minus 6 degrees in the spring when the sap is actually rising. This remarkable *Weinperle* produces an abundant crop of grapes, and the wine made from them is soft and flowery. It also matures early. It was introduced by Dr Breider, who may have more surprises in store for the viticultural experts of the future.

All these and a few other grapes are grown for the production of white wines. But there are also black grapes, which the Germans rightly call blue, grown for the production of red wines. Here is the full list, taken from the *Bundessortiment*.

BUNDESSORTIMENT

List of admitted vines for planting out.

a)   *Vines for wine production*

1. Helfensteiner (Blauer Weinsberger)
2. Freisamer (Freiburger)
3. Heroldrebe
4. Morio-Muskat
5. N I 11–17 (Mainriesling)
6. Perle
7. Scheurebe
8. Siegerrebe
9. Siegfriedrebe (for export only)
10. Auxerrois
11. Aris (for export only)
12. Blauer Portugieser (red)
13. Blauer Spätburgunder (red wine)
14. Blauer Trollinger (red)
15. Gelber Muskateller
16. Grauer Burgunder

17. Grüner Silvaner
18. Müller-Thurgau
19. Muskat-Ottonel
20. Roter Gutedel
21. Roter Muskateller

22. Roter Traminer
23. St Laurent (red)
24. Weisser Burgunder
25. Weisser Gutedel
26. Weisser Riesling

b) *Root stock*

27. Dr Decker-Rebe
28. 5 C Geisenheim
29. Geisenheim 26
30. Selektion Oppenheim 4

31. Sori
32. Berlandieri × Riparia Kober 5 BB
33. Berlandieri × Riparia Kober 125 AA
34. Riparia × Rupestris 3309 Couderc

THE WINES OF
THE MOSELLE—SAAR—RUWER

It must have been in Olympus, long ago, that a marriage was arranged between pretty Moselle and handsome Rhine. Both flow for many miles in the same northerly direction but not within speaking distance, the Moselle west and the Rhine east of the Vosges Mountains. For a long time the Moselle is a reluctant bride, twisting and curling fretfully in a most feminine and capricious manner, but when she leaves Lorraine at Thionville and enters Luxembourg she turns resolutely towards the east as if her mind were at last made up to surrender. Yet even then the Moselle does not appear to be in any great hurry as she meanders softly through the rich meadows and gentle hills of Luxembourg and its old-world cities, Remich, Wormeldange and Grevenmacher. The Moselle leaves Luxembourg at Wasserbillig, passes through imperial Trier seven miles further on, and then seems to become timorous of the approaching meeting with her groom. The last lap of her course, until she slips finally into his bed at Koblenz, is made up of miles of hair-pin turns and loops, often rushing due south-west back almost to the point she has just left.

Whenever there are hills, plenty of air and sunshine, grapes will grow and give us wine, which may be fair or fine according to the weather each year. If anybody has any doubts, however, regarding the relative importance of sun and soil for the making of fine wine, the Moselle is there to show that the soil holds first place. The Moselle vineyards, during the river's long run through France, get their full share of sunshine and are protected by the Vosges Mountains from those blasting east winds which the vines hate as much as we do. But the soil is not right. It brings forth grapes in plenty, but the wine made from them is just plain wine; it is refreshing, it is sharp and wholesome, splitting fats, removing stains and stimulating the bladder—but not the brain.

Plate 10. Leinsweiler, in the Palatinate.
Plate 11. Kiedrich, in the Rheingau.

There is nothing anybody can do about it. The soil is not, and never can be, the soil to give us fine wine.

Then the Moselle enters Germany, and it is on her way from Trier to Koblenz that her vineyards bring forth truly remarkable white wines, wines possessing an enchanting perfume, slender of body yet by no means thin, wholly admirable. The Riesling grape is, of course, responsible for a great deal but not for everything: it cannot possibly give us anywhere else any wine comparable in charm to the finer Moselle, Saar and Ruwer wines. These are made from Riesling grapes grown fairly high up the steep hill-sides of those favoured rivers, and the slate which is the peculiar geological formation of those hills is of the utmost importance and value.

During the first seven miles of her course in Germany, from Wasserbillig to Trier, the Moselle passes through a number of vineyards which yield a fair amount of useful but quite undistinguished wines; yet the Saar, the largest German tributary of the Moselle, which it enters about three miles above Trier, is able to boast vineyards whose wines are as fine as the finest wines of the Moselle proper. This does not mean, unfortunately, that all Saar wines are wonderful: they are not. Riesling and soil will not show how good their wines can be unless the sun shines long enough and at the right time: the upper Saar Valley has the blast furnaces of heavy industry to keep it warm day and night, but the lower Saar Valley is a very cold corridor where grapes find it difficult to ripen every year. When the sun does oblige, however, the superlative excellence of the Saar wines richly rewards the obstinate optimism of the *vignerons* who refuse to be beaten by the weather.

As one comes down the Saar towards the Moselle, the first vineyards of any note are those of SERRIG, a village straight out of Grimm's fairy tales, sheltering at the foot of a line of wooded bluffs with a chapel on the cliff's edge, the König Johann Berg, where they laid the bones of the blind king of Bohemia who was killed at Creçy in 1346. The remains of King John were transferred, in 1947, to the Cathedral of Luxembourg where they have been given the place of honour of a national memorial.

The best vineyards of Serrig are as follows. (Names in SMALL CAPITALS, here and below, are those sites or vineyards reputed to produce the best wines.)

Antoniusberg	Saarstein	Wingertsheck
Hindenburglay	Schloss Saarfelser	Würzburger Helenenberg
Kupp	VOGELSANG	Würzburger Marienberg

SAARBURG is only a small town but it is the most important of the lower course of the Saar; it has only a few vineyards of its own, and none of great merit, but it has incorporated the vineyards of Niederleuken nearby, the best of them being:

Antoniusbrunnen	Layenkaul	Rausch
Klosterberg	MÜHLENBERG	Schlossberg

OCKFEN's vineyards do produce some quite outstanding wines—if and when the sun is kind! Most of them were planted by the Abbey of St Martin, Trier, which owned the site from 1037 to 1803.

BOCKSTEIN	Heppenstein	St Irminer
Geisberg	Herrenberg	

AYL is a small village, on the left bank of the Saar, with a beautiful fanlike stretch of vineyards facing south, most of them still ecclesiastical property, the property of the Bischof Konvikt and Bischof Priesterseminar of Trier.

Euchariusberg	KUPP	Scheidterberg
Herrenberg	Neuberg	Silberberg
Junkerberg	NIEDERMENNIG	Sommerberg
KRETTNACH		

KONZ is a modest village, so modest that it does not give its name to the wines made from its vineyards; most of them are sold as *Oberemmeler* and some as *Falkenstein*, the only Konz vineyard of any importance, which is owned by the Friedrich Wilhelm Gymnasium.

OBEREMMEL is not actually in the Saar Valley but in a tributary valley close by, adjoining Wiltingen.

Agritiusberg	Hütte	Raul
Altenberg	Karlsberg	Rosenberg
Eltzberg	Lauterberg	SCHARZBERG

WILTINGEN is on the right bank of the Saar and its vineyards produce both more and better wines than any of the other Saar vineyards. The pride of Wiltingen are the wines of the *Scharzhof* and *Scharzberg*. The *Scharzhof* itself is a fine old mansion, the home of the Egon Müller family for many years, and its vineyard is divided into three strips which belong to Egon Müller, Apollinar Joseph Koch and Trier Cathedral: the first two sell their wine as *Scharzhofberger*, without any mention of Wiltingen; the Trier Cathedral sell theirs as *Dom Scharzhofberger*. The *Scharzberg* vineyard adjoins the Scharzhofberg and overflows into the adjacent territory of Oberemmel, but Scharzberg wine, one of the truly great wines of the world, is sold as Scharzberger without any mention of either Wiltingen or Oberemmel.

Braune Kupp	Johannisberg	Rosenberg
Braunfels	Klosterberg	SCHARZBERG
Dohr	Kupp	SCHARZHOFBERG
Gottesfuss	Neuberg	Schlangengraben

The following are proprietors of Scharzhofberg:

Egon Müller (largest owner)	v. Volxem
Hohe Domkirche (second largest owner)	Rautenstrauch
Vereinigte Hospitien	Kesselstadt
Apollinaris Koch	v. Hövel

According to a local saying, a vintage is a good vintage when there are 1,400 Fuder of wine made from Wiltingen vineyards, that is, as many Fuder as there are inhabitants.

KANZEM or CANZEM is an important village built on the west or left bank of the Saar, facing north, but its vineyards are up on a slope of the hill, facing south, on the other side of the river.

Altenberg	Kelterberg	Unterberg
Berg	Ritterpfad	Wolfsberg
Hörecker	SONNENBERG	

WAWERN is a small village below Kanzem and on the same left bank of the Saar, and its vineyards adjoin those of Kanzem, but there are not so many of them.

Goldberg	Jesuitengarten	Ritterpfad
Herrenberg		

FILZEN is the last village of the Saar Valley before this river joins the Moselle: its vineyards are not important, and their wine is not of any particular merit, unless of an exceptionally hot vintage.

Neuberg	Urbelt	VOGELBERG
Pulchen		

TRIER is a most interesting city from an antiquarian, an ecclesiastical, or an artistic point of view, but it has also been for centuries past and still is the very heart of the vineyards of the Moselle, Saar and Ruwer. Its own vineyards are almost negligible, barely fifty acres of Riesling-planted slopes:

Herrenberg	Klosterberg	Neuberg

Its municipal cellars, however, can, and often do, house 30,000 Fuder, or over 6½ million gallons of Moselle, Saar and Ruwer wines. In the past the archbishops of Trier were among the greatest owners of vineyards as well as most generous in their gifts of vineyard sites to religious orders; to this day the Trier Cathedral Chapter, and several episcopal colleges and hospitals, could not meet ever-rising costs if they did not have an assured revenue from the sale of some of the finest white wines of the Moselle, Saar and Ruwer wines of their own vineyards. Trier is also today, as it has been since medieval times, noted for those famous annual public auctions at which great quantities of newly made wines, and some of the older wines as well, are sold. It is also the seat of the provincial *Weinbaulehranstalt* (viticultural college), a seat of wine lore and learning, responsible in no small measure for the high standard of the quality of the Moselle, Saar and Ruwer wines.

Here, too, are the headquarters of the five famous ecclesiastical, charitable, educational and state organisations. A list of the widely distributed vineyards owned by them:

Bischöfliches Priesterseminar

Ayler Kupp	Kanzemer Altenberg	Ürziger Würzgarten
Dhronhofberger	Kaseler Nies'gen	Wiltinger Kupp
Erdener Treppchen	Trittenheimer Apotheker	

Hohe Domkirche

Dom Avelsbacher Herrenberg	Dom Scharzhofberger

Vereinigte Hospitien

Braunfels	Saarfelser Vogelsang	Wiltinger Holle
Kanzemer Kellerberg	Scharzhofberger	Wiltinger Kupp
Piesporter Goldtröpfchen	Serriger Schloss	

Friedrich Wilhelm Gymnasium

Bernkasteler Rosenberg	Jesuitenhofberg	Ockfener Geisberg
Dhroner Hofberg	Mehringer Treppchen &	Trittenheimer Altärchen
Falkensteiner Hofberg	Zellerberg	Zeltinger Sonnenuhr
Graacher Abtsberg	Neumagener Rosengärtchen	

State Domain

Avelsbacher Hammerstein	Ockfener Bockstein	Serriger Heiligenborn
Avelsbacher Kupp	Ockfener Heppenstein	Serriger Höppslei
Avelsbacher Rotlei	Ockfener Oberherrenberg	Serriger Vogelsang
Avelsbacher Thielslei	Serriger Findenburglei	Serriger Wingertsheck
Avelsbacher Vogelgesang		

There are practically no fine wines made from the vineyards of the Moselle between the Saar and the Ruwer above and below Trier. One exception should be made, however, for the vineyards and wines of AVELSBACH, close to Trier. Its best vineyards are owned by the Trier Cathedral and the Rheinland-Pfalz State; the first sold as Dom-Avelsbacher with the site name added. The State sells the wine of its HAMMERSTEIN vineyard which owes its existence, if not its excellence, to convict hard labour.

A little more than two miles downstream from Trier, the Moselle welcomes yet another tributary from the east, the Ruwer, a brook rather than a river, its clear waters babbling and tinkling as they flow faster than do the trains on the ancient narrowgauge railway which follows its course. As one leaves the village of Ruwer, where the

Plate 12. Grape press of 1619 at Schloss Vollrads

two rivers meet, one sees from the road a broad curving slope of serried vines, like a segment of an enormous amphitheatre facing the sun. They are the vines of EITELS-BACH, on the right bank of the Ruwer. The Karthaus Hof was originally a Dominican property, but it was owned by the Carthusians from the fourteenth century until 1802, when Napoleon gave it to the Rautenstrauch family, who have owned it ever since; it is now under the direction of the present Rautenstrauch's son-in-law, Herr von Tyrell. Whenever the sun obliges (as in 1959), he makes wines of quite outstanding excellence which are sold under the name of *Eitelsbacher Karthäuserhofberg*. The other vineyards of Eitelsbach are:

Dominikanerberg	Kehrnagel	Paulinsberg
Hitzlay	Kohlenberg	Sonnenberg
Katharinenberg	Lorenzberg	Steininger
Käulen	Nieschen or Nies'gen	Taubenberg

MERTESDORF-GRÜNHAUS is the village which faces Eitelsbach on the opposite bank of the river. Grünhaus is the beautiful residence of the von Schubert family who own the narrow tree-crested slope on which is grown the famous Maximin-Grünhauser.

ABTSBERG	Johannisberg	Spielberg
BRUDERBERG	Lorenzberg	Treppchen
Herrenberg		

KASEL or CASEL, a little higher up the valley, is the largest of the wine-producing villages of the Ruwer, and its vineyards are also the most important: they produce some very fine wines, although not the peers of the Karthäuserhofberger or Maximin-Grünhauser. One of its vineyards—KATHARINENBERG—is the property of the City of Trier on behalf of its School of Viticulture and Wine-Making. Other Kasel vineyards are:

Dominikanberg	Kohlenberg	Paulinsberg
HITZLAY	Lorenzberg	Steininger
Käulgen	NIESCHEN or NIES'GEN	Taubenberg
KEHRNAGEL		

WALDRACH, at the back of Kasel, has but one vineyard of any note, Waldracher Doktor.

Coming now to the vineyards of the Moselle proper, travelling from the Ruwer to the Rhine, we find a considerable number on both banks of the river. They produce each year a great deal of wine, some of quite outstanding excellence, some of very fair quality, and some, of course, in the plain or *ordinaire* category. The many twists and loops of the Moselle are due to the number of hills which throw their spurs in the way of the river at all sorts of different angles, forcing it to alter its course all the time, but also providing a much greater number of suitable sites for vineyards facing the sun and protected from cold winds. All the finest Moselle wines come from vineyards of the Middle Moselle, from Leiwen to Enkirch, but there are some very pleasant wines made, in good sunny years, from the vineyards of the other territories above Leiwen and below Enkirch. Here is a list of wine-producing villages, and their vineyards, as one journeys downstream from the Ruwer to the Rhine, a journey through some of the most beautiful vinelands of the world.

LONGUICH (*longus vicus*—the long village)

| Herrenberg | Kirchberg | Maximiner-Herrenberg |

MEHRING

| Goldkupp | Hüxlay | Plattenberg |
| Heidenkupp | Kuckuckslay | ZELLERBERG |

DETZEM (*decima lapis*—ten miles mark)

| Königsberg | Maximiner-Klosterlay |

THÖRNICH

| ENGÄSS | RITSCH | Schiess-Lay |
| Ley | | |

KLÜSSERATH

| BRUDERSCHAFT | Königsberg | St Michel |

LEIWEN

| Klostergarten | LAURENZIUS LAY | Ohligsberg |

Before reaching Trittenheim, the Moselle meanders through the rich fields, orchards and gardens of half a dozen villages, some of them near the river, and others a short distance away. Of course, there are vineyards also, but their wines are practically all consumed locally, possibly because they are so good that *vignerons* hate to let them go, but more likely because they are so homely that they do not attract or retain the attention of merchants.

TRITTENHEIM owes its name to Trithemius, a saintly fourteenth-century Abbot of Spanheim, who was renowned for his learning. It is built upon a rock on the left bank of the Moselle, opposite to Leiwen, its slopes covered with vineyards and crowned by a small chapel dedicated to St Lawrence, hence the LAURENZIUS LAY vineyard of Leiwen and LAURENZIUSBERG of Trittenheim.

The better vineyards of Trittenheim are:

ALTÄRCHEN	LAURENZIUSBERG	Sonnteilen
APOTHEKE	Neuberg	Vogelsang
Clemensberg	Olk	Weierbach
Falkenberg	Sonnenberg	

NEUMAGEN (*Novigamus*) A little way down the Moselle, on the opposite bank, Neumagen, one of the oldest villages of the Moselle, stands upon the high ground which rises where the little River Dhron flows into the Moselle. Its vineyards do not produce any wines of remarkable quality and Neumagen is chiefly noted for the interesting Roman remains which have been unearthed there.

ENGELGRUBE	Lasenberg	Pichter
Hengelberg	LAUDAMUSBERG	Rosengärtchen
Kirchenstück	Pfaffenberg	Thierlay

DHRON lies behind Neumagen along a little tributary valley.

Grosswingert	Kandel	ROTERD
Hengelberg	Pichter	Sangerei
HOFBERG		

PIESPORT is said to derive its name from *Pepini Portus* (the Gate of Pepin), Pepin being the first king of the Carolingian dynasty (A.D. 752)—although it is difficult to imagine of what military value Piesport could ever have been. It consists of a straggling row of houses squeezed between the river and a mountain with tier upon tier of vineyards rising in great curves facing south, above the north bank of the Moselle. The wines of Piesport are among the very best of the Moselle.

Bildchen	Hohlweid	Schubertslay
Falkenberg	Lay	Taubengarten
GOLDTRÖPFCHEN	Michelsberg	Treppchen
Gräfenberg	Pichter	Weer
Güntherslay		

MINHEIM

Grauberg	Lay	Rosenberg

WINTRICH, a village round the bend of the Moselle, sits unafraid below the butt-ressed terrace walls of its vineyards along the very face of the rock.

Geierslay	Ohligsberg	SIMONSBERG
Grosser Herrgott	Rosenberg	Sonnseite
Neuberg		

KESTEN

Herrenberg	Niederberg	Paulinshofberg

BRAUNEBERG is a former settlement of the Romans, who planted its first vineyard and called the hill *Dulcis Mons*, hence Dusemond, which was its name until 1920 when it took the better-known name of Brauneberg, the Brown Hill. It owes its fame to the very high quality of its wines. It is a steep and lofty hill facing south-east and completely covered with vines—all of them Rieslings, of course.

Bürgerslay	JUFFER	Obersberg
Falkenberg	Kammer	Sonnenuhr
Hasenläufer	Lay	

MÜLHEIM

Bitsch	Kloster	Sonnenlay
Johannisberg		

VELDENZ is about two miles to the east of the Moselle in the valley of the Veldenz, one of the Moselle's many small tributaries.

Carlsberg	Geisberg	Neuberg
Elisenberg	Kirchberg	

LIESER is a very small village with a fine modern château, one of the residences of the von Schorlemer family, with an important stretch of very fine vineyards behind it.

Kirchberg	Paulsberg-Niederberg	Rosenberg
Niederberg	Pfaffenberg	Schlossberg

BERNKASTEL is the chief city of the Middle Moselle, not a great city in size, but greater than most in fame. Viewed from the topmost of the vineyards which rise from its old houses with roofs of variegated colours on three sides, Bernkastel is one of the most picturesque and attractive little towns imaginable, with the Moselle lying like a silver girdle around it. Across the bridge, on the left bank of the river, is KUES or CUES, also with vineyards all around. By far the best known vineyard of Bernkastel is the DOKTOR, owned by Dr H. Thanish, Deinhard of Koblenz, and Lauerburg. Unfortunately, the fame of Bernkastel Doktor has grown to such an extent that the demand has completely outrun the supply. The heirs of the original Dr Thanish have met the difficulty by offering their Doktor wine under the label *Doktor und Graben*, GRABEN being the vineyard next to the *Doktor*. Messrs Lauerberg sell their wine under the label of *Bernkasteler Doktor und Bratenhöfchen*, and Deinhard, the third part-owners, sell theirs as *Doktor und Badstube*. There are a number of other good vineyards of both Bernkastel and Kues, that is on the right and left banks of the Moselle, such as:

BERNKASTEL

BADSTUBE (includes Eich, Theurenkauf, Olk, Lay and Kirch-grabe)	BRATENHÖFCHEN (includes Held, Rosenberg, Pfalz-graben)	DOKTOR JOHANNISBRÜNNCHEN Schlossberg SCHWANEN

KUES

| Kardinalsberg | Rosenberg | Weissenstein |

GRAACH The Moselle changes its course from east to west as it leaves Bernkastel for Graach and Wehlen, which is why the vineyards of those two famous growths are on the right bank of the river. The Weingut *Josephshof* wines of Graach are sold under the name of the Estate *Josephshöfer* without the name of Graach or site names. Sites:

Abtsberg	HIMMELREICH	Münzlay
Bistum	Hömberg	Petrus
DOMPROBST	Kirchlay	Rosenberg
Goldwingert	Lilienpfad	Stablay
Heiligenhaus	Münich	Tirlei

WEHLEN can pride itself on having the finest vineyard of the Moselle in its SONNEN-UHR (which takes its name from the sun-dial fixed in the heart of this steep, sun-drenched, hillside vineyard). The greatest owner of Wehlen vineyards is Zach. Berg-weiler-Prüm, who for some years has refused to use the cream of his vineyards for *Beeren-* or *Trockenbeerenauslesen*; but his *Spätlesen* and *Auslesenweine* are most refined and distinguished wines.

Abtei	LAY	Rosenberg
Feinter	Münzlay	SONNENUHR
Klosterlay	NONNENBERG	Wertspitz

ZELTINGEN is a small town of no great interest in itself but with a wonderful expanse of vineyards, nearly five hundred unbroken acres of Rieslings, rising sharply behind it: they produce a very large quantity of wine, some of which is excellent, the peer of the best wines of Wehlen or Bernkastel, whilst a good deal of plain Zeltinger is definitely *plain*.

Bickert	Kirchlay	Sonnenuhr
HIMMELREICH	Rotlay	Stefanslay
Hirzlay	SCHLOSSBERG	Steinmauer
Kirchenpfad	Schwarzlay	Welbersberg

ERDEN is a small village perched on a narrow ledge above the right bank of the Moselle. Its vineyards, at the rear, climb a cliff as nearly perpendicularly as any vine can possibly grow.

Buslay	Herzlay	Rotkirch
Filiusberg	Hötlay	Schönberg
Franklay	Kaufmannsberg	TREPPCHEN
Herrnberg	Prälat	

ÜRZIG is a more important village than nearby Erden, and its vineyards rise steeply behind it at a safe distance from the flood waters of the Moselle which, nevertheless, find their way occasionally into the cellars, and even into the livingrooms, of its old stone houses.

KRANKLAY	Schwarzlay	WÜRZGARTEN
Lay		

From Ürzig the Moselle changes its course once more from west to east, and leaves behind it those vineyards which are responsible for all truly great Moselle wines. The next villages are:

KINHEIM

Eulenberg	Löwenberg	Rosenberg
Hubertusberg	Peterberg	

KRÖV or CRÖV

Halsbach	Niederberg	Petersberg
Heislay	Paradies	STEFFENSBERG

The most popular wine of Kröv, in Germany, is that which is sold under the label *Nacktarsch*, showing a bare-bottomed boy.

WOLF

Goldgrube	Herrenberg	Sonnenlay

TRABEN–TRARBACH are little twin towns, Traben on the left and Trarbach on the opposite bank of the Moselle. The vineyards of Trarbach are on the lower slopes of the Grafenburg and produce better wines than those of Traben.

TRARBACH

Burgberg	Hühnerberg	Ungsberg
Halsberg	SCHLOSSBERG	

TRABEN

Backhaus	KRÄUTERHAUS	Steinbacher
Bergpächter	Rickelsberg	WÜRZGARTEN
Geispfad		

ENKIRCH, the next village, is most picturesque and its vineyards produce some pleasant wines, although it is at the limit of the Middle Moselle, beyond which few wines possess real merit except in unusually hot years.

Edelberg	Hinterberg	STEFFENSBERG
Herrenberg	Monteneubel	Weinkammer

REIL

Heissenstein   Görlay

From here to Koblenz, where the Moselle meets the Rhine, the only places with vineyards responsible for some fair white wines are as follows:

PÜNDERICH

Farlay	Marienburg	Rosenberg
Goldlay	Peterslay	Staaden

ZELL

Burglay	Nossberg	Schwarze Katz
Domherrn		

The Schwarze Katz (Black Cat) has, like the Kröver Nacktarsch, achieved great popularity in Germany.

COCHEM

Langenberg   Pinnerberg   Schlossberg

POMMERN

Goldberg	Kapellenberg	Rosenberg
Greismund		

KOBERN

Fahrberg   Uhlen   Weissenberg

WINNINGEN

Hamm	Röttgen	Uhlen
Rosenberg		

The vineyards of the Moselle, Saar and Ruwer cover some 20,000 acres, but fully two-thirds produce none but the commoner sort of table wine, refreshing and pleasant enough and above all cheap enough to be within the means of all but the really poor. The vineyards responsible for the great white wines of the Moselle, Saar and Ruwer, wines whose superlative excellence commands also superlative prices in the world's markets, do not add up to more than about 6,200 acres.

Before leaving the Moselle, just a few words about *Moselblümchen*. *Moselblümchen* —the flower of the Moselles—how many promises does it contain to the occasional wine drinker! But in reality, generally speaking, *Moselblümchen* is the cheapest of all Moselles listed; it is a fancy name for a Moselle wine which is legally not entitled to a geographical name, or it comes from an unknown place, in most cases from the Upper Moselle.

The wine drinker who is looking for value should always remember that all expenses

—from the gathering of the grapes to the bottling, for packing, dispatch and freight, not to forget the duty—are in most countries much the same for *all* table wines. A wine which costs only a fraction more, represents therefore a much greater quality.

THE WINES OF THE RHEINGAU

When the Rhine decides to turn its back on its native Switzerland at Basle, it keeps a remarkably straight course to the north until the River Main joins it opposite Mainz. From there to Bingen, where it is joined by another river, the Nahe, the Rhine is forced to change its course from north to west by the massive barrier of the Taunus Mountains. The Rheingau is the name given to the strip of land which lies between the right bank of the Rhine and the Taunus foothills and extends a few miles both north and east. Its vineyards are by no means as extensive as those of Rheinhessen, on the opposite bank of the Rhine, from Mainz to Bingen, but they are responsible for a greater proportion of fine wines, as well as for some which may rightly claim to be among the greatest of the great white wines of the world. The great white wines of the Rheingau possess an intensity of bouquet which can be almost overpowering, a fullness of body which is entirely free from coarseness, and above all an aristocratic distinction or "breeding" which is impossible to describe but as admirable as it is rare. Of course, not all Rheingau wines are aristocrats; they are not all Riesling and hillside wines, but it may be said that of the 5,500 acres of Rheingau vineyards, fully one third produce really great wines—an exceptionally high proportion—one third produce quite good wines; and one third produce commoner beverage wines which are consumed locally and never exported.

Going downstream from the Main to the Nahe, the vineyards of the Rheingau are as follows.

HOCHHEIM The vineyards of this old city, some three miles upstream on the river Main before it joins the Rhine, are quite remarkable in one respect: they are the only vineyards of the Rheingau planted on what is practically flat ground. Yet their wines are not only good wines but the best of them possess the distinctive personality of the best Rheingau wines. This is evidently the reason why Hochheim has always been included in the Rheingau, although it is over ten miles from the Taunus foothills and the Rheingau proper.

Hochheim and its vineyards were sold by the Chapter of Cologne Cathedral in 1273 to the Chapter of Mainz Cathedral, which owned the best vineyards of Hochheim until 1803. Today the two best vineyards of Hochheim still bear their original ecclesiastical names, Domdechaney (cathedral deanery) and Kirchenstück (church piece), the first being much better known than the second. The greater share of the Domdechaney vineyard is owned by the *Domdechant Wernersches Weingut*, but the State Domains, the city of Frankfurt-on-Main, and Graf von Schönborn also own parts of it. Another of the

Plate 13. Vineyards of the Ahr in autumn.

fine ecclesiastical vineyards near Hochheim's old church is named Hölle. Hölle is derived from the Old German *Halda* or *Helda* which meant the slope of a hill: it stands for "hillside" and not "hell", as it is sometimes wrongly translated. It belonged to the Carmelites until 1803, when the city of Frankfurt-on-Main finally acquired it. To this day, Hochheimer Hölle is the municipal tipple at Frankfurt's famous *Ratskeller*.

Just a word about the estate known as the "Queen Victoria Vineyard" (Königin-Viktoria-Berg). This vineyard was christened after Queen Victoria. In 1850 she paid a visit to the vineyard which produced her favourite wine, as a result of which permission was asked of the Royal Court to give the "Lage" the new name. It displays a monument to her within its own precincts, and on December 5, 1950, the town of Hochheim celebrated the centenary of the Lage "Königin-Viktoria-Berg".

Other Hochheim vineyards:

Bein	Kohlkaut	Stein Kreuz
Bettelmann	Neuberg	Stiehlweg
Daubhaus	Raber	Wandkaut
Domdechaney	Rauchloch	Weid
Gehitz	Sommerheil	Weisserd
Hölle	Stein	Wiener
Kirschenstück		

WALLUF When we reach the little Rhine harbour of Nieder-Walluf we set foot on old Rheingau territory and, turning our back on the river, soon come to the vineyards of Ober-Walluf, in a narrow valley leading to Martinsthal. Although there is still a lower and an upper village, the *Nieder* and *Ober* are no longer used and the name of Walluf applies to both.

Bildstock	Oberberg	Steinritz
Gottesacker	Röderweg	Unterberg
Langenstück	Sonnenberg	Walkenberg
Mittelberg		

MARTINSTHAL is the new name of a very old village which grew tired of being called *Neudorf*—New Village: its vineyards on the foothills of the Taunus Mountains produce some very fair wines, although none of outstanding merit.

Geisberg	Oberrödchen	Steinberg
Heiligenstock	Pfaffenberg	Wildsau
Langenberg	Sand	

KIEDRICH, like Martinsthal and Rauenthal (see below), lies back in the hills above Eltville, and its vineyards are mostly in a sheltered valley dominated by the Scharfenstein, the ruins of a medieval castle. Their wines are superior to those of Martinsthal, most of them being the peers of the second-best wines of nearby Rauenthal. The famous church, known as "the house of Our Good Lady", contains many gifts from

Sir John Sutton, Bt, of Norwood Park, who loved the "wine village" of Kiedrich and its church. It contains the oldest German organ (1630) and a second one with pipes of the fourteenth century. It was the reason why Sir John Sutton came to Kiedrich in 1857, to stay and become a Maecenas who during the sixteen years until his death donated no less than 240,000 guilders.

Berg	Heiligenstock	Turmberg
Brück	Klosterberg	Wasserros
Dippenerd	Langenberg	Weihersberg
Gräfenberg	Sandgrube	

RAUENTHAL is a small village and its vineyards produce less wine per acre than any other vineyards in the Rheingau, which in all likelihood is the reason why the wines of Rauenthal are certainly among the best, and known as such in overseas markets.

BAIKEN	Herberg	Pfaffenberg
Burggraben	Hilbitz	Siebenmorgen
Ehr	Hünnerberg	Steinmächer
Eisweg	Kesselring	Wagenkehr
Gehrn	Langenstück	Wieshell
Geierstein	Maasborn	Wülfen
Grossenstück	Nonnenberg	

ELTVILLE Returning to the Rhine we come to Eltville, no longer the important city it once was, but still the largest of the Rheingau towns. Here are the headquarters or administrative offices of the former Prussian domains, now and since 1945 the Hessian domain. They originally formed the bulk of the Duke of Nassau's vineyards, and even today they remain the largest stretch of vineyards under one ownership in the Rheingau, the domain being predominant particularly in the following vineyards:

Albus	Kalbpflicht	Sandgrube
Alte Bach	Klümbchen (sole	Schlossberg
Bunken	property of	Setzling
Freienborn	Schloss Eltz)	Sonnenberg
Grauer Stein	Langenstück	Steinmächer
Grimmen	Mönchhanach	Taubenberg
Hahn	Posten	Weidenborn
Hanach Hühnerfeld	Rheinberg	

ERBACH Only about half a mile downstream from Eltville, we come to Erbach, the most famous vineyard of which, MARCOBRUNN, is a narrow strip of vines alongside river, road and rail as far as the next village of Hattenheim; which is why the vineyard is called Marcobrunn, the "boundary fountain"—*Marke* being in Old German a boundary. The best wines of Erbach are among the greatest of all Rheingauers, that is to say, the greatest white wines of the world. Although St Mark happens to be the patron saint of Erbach's parish church, his name has nothing to do with Marcobrunn. Five proprietors own the Marcobrunn vineyard: Baron von Simmern, Hessian Domain, Prince Friedrich of Prussia, Baron von Ötinger, and Graf Schönborn.

Brühl	Kalig	Seelgass
Gemark	Langenwingert	Siegelsberg
Herrnberg	Michelmark	Steinchen
Hinterkirch	Pellet	Steinmorgen
Hohenrain	Rheinhell	Wormlock
Honigberg		

HATTENHEIM, which is close to Erbach, is a much more important as well as a more picturesque village, almost a little town, with green meadows sloping gently to the Rhine in front of its old houses and high mountains behind them, with vines, of course, everywhere, on both low and high ground. The low level vineyards are practically the continuation of the Marcobrunn vineyard of Erbach, from the "boundary fountain" westwards to the first houses of Hattenheim. However, good as the wines of the low level of Hattenheim may be—and they are quite good—their fame is eclipsed by that of the *Steinberger*, the wine of a wonderful vineyard of 62 acres which was originally planted and walled in by the Cistercian monks, and is now owned by the Hessian State. Steinberg is just about a mile from Hattenheim and so is Kloster Eberbach close by: this is an ancient monastery wonderfully well preserved, and housing a remarkable collection of old wine presses; its great hall is used for wine auctions and its cellars are a most fitting home for the Steinberg wines to lie and mature in peace. The great advantage of undivided ownership of a large vineyard is the consistently dependable quality of all its wines: there is no such dependability, for instance, in the wines of Clos Vougeot. There are, however, quite a number of different Steinbergers of one and the same vintage, because the wines which are made each day are never blended with those of the day before or the day after, as is done at the great Sauternes *châteaux*. The less remarkable wines of Steinberg are labelled plainly *Steinberger*, and the better ones *Steinberger Kabinett*, with the addition of Spätlese, Auslese, Beerenauslese or Trockenbeerenauslese, as the case may be, and with the number of the individual cask in which the wine was reared.

Among the other fine vineyards of Hattenheim, the following deserve notice:

Aliment	Gasserweg	Pfaffenberg
Bergweg	Geiersberg	Pflänzer
Bitz	Hassel	Rothenberg
Boden	Hinterhausen	Schützenhäuschen
Boxberg	Kilb	Stabel
Deutelsberg	Klosterberg	Weiher
Dillmetz	Mannberg	Willborn
Engelmannsberg	NUSSBRUNNEN	Wisselbrunnen

HALLGARTEN is one of the upland villages of the Rheingau: it is sheltered from the east by the towering height of the *Hallgartener Zange* (Hallgarten Pincers) and its vineyards are close to the famous Steinberg, immediately to the west: they produce wines of superlative excellence.

Biegels	Hitz	Reuscherberg
Deutelsberg	Jungfer	Rosengarten
Egersberg	Kirchenacker	Sandgrub
Frühenberg	Mehrhölzchen	Schönhell
Geiersberg	Neufeld	Würzgarten
Hendelberg		

Hallgarten has four co-operatives:—the English, the Boers, the Germans and the Boxers. The first was established at the time of the Boer War, and was composed of the wealthier growers. They were dubbed "the English" by the poorer growers, who were excluded—and whose co-operative, in turn, became "the Boers". The "Germans" were a third group of growers, excluded from the first two, who formed their own co-operative shortly afterwards. The names have since come to be used officially. The Boxers, formed a few years ago, took their "period" name from the Chinese Boxer Rebellion.

Close together below and west of Hallgarten there are three other wine-producing villages: Östrich, Mittelheim and Winkel.

ÖSTRICH's vineyards slope gently in a semi-circle from the vineyards of Hallgarten down to the Rhine.

Aliment	Klosterberg	Pflänzen
Deez	Klostergarten	Räuscherberg
Doosberg	LENCHEN	Rheingarten
Eiserberg	MAGDALENENGARTEN	Rosengarten
Hölle	Mühlberg	St Gottesthal
Kellerberg	Pfaffenpfad	St Nikolaus
Kerbesberg		

MITTELHEIM's vineyards produce wines of fair to fine quality.

EDELMANN	Magdalenenacker	St Nikolaus
Goldberg	Neuberg	Schlehdorn
Gottestal	Oberberg	Stein
Honigberg	Rheingarten	

WINKEL adjoins Mittelheim, but its vineyards produce some very remarkable wines, none finer nor more famous than the great wines of SCHLOSS VOLLRADS, the property of the noble Matuschka-Greiffenclau family. Its 81 acres of vines are the largest

Plate 14. Sculpture with bottles

privately owned vineyard of the Rheingau. The estate-bottled wines of Schloss Vollrads are today, in good vintages, among the best of the Rheingau schloss wines and they are sold under five capsules of different colours (according to their individual standard of excellence), as follows. The colours in brackets are sub-divisions of the five grades, each in ascending order of quality.

Schloss Vollrads, green capsule (green, green-silver)
Schloss Vollrads Schlossabzug, red capsule (red, red-silver, red-gold)
Schloss Vollrads Kabinett, blue capsule (dark blue, light blue, blue-silver, blue-gold)
Schloss Vollrads Auslese, pink capsule
Schloss Vollrads Beerenauslese, white capsule (Trockenbeerenauslese: white-gold plus neck label showing the tower of Schloss Vollrads)

All the above wines, bottled on the estate of the Schloss Vollrads, bear, in addition to the name, the statement: *Originalabfüllg Graf Matuschka-Greiffenclau'sche Kellerei und Gutsverwaltung* ("Genuine produce of the cellars and estate of Count Matuschka-Greiffenclau"). It is noteworthy that the Auslese and higher qualities are not called *Kabinett* wines. This variety of qualities is of course produced in excellent vintages only. In some vintages no other than the ordinary Schloss Vollrads or *Schlossabzug* are produced. Wine which does not come up to the necessary standard, and which has to be improved, is sold without the right to the use of its name of origin and goes to Sekt-manufacturers.

Among the other fine vineyards of Winkel are the following:

Ansbach	Gutenberg	Kläuserberg
Bienengarten	HASENSPRUNG	Kreuzberg
DACHSBERG	Honigberg	Oberberg
Eckeberg	Jesuitengarten	Plankener
Ensing	Klaus	Steinchen

A short distance westwards, one is bound to stop and admire from the river road the most spectacular vineyard in all Germany, JOHANNISBERG, an immense symmetrical, really beautiful amphitheatre of vines, crowned by the Schloss. From this point there is no sign of the little village of Johannisberg which hides behind the Schloss. There never could be a more ideal site for a vineyard, but, contrary to popular belief, there is no evidence that Charlemagne was responsible for its first vines. It is known, however, that Archbishop Ruthard of Mainz (1088 to 1109), gave the site to the Benedictines; they built a monastery and planted the first vineyard on the hill which was called at the time Bischofsberg. Napoleon gave it to his Maréchal Kellerman, but at the Congress of Vienna in 1815 it was given to the Emperor of Austria, who in turn presented it to the Fürst von Metternich of the day, whose descendants still own it today, but the Habsburgs have still reserved the right of a tenth of the crop.

In most years there are three different *cuvées* made at Schloss Johannisberg. Here is the classification of the 1959 vintage: the first *cuvée* is of the wines of ordinary quality and is bottled at the estate with a red seal; the second *cuvée* is of better-quality wines and bottled at the estate with a green seal; the third *cuvée* is made up of Spätlese wines and bottled with a pink seal. In good vintages, when it is possible to make Auslese, Beerenauslese and Trockenbeerenauslese wines, these are not made into *cuvées*, but each cask is kept separately and bottled individually at the estate, also with a pink seal.

In each category of the Schloss Johannisberg wines there are some which are selected to be bottled as *Kabinett* wines: the ordinary wines are bottled with either a white or an orange seal, the *Spätlesen* and *Auslesen* with a blue seal, the *Beerenauslesen* and *Trockenbeerenauslesen* with a gold seal. Unfortunately, Schloss Johannisberg, despite its position on such a favoured site, was unlucky in 1959 and did not produce a Beerenauslese or Trockenbeerenauslese wine; but the memory of great wines produced there in 1943, 1945 and 1949 lingers on.

All other wines of Johannisberg are sold either as "Johannisberger and site name" or as "Dorf Johannisberger".

The other vineyards of Johannisberg are as follows:

Erntebringer	Klaus	Steinacker
Goldatzel	Kläuserberg	Steinhölle
Hansenberg	Kochsberg	Sterzelpfad
Hölle	Mittelhölle	Unterhölle
Kahlenberg	Nonnenhölle	Vogelsang
Kerzenstück	Schwarzenstein	Weiher

GEISENHEIM is next: an old town by the Rhine famous for its viticultural training college and its extensive vineyards stretching practically from those of Johannisberg in the east to those of Rüdesheim to the north and west, a distance of nearly two miles.

A memorial to Longfellow, in the form of a fountain of Nassau marble, stands on the Bishop Blum Platz, at the foot of the Rheingau "Dom" (cathedral) whose bells inspired Longfellow to write the closing stanzas of his *Golden Legend*. Laid into the walls are marble plaques on which is inscribed the verse referring to the Geisenheim Bells.

> What bells are those that ring so slow,
> So mellow, musical, and low?
> They are the bells of Geisenheim,
> That with their melancholy chime
> Ring out the curfew of the sun.

The vineyards of Geisenheim produce a great deal of wine from fair to fine (on occasion very fine), and none better than the wines from the vineyards owned by the School of Viticulture:

Altbaum	Kapellengarten	Marienberg
Backenacker	Katzenloch	Mäuerchen
Decker	Kilsberg	Monchpfad
Fegfeuer	Kirchgrube	Morschberg
Fuchsberg	Kläuserweg	Rosengarten
Hinkelstein	Kosakenberg	Rothenberg
Hoher Decker	Kreuzweg	Schlossgarten
Hoher Rech	Lickerstein	Steinacker

RÜDESHEIM, opposite Bingen, with its wine museum in the Brömserburg, is the westernmost town of the viticultural Rheingau proper, its houses strung in a long line by the Rhine, and its many vineyards occupying terraces cut into the face of the steep mountainside—the Berg—high past the ruins of the Ehrenfels Castle. The wines of Rüdesheim, more particularly those of the Berg vineyards, are among the best of the Rheingau wines.

Rüdesheim, too, is something of a pleasure resort with many good hotels and pensions along the Rhine. The Rhenish wine taverns flourish along the world-famous *Drosselgasse*, an excellent venue for tasting all Rheingau wines to the sound of music and feasting, although it is not recommended for contemplation.

Berg Bronnen	Berg Mühlstein	Berg Stumpfenort	Häuserweg
Berg Burgweg	Berg Pares	Berg Zinnengiesser	Hinterhaus
Berg Dickerstein	Berg Platz	Berg Zollhaus	Kiesel
Berg Engerweg	Berg Rammstein	Bienengarten	Linngrub
Berg Hellpfad	Berg Roseneck	Bischofsberg	Mühlstein
Berg Katerloch	Berg Rottland	Dickerstein	Wilgert
Berg Kronest	Berg Schlossberg	Engerweg	Wüst
Berg Lay	Berg Stoll	Hasenläufer	

The following are among the most noteworthy winegrowers in the Rheingau:

Verwaltung der Staatsweingüter im Rheingau, Eltville.

Gräfl. Eltz'sche Gutsverwaltung, Eltville.

Graf von Schönborn-Wiesentheid'sches Domänen-Weingut, Hattenheim.

Weingut Dr R. Weil, Kiedrich.

Graf Matuschka-Greiffenclau'sche Kellerei- und Güterverwaltung "Schloss Vollrads", Winkel.

A. von Brentano'sche Gutsverwaltung, Winkel.

Fürst von Metternich; Winneburg'sches Domäne-Rentamt "Schloss Johannisberg", Johannisberg.

Staatl. Lehr- und Forschungsanstalt für Wein-, Obst- und Gartenbau, Geisenheim.

Domdechant Werner'sches Weingut, Hochheim.

Geh.-Rat Aschrottsche Gutsverwaltung, Hochheim.

The first three growers own vineyards in a number of communities, viz:

State-owned Domains

Hattenheim:	Engelmannsberg, Steinberger
Erbach:	Marcobrunn
Kiedrich:	Grafenberg
Rauenthal:	Baiken, Gehrn, Grossenstück, Langenstück, Pfaffenberg, Steinhaufen, Wieshell
Hochheim:	Domdechaney, Kirchenstück
Rüdesheim:	Bischofsberg, Hinterhaus, Klosterkiesel, Berg Roseneck, Berg Rottland, Schlossberg, Wilgert
Assmannshausen:	Höllenberg (red hock)

Graf Eltz'sche Gutsverwaltung

Eltville:	Klümbchen, Langenstück, Mönchhanach, Sonnenberg
Kiedrich:	Sandgrub
Rauenthal:	Baiken, Burggraben, Gehrn, Herberg, Siebenmorgen, Wieshell

Graf von Schönborn-Wiesentheid'sches Domänen Weingut

Hochheim:	Stein, Kirchenstück, Domdechaney
Johannisberg:	Klauser Garten, Klauser Berg
Geisenheim:	Rothenberg
Hattenheim:	Wisselbrunnen, Hassel, Pfaffenberg
Rüdesheim:	Berg Bronnen, Roseneck

THE WINES OF RHINEHESSIA

Although there are in Rhinehessia some 30,000 acres of vineyards to the Rheingau's 5,000, and over 150 wine-producing localities to the Rheingau's twenty-five, the average quality of its wines is not comparable to that of the Rheingau wines. This is due to the richer soil of Rhinehessia, mostly red sandstone along the left bank of the Rhine and a good deal of clay further away from the great river; also to the fact that not more than 10 % of the Rhinehessia vineyards are planted with Riesling grapes. Rhinehessia, in shape, is a rectangle some 30 miles in length and 20 miles in width, clearly marked on the north and east by the bend of the Rhine, from Mainz to Bingen, on the west by the Nahe and on the south by the Pfalz.

Rhinehessia is divided into a number of wine-producing administrative areas (*Kreise*, or districts): Mainz, Oppenheim, Worms, Bingen and Alzey are the five most important of these, all of them on or near the left bank of the Rhine.

MAINZ

Mainz is the least important of the five districts from a wine-producing point of view, but it is the first city of the Province and, incidentally, the birth-place of Gutenberg, traditionally the father of printing.

In Mainz is situated the head office of the Rhinehessian Domain—the greatest vineyard owner in Rhinehessia with vineyards in the following villages:

Bingen	Nackenheim	Oppenheim
Bodenheim	Nierstein	

There are fifteen localities in the Mainz district with vineyards, but none of them produce any wine of real merit, unless one is willing to make an exception for LAUBENHEIM (Edelmann, Hitz, Kalkofen, Johannisberg, Klosterberg, Neuberg) and GAUBISCHOFSHEIM (Gickelsberg, Glockenberg, Herrnberg, Kellerberg, Kreuzwingert, Pfaffenweg, Pflänzer).

OPPENHEIM

Oppenheim is by far the most important *Kreis* of Rhinehessia. There are in the Oppenheim *Kreis* no fewer than 43 wine-producing localities, including Nierstein, the vineyards of which produce more and far better wines than the vineyards of any of the other 42 localities, though four of these situated on the "Rheinfront" are responsible for some fine quality wines: Bodenheim, Dienheim, Nackenheim and Oppenheim. Here is a list of the best vineyards of these five Rhinehessian localities:

BODENHEIM

Bock	Hoch	Mönchpfad
Braun	Kahlenberg	Neuberg
Burgweg	Kapelle	Rettberg
Ebersberg	Leidhecke	Silberberg
Heitersbrünnchen	Leistenberg	WESTRUM

NACKENHEIM

Engelsberg	Kapelle	Rotenberg
Fenchelberg	Kirchberg	Sommerwinn
Fritzenhölle	Rheinhahl	Spitzenberg

NIERSTEIN

REHBACH This name comprises the following site names as registered in the Land Register:

Floss, Hinkelstein, Obere Rehbach, Untere Rehbach, Rehbacher Steig, Sommerseite

Spiegelberg comprising:

Bettzüge, Böllengewann, Diebsweg, Domtal, Findling, Flossgewann, Geisenberg, Grasweg, Hessbaum, Kindswiese, Klauer, Klostergewann, Loch, Lörzweilerweg, Mittelgewann, Mommenheimer Weg, Nackenheimer Loch, Nassgewann, Ohrenberg, Ohrenbrunnen, Ohrenfloss, Pulver, Hoher Rechen, Über der Rehbacher Steig, Vorderer Rolländer, Hinterer Rolländer, Hintere Schmitt, Leimen Schmitt, Steinrutsch, Warte.

Fockenberg comprising:

      Brudersberg, Fockenberg, Fritzenhölle, Ober der Fläschenhahl, Vorderer Rosenberg, Hinterer Rosenberg, Schappenberg, Schmitt, Kleiner Schmitt, Stumpfenloch, Weisenberg.

HIPPING comprising:

      Eselspfad, Fläschenhahl, Fuchsloch, Unterer Hipping, Oberer Hipping, Hinterer Hipping, Kehr, Pfütze, Sommerbirnbaum, Tal.

ST KILIANSBERG comprising:

      Bergkirche, Dorf, Oberer Granzberg, Unterer Granzberg, Kiliansweg, Kiliansäcker, Kreuz, Langgewann, Mockenberg, Reisenberg.

AUFLANGEN comprising:

      Unterer Auflangen, Oberer Auflangen, Hinter den Häuser, Löhgasse, Pfuhlweg, Rohr, Hinter Saal, Ober der grossen Steig.

Ölberg comprising:

      Ölberg, Oberer Ölberg, Schiessmauer, Schlangenberg, Steig, Streng, Warte.

HEILIGENBAUM comprising:

      Bruch, Entenpfuhl, Heiligenbaum, Kelterbaum, Orbel, Riedmühle, Schwabsburger Weg, Stall.

Bildstock comprising:

      Bildstock, Bleiche, Brückchen, Daubhaus, Fäulingsbrunnen, Heugasse, Hörsterweg, Läusbrunnen, Mittel, Muhl, Die Neunmorgen, Oberdorf, Ostergärten, Ried, Riedmühle, Rossberg, Säuloch.

Paterberg comprising:

      Brückchen, Brudersberg, Dalheimer Brunnen, Ober dem Dalheimer Brunnen, Burgrechen, Burgweg, Dauzklauer, Essigkaut, Fahrt, Galgenberg, Galgenhohl, Gemarkrech, Die Glöck, Haasenwörth, Heuwiese, Hölle, Hummertal, Ober dem Hummertal, Hummertaler Hohl, Kanal, Ketzenrechen, Monzenberg, Die 13 Morgen, Auf den 16 Morgen, Oppenheimer Strasse, Ottenberger Gewann, Ober dem langen Rech, Scheinbügel, Das Taubennest, Taubhaus, Wiesengewann, Die zehn Morgen.

"Gutes Domtal" is the generic name for all Nierstein sites.

OPPENHEIM (Seat of a viticultural college)

Daubhaus	Kreuz	SACKTRÄGER
Goldberg	Krötenbrunnen	Schlossberg
Herrenberg	Kugel	STEIG
Herrenweiher	REISEKAHR	Zuckerberg
Kehrweg	Saar	

DIENHEIM

Goldberg	Krötenbrunnen	Silzbrunnen
Guldenmorgen	Rosswiese	Tafelstein

And here are the better-known wine-producing villages (with vineyards shown in brackets) of the Oppenheim *Kreis*:

Armsheim

Bechtolsheim

Biebelnheim

Dalheim

Dexheim (Doktor, Hölle, Königsberg)

Dolgesheim

Eichloch

Eimsheim

Enshcim

Friesenheim

Gabsheim

Gau-Bickelheim (Frongewann, Gans, Goldberg, Hollerstrauch, Kapelle, Kaus, Ober-intersteig, Saukopf)

Gau-Weinheim

Guntersblum (Authental, Bornpfad, Dreissigmorgen, Eiserne Hand, Enggass, Gänsweide, Haseweg, Himmelthal, Kachelberg, Kehl, Kellerweg, Kreuz, Neuweg, Neubaum, Oppenheimerweg, Rost, Sonneberg, Spiegel, Steig, Steinberg, Vogelsrech, Vogelsgärten, Wohnweg)

Hahnheim

Hillesheim

Köngernheim a.d. Selz

Lörzweiler

Ludwigshöhe (Appenthal, Geierscheiss, Honigpfad, Modern, Rheinpfad)

Mommenheim

Nieder-Saulheim

Ober-Saulheim

Partenheim

Schimsheim

Schornsheim

Schwabsburg (Birkenauer, Ebersberg, Federberg, Heileck, Domtal, Kirschplatte, Kupferbrunnen, Neuberg, Schlossberg, Schnappenberg, Tafelstein)

Selzen

Spiesheim

Sulzheim

Udenheim

Undenheim

Vendersheim

Wald-Ülversheim

Wallertheim

Weinolsheim

Wintersheim

Wörrstadt

Wolfsheim

WORMS

Worms (Katterloch, Liebfrauenstift, Luginsland, Maria Münster), is famous in wine history above all for its *Liebfrauenkirche* (the Church of Our Lady) and its *Liebfrauenstiftswein*, the wine from the Liebfrauenstift vineyard which adjoins the church. Here the original vineyards still flourish up to the very walls of the church. Here too, originated the name "Liebfraumilch", a term whose meaning is explained by Dr E. G. Zitzen in *Der Wein in der Wort- und Wirtschaftsgeschichte* (Bonn, 1952):

Liebfraumilch is not a geographical denomination, but a fancy name applicable to all Rhine wines of good quality and pleasant character. The name originated from the vineyards round the Liebfrauenkirche in Worms—the vineyard of the Monks of the Liebfrauenstift. In former days the name of the wine was not Liebfraumilch, but Liebfrauenminch. The word "Minch" is developed from "Münch" which later on became "Mönch". Minchgärten, Minchwege, Minchgassen and Minchpfade, which were formerly in Worms and in other Rhenish wine-villages, were all situated within the walls of old cloisters and belonged to the gardens of the monks. In other words, the term Liebfraumilch arises out of the natural development of the language, and the "milk" in this name has nothing whatsoever to do with the nourishing beverage which we all enjoy in one way or another, and which was not in the minds of the originators of the name Liebfraumilch. It is certainly wrong to translate Liebfraumilch, as it has been translated, as "Milk of Our Lady". In other words, when I say that the name Liebfraumilch originated in Worms, I want to emphasize that the name is the result of shifting of consonants of the spoken word, a phenomenon common to the development of all languages.

The name Liebfraumilch is now given to a considerable quantity of German white wines of very different standards of quality; it may come from any part of the Rhine wine districts—Rhenish Palatinate, Rhinehessia, Rheingau, Nahe, Middle-Rhine—or may be a blend of wines from one of these or even all the districts, and may contain wines of the hinterland only or of the finest vineyards. Under the name Liebfraumilch may be hidden a number of sins; hence the importance of the name of a shipper of repute, or of its registered brand, appearing on the Liebfraumilch labels.

Here, in alphabetical order, are the localities within the administrative boundaries of Worms which have vineyards of their own producing pleasant white table wines which, in good vintages, attain an astonishingly high quality:

Abenheim	Bermersheim	Heppenheim a.d. Wiese
Alsheim mit Hangenwahl-	Dalsheim (Bürgel, Heck,	Herrnsheim
heim (Fischerpfad,	Hubacker, Sauloch,	Hessloch
Friedrichsberg, Früh-	Wachenheimer-Weg,	Hohen-Sülzen
messe, Goldberg,	Wingertstädten,	Horchheim
Ohligstück, Rheinblick,	Zellerweg)	Ibersheim
Römerberg, Rosenberg,	Dittelsheim	Kriegsheim
Sommerhäuschen,	Dorn-Dürkheim	Leiselheim
Sonnenberg)	Eppelsheim	Mettenheim (Goldborn,
Bechtheim (GEYERSBERG,	Frettenheim	Hellborn, Kandelberg,
Rosengarten, Hasen-	Gimbsheim	MICHELSBERG, Mittel-
sprung, Löwenberg,	Gundersheim	berg, SCHLOSSBERG)
Pilgerpfad, Wölm und	Gundheim	Mölsheim
Stein)	Hangen-Weisheim	Monsheim

Plate 15 (overleaf). Baden vineyards near Neuweier,
in the Black Forest.

Monzernheim
Nieder-Flörsheim
Osthofen (Goldberg,
  Hasenbiss, Köhm,
  Lerchelsberg, Leckz-

apfen, Liebenberg,
  Neuberg, Schnapp,
  Wölm)
Pfeddersheim
Wachenheim

Westhofen (Dautensatz,
  Erkelnest, Gries,
  Hackgraben, Prob,
  Schenk, Stassbühl)
Worms a. Rh.

BINGEN

Bingen, on the left bank of the Rhine, facing Rüdesheim across the river, is at the mouth of the River Nahe but officially in Rhinehessia. It has now absorbed and hyphenated with its own name its two nearest neighbours, Bingen-Büdesheim (Nahe) and Bingen-Kempten. Behind Bingen and running eastwards rises the Rochusberg with vineyards practically everywhere, those of Scharlachberg, or Scarlet Hill, a name they owe to the reddish colour of the soil at its western end. The best wines of Bingen are those of the Scharlachberg.

Here are some of the other vineyards of Bingen, with a list of the other twenty-two wine-growing localities within its administrative *Kreis*.

BINGEN

EISELBERG
Mainzerweg
Ohligberg

Rochusberg
Rosengarten

Schlossberg
Schwätzerchen

Bingen Kreis

Appenheim
Aspisheim
Bingen-Kempten (Berg, Lies,
  Pfarrgarten)
Bubenheim
Dietersheim
Dromersheim
Elsheim
Engelstadt
Gau-Algesheim
Gaulsheim
Gensingen

Grolsheim
Gross-Winternheim
Horrweiler
Jugenheim
Nieder-Hilbersheim
Nieder-Ingelheim
  (Famous for red wines)
Ober-Ingelheim
Ockenheim
Schwabenheim
Sponheim
Wackernheim

ALZEY

Alzey has within its district no less than 40 wine-producing localities, all of them further away from both the Rhine and the Nahe, and they produce vast quantities of wine, both red and white, none of which is deserving of the connoisseur's attention:

Albig
Alzey
Badenheim
Bermersheim
Biebelsheim
Bornheim
Bosenheim
Dautenheim
Eckelsheim
Erbes-Büdesheim
Flonheim
Framersheim
Frei-Laubersheim
Fürfeld
Gau-Heppenheim
Gau-Odernheim
Gimbsheim
Hackenheim
Heimersheim
Ippesheim

Lonsheim
Neu-Bamberg
Offenheim
Pfaffen-Schwabenheim
Planig
Pleitersheim
St Johann
Siefersheim
Sprendlingen
Stein-Bockenheim
Tiefenthal
Uffhofen
Vollheim
Wahlheim
Weinheim bei Alzey
Welgesheim
Wendelsheim
Wöllstein
Wonsheim
Zotzenheim

The most important growers of quality wines in Rhinehessia, next to the Domains, are:

Franz Karl Schmitt, Nierstein
Anton Balbach Erben, Nierstein
Weingut Baron Heyl. z. Herrnsheim, Nierstein
Weingut Reinhold Senfter, Nierstein
Gunderloch-Lange'sche Weingutsverwaltung, Nackenheim
Weingut Gunderloch-Usinger, Nackenheim
Weingut Oberst Schultz-Werner, Gaubischofsheim b. Mainz
Oberstleutnant Liebrecht'sche Weingutsverwaltung, Bodenheim am Rhein
Weingut Kommerzienrat P. A. Ohler, Bingen am Rhein
Weingut "Villa Sachsen", Commerzienrat Curt Berger Erben, Bingen am Rhein

THE WINES OF THE PALATINATE
(RHEINPFALZ)

The Bavarian Pfalz was the name given in 1816, at the time of the re-shuffling of the kingdoms, duchies and principalities of Europe when Napoleon's reign had come to an end, to the major part of the lands long held by the Pfalzgrave or Pfalzgräf north of Alsace, east of Lorraine, south and west of Hessia. The outstanding features of the Palatinate are its wonderfully mild climate, the fertility of its soil, and the range of the Haardt Mountains, a northern extension of the Vosges. The Haardt Mountains protect the great Palatinate plain from icy winds from the north as well as from rain and snow from the west: their lower slopes are covered with vineyards which have also invaded the plain: acre upon acre of undulating land 600–700 feet above the level of the Rhine, which flows some ten miles to the east.

The vineyards of the Palatinate cover an area seven times as great as that of the Rheingau. They produce more wine per acre than any of the other German vineyards, but a smaller quantity of fine quality wine than either the Rheingau, Rhinehessia, or Moselle vineyards. The fine quality wines of the Palatinate, however, are of quite remarkable excellence, the peers of the greatest white wines of the Rheingau or of the world.

The Palatinate is divided into three unequal parts, known as Oberhaardt, Mittel-haardt and Unterhaardt. The Oberhaardt or Upper Haardt is the largest; it stretches from the French frontier in the south to Neustadt in the north. The Mittelhaardt or Middle Haardt stretches from Neustadt to Herxheim along the *Weinstrasse* or Wine Road. The Unterhaardt or Lower Haardt is the smallest of the three; it stretches from Herxheim to Zell in Hessia.

There are in the Upper Haardt over a hundred wine-producing localities, the more important of them being Maikammer (1,500 acres), Edenkoben (1,100 acres), Hambach (825 acres), Diedesfeld (700 acres), Kirrweiler (650 acres), Edesheim (600 acres), St Martin (600 acres), Hainfeld (480 acres), Godramstein (450 acres), Bürrweiler (450 acres) and Ilbesheim (400 acres). The Upper Haardt produces more wine, both red and white, than all the rest of the Palatinate vineyards.

The Middle Haardt vineyards produce all the greatest Palatinate wines. There are some 40 different wine-producing localities, the largest being Bad Dürkheim (2,200 acres), Mussbach (1,100 acres), Wachenheim (1,000 acres), Deidesheim (1,000 acres), Ruppertsberg (800 acres), Neustadt (760 acres), Ungstein (700 acres), Kallstadt (600 acres), Freinsheim (575 acres), Ellerstadt (550 acres), Weisenheim a. Sand (530 acres), Forst (530 acres), Herxheim (400 acres), Gimmeldingen (400 acres), Weisenheim a. Berg (400 acres) and Haardt (375 acres).

The Middle Haardt is about 18 miles in length, and the four villages whose vineyards produce the greatest wines of all—Ruppertsberg, Deidesheim, Forst and Wachenheim—are in the very centre; one other, Königsbach, south of Ruppertsberg, and three more, Bad Dürkheim, Ungstein and Kallstadt, north of Wachenheim, are responsible for the next best wines of the Palatinate.

The best vineyards of the principal localities are as follows:

KÖNIGSBACH

Bender	Jesuitengarten	Mückenhaus
IDIG	Ölberg	

RUPPERTSBERG

Goldschmitt	LINSENBUSCH	Reiferpfad
Hoheburg	Mandelacker	Spiess
Kreuz	NUSSBIEN	Weinbüchel

DEIDESHEIM

Geheu	KIESELBERG	Mühle
Grain	Klostergarten	Petershöhle
Grainhübel	Kränzler	RENNPFAD
Hahnenböhl	Langenböhl	St Michelsberg
Herrgottsacker	Langenmorgen	Sonneneck
Hofstück	Leinhöhle	Weinbach
Hohenmorgen	Linsenbusch	
Kalkofen	Maushöhle	

"Paradiesgarten" is the generic name for all Deidesheim wines.

FORST

Alser	JESUITENGARTEN	Langkammert
Altenburg	KIRCHENSTÜCK	LINSENSTÜCK
Elster	Kranich or Granich	MUSENHANG
Fleckinger	Langenacker	Pechstein
Freundstück	Langenböhl	UNGEHEUER
Gerling	Langenmorgen	

WACHENHEIM

Altenburg	Goldbächel	Luginsland
Bächel	Goldberg	Rechbächel
Böhlig	Königswingert	Schenkenböhl
Gerümpel	Mandelgarten	Schlossberg

What were formerly some seventy sites have recently been combined to form these twelve.

BAD DÜRKHEIM

Feuerberg	Hochbenn	MICHELSBERG
Forst	Hochmess	Schenkenböhl
Fuchsmantel	Klosterberg	SPIELBERG

UNGSTEIN

Herrenberg	Michelsberg	Vogelsang
Honigsäckel	Spielberg	

KALLSTADT

Annaberg	Kreuz	SAUMAGEN
Horn	Kronenberg	Steinacker
Kobnert	Nill	

FREINSHEIM

Goldberg	Musikantenbuckel	Oschelskopf
Gottesacker		

FRIEDELSHEIM

Feuerberg	Letten	Roscngarten
Forster Neuberg	Neuberg	Schlossgarten
Gerümpel	Neumorgen	Tiergarten

GIMMELDINGEN

Bienengarten	Hofstück	Meerspinne
Fürstenwcg	Kirchenstück	

HAARDT

Herrenletten	Mandelring	Ritter
Herzog	Paradies	Schlossberg
Kirchpfad		

MUSSBACH

Bischofsweg	Johannismorgen	Spiegel
Eselhaut	Kurfürst	

HERXHEIM

Berg	Himmelreich	Mahlstein
Blume	HONIGACKER	Sommerseite
Felsenberg	Kirchenstück	Steinberg
Goldberg		

NEUSTADT

Erkenbrecht	Hag	Ritterberg
Grain	Klosterberg	Rosengarten
Guckins Land	Mandelgewann	Vogelsang

NIEDERKIRCHEN

| Kirchgarten | Martenweg | Rittershöhe u.a. |
| Klostergarten | | |

The proportion of Riesling grapes (which are responsible for quality wines) to commoner grapes (from which the more ordinary beverage wines, both red and white, are made) varies very much, as these approximate figures show:

Forst	70%	Wachenheim	24%
Deidesheim	62%	Ruppertsberg	23%
Königsbach	31%	Ungstein	18%

All Palatinate wines made from Riesling grapes in a good year possess a family likeness, in body, bouquet and breeding, and a richness of flavour which is quite distinctive. There are, however, appreciable differences of bouquet and taste among them, and also of sweetness, of course, according to whether the wine is an Auslese, a Beerenauslese or a Trockenbeerenauslese, the last-named being the most remarkable of all natural sweet white wines in the world. Most good judges agree that of all the finest Palatinate wines those of Forst deserve the first place. One cannot, however, agree with such a categoric statement. It very much depends upon the vintage. In some vintages, Forst is supreme; in others, Deidesheim.

In the Lower Haardt there are some fifty wine-producing localities, but only a very small proportion of their wines, even in good vintages, have attracted wine lovers outside their native Palatinate. Many of them, however, are quite fair beverage wines which are not merely acceptable, but very enjoyable upon a hot summer's evening.

An alphabetical list of the wine-producing localities of the Unterhaardt:

Affenberg (Fuchsloch,
   Hochgewann, Himmelsreich,
   Jesuitenhofgarten)
Albisheim a.d. Pfrimm
Albsheim a.d. Eis
Asselheim
Bennhausen
Bissersheim
Bolanden
Bubenheim
Colgenstein-Heidesheim
Einselthum
Eisenberg-Stauf
Gauersheim
Gerolsheim

Grossniedesheim
Grünstadt
Harxheim
Hessheim
Heuchelheim
Immelsheim
Jakobsweiler
Kerzenheim
Kindenheim
Kirchheim a.d. Eck
Kirchheimbolanden
Kleinbockenheim
  (Burggarten, Dom,
  Gretenbrunnen,
  Kieselberg)

Kleinniedesheim	Obrigheim
Laumersheim	Orbis
Mauchenheim	Ottersheim
Mertesheim	Quirnheim
Mörsfeld	Ridzheim
Mühlheim a.d. Eis	Rittersheim
Niefernheim	Rüssingen
Obersülzen	Sausenheim

A further part of the Palatinate north of the Unterhaardt is the *Zellertal* with the village Zell and its sites, which include Philippsbrunnen and Schwarzer Herrgott.

The most important wine-growers of the Palatinate are von Buhl, Bürklin-Wolf and Bassermann-Jordan.

THE WINES OF THE NAHE

The valleys of the River Nahe and its tributaries, from the valley of the Alsenz which branches off from the Nahe into the northern tip of the Palatinate, down to Bad Kreuznach (the geographical, historical and commercial centre of the Nahe), must be reckoned among the most picturesque and beautiful vinelands of the world. From Bad Kreuznach down to Bingen, where it joins the Rhine, the Nahe flows mostly through rich meadows and agricultural land, dotted with vineyards and orchards wherever there is a clump of houses or a village. The area of the Nahe vineyards is about a thousand acres more than that of the Rheingau and the average yield of Nahe wines is about 1,500 hectolitres more than that of the Rheingau. Unfortunately, if we turn from quantity to quality, the Nahe vineyards do not produce more than one third of the proportion of quality wines produced by the Rheingau vineyards. But they do produce a fair number of quality wines of superlative excellence which deserve the attention of the more fastidious among wine lovers: they always deserve their attention, and they often also deserve their whole-hearted praise.

The Nahe district is easily subdivided into eleven viticultural regions. The most important communities and sites are as follows:

Left bank of the Nahe up to Bad Kreuznach

Martinstein	Burgwingert
Monzingen	Auf der Lay, Auf der Fels, Rosenbaum, Kronenberg, FRÜHLINGSPLÄTZCHEN
Waldböckelheim	Königsfels, Mühlberg, Welschberg
Schloss Böckelheim	KUPFERGRUBE, Felsenberg, Mühlberg
Niederhausen	Steinberg, Hermannshöhle, Rossel, Rosenheck, Steier, HERMANNSBERG

Hüffelsheim	Gutenhöll, Brauneberg, Hipprich
Norheim	Kafels, Hinterfels, Dellchen
Bad Münster am Stein	Kirschheck, Oberberg, Schmalberg, Rotenfels, Höll, Felsen-eck
Bad Kreuznach	Kauzenberg, Kronenberg, Hinkelstein, Forst, Narrenkappe, BRÜCKES, Steinweg, Kahlenberg, Galgenberg, Kehren-berg, Monau

Ellerbachtal

Weinsheim	Kellerberg, Frohnberg, Schafskopf
Mandel	Kranzwingert, Schlossberg, Dellchen, Rosengarten
Rüdesheim	Rosengarten, Wiesberg

Gräfenbachtal

Dalberg	Schlossberg, Wingertsberg
Hergenfeld	Mayen, Herrschaftsacker, Münchrech
Wallhausen	Johannisberg, Pastorenberg, Hahnenbach, Rebsgrund
Braunweiler	Weingarten, Heide
Sommerloch	Steinrossel, Lett, Neuberg, Kaul
St Katharinen	Berg, Heide, Steinig
Gutenberg	Schlossberg, Stein, Heide, Fels, Vogelgesang
Roxheim	Birkenberg, Mühlenberg, Hüttenberg, Neuenberg, Bangert

Valley of the Nahe up to the estuary of the Guldenbach

Winzenheim	Rosenheck, Honigberg, Metzler
Bretzenheim	Manik, Kronenberg, Vogelgesang

Guldenbachtal

Schöneberg	Schäfersley, Eichenreis, Hölle
Schweppenheim	Steyerberg, Hölle, Homberg, Hardt
Windesheim	Hölle, Hüttenberg, Sonnenmorgen, Hinkelstein, Rosenberg, Römerberg
Waldhilbersheim	Rödern, Apostelgraben, Butterberg, Kilb
Heddesheim	Kilb, Hipperich, Geisemann, Bemerich, Honigberg, Gold-loch, Höll, Huttenberg, Scharlachberg, Rosenburg, Rörnerberg, Sonnenmorgen
Waldlaubersheim	Domberg, Rosenberg, Wingertsberg
Genheim	Genheimer Berg

Valley of the Nahe upwards to the mouth of the Rhine

Langenlonsheim	Rotenberg, Borngraben, RIETH, Grems, Sonnenborn, Löhr
Laubenheim	Karthäuser, Hörnchen, Löhr, Remicher, Vogelgesang
Dorsheim	Burgberg, Goldloch, Pittermännchen, Honigberg

Plate 16.   Schloss Vollrads bottles.

Rümmelsheim	Honigberg, Hölle, Hirschhorn, Rotenberg
Sarmsheim	Mühlberg
Münster bei Bingerbrück	Pittersberg, Kapellenberg, Mönchberg, Dautenpflänzer
Weiler	Rechte Mühe, In der Lay, Hungerborn
Bingerbrück	Elisenhöhe, Mühe, Hörnchen

Valley of the Nahe upwards to the mouth of the Glan

Becherbach	Rotenberg
Krebsweiler	Delberg
Meckenbach	Weidentell
Merxheim	Vor der Burg, Aresberg, Hinterberg
Kirschroth	Sand, Nauenberg
Meddersheim	Altenberg, Scherendell, Eisendell
Staudernheim	Hohrech, Grube, Kauzenberg

Valley of the Glan

Offenbach	Hinterberg, Kellenbach, Freifrauenloch
Medard	Rattenfels, Götzennell
Meisenheim	Altenberg, Heimbach
Raumbach	Raumberg, Allenberg
Lauterecken	Schäfersberg, Oberberg
Odenbach	Bornberg, Leckberg
Callbach	Fastenberg, Im Mai, Delbchen
Rehborn	Raumberg, Eschbach, Hahn
Odernheim	Klosterberg, Sonnenberg

Valley of the Nahe up to the mouth of the Alsenz

Duchroth Oberhausen	Vogelschlag, Kaisergrund
Ebernburg	Schlossberg, Weidenberg, Erzgrube, Zennerrech

Valley of the Alsenz

Hochstätten	Häuserweg, Glückerberg
Feil-Bingert	Kahlenberg, Hochstätterberg
Altenbamberg	Rothenberg, Schlossberg, Treuenfels

Valley of the Nahe right bank up to where the Nahe meets the Rhine

Hackenheim	Galgenberg, Heide
Bosenheim	Bosenberg, Honigberg
Planig	Frenzenberg, Rieth
Ippesheim	Steiler, Baumann
Gensingen	Mühlenberg, Kirchberg
Grolsheim	Nauenberg
Dietersheim	Pfingstweide

| Bingen-Büdesheim | SCHARLACHBERG, Steinkautweg, Rosengarten, Rochusberg, Kieselberg |
| Bingen (adjoining the Rhinehessian district) | Eisel |

The best of these are definitely the wines grown on the left bank up to and including Bad Kreuznach, and among them first place is taken by Schloss Böckelheim—which is, surprisingly, the name of a village. Here is the seat of the State Domain. The volcanic and slate soils produce wines of elegance, flavour and breeding.

The vineyards of the State Domain were carved out of the hillsides, terraced and planted by convict labour only some seventy years ago. This may be the latest of the Nahe vineyards, but the first were planted some 2,000 years ago, and the considerable quantity of Roman remains from excavations in and near Bad Kreuznach leave no doubt about the early settlement of the valley by the Romans.

The 7,500 acres of the Nahe are planted mostly with Sylvaner and only to a small extent with Riesling grapes. In their character the wines of the Nahe are considered first cousins of the Rhine and the Moselle wines. Wines of the Upper Nahe (between Martinstein and Boos) remind one of the Saar wines, wines of the Glan valley, and of some Palatinate wines. They range from the simple luncheon wine of Rüdesheim (Rosengarten) in the Ellerbachtal to kings of wine like the 1945 Schloss Böckelheimer Kupfergrube Trockenbeerenauslese or the 1959 Kreuznacher Brückes Trockenbeerenauslese. Of the 1953 Nahe wines it was said: "They are real beauties. They have the charm of a good Moselle, the aroma of a Rheingau and the fruit of a Rhinehessian wine." The 1959 vintages even surpass the 53's!

A list of some proprietors owning vineyards in various villages:

Weingut August Anheuser	Kreuznach, Schloss Böckelheim, Niederhausen
Paul Anheuser	Kreuznach, Schloss Böckelheim, Monzingen, Niederhausen, Norheim
Landesweinbaulehranstalt	Kreuznach, Norheim, Niederhausen
State Domain	Schloss Böckelheim, Niederhausen, Münster am Stein

THE WINES OF FRANCONIA (FRANKEN)

Franconia was once an independent duchy within the Holy Roman Empire, but it has long since been dismembered. Parts of the former duchy are now in Bavaria, Württemberg, Baden and Hessia. Happily, the vineyards of Franconia have survived all political upheavals and administrative partitions. They still flourish along practically the whole of the many curves of the river Main from east of Frankfurt to Bamberg, producing a great variety of wines, most of which possess a very distinctive character.

The great majority of the wines of Franconia are plain beverage wines made from Sylvaner, some red, others white; but there are a number of white Franconian wines which are truly fine wines, possessing body, breeding and a fine bouquet that are all their own. The fine white wines of Franconia are well-balanced wines, and this rare quality gives them a better chance to withstand the changes of temperature and the usually rough handling which so many wines resent on long journeys by land and sea. This is why the wines of Franconia were so popular in England from an early date and why the demand for them has been steadily growing since the last war, in both the British Isles and the United States.

Of the three administrative divisions of Franconia—Lower, Middle and Upper—some 95% of the vineyards are in Lower Franconia, in Bavaria, and the best of the Franconian wines are those from the vineyards of Würzburg, Randersacker, Iphofen, Escherndorf and Hörstein.

The vine is no newcomer to Franconia: it was first planted near Würzburg in the eighth century, when St Kilian first brought the Gospel and the grape to the heathen populations of the Upper Main valleys. Today some 520 acres of vineyards are within the administrative bounds of Würzburg, which is more than any other locality possesses in Franconia. What is of greater importance is that the vineyards of Würzburg are responsible for some of the finest white wines of Franconia, including especially the wines from the Stein vineyard, the only ones legally entitled to the name of *Steinweine*. This vineyard and the *Leisten* vineyards were planted, according to tradition, by order of Charlemagne; since then, they have been enlarged and improved without any doubt by successive princes and bishops of Würzburg. They now belong mostly to the Bavarian State, the Würzburg Municipality and two Würzburg hospitals (Bürgerspital and Juliusspital). We may be quite sure that they are tended with as much care and love as ever before, as well as with a greater measure of scientific knowledge.

Experts have called the Würzburger Stein the most beautiful site in all Germany. There are parts or strips of the original Stein vineyard which have been given different names for the sake of differentiation and identification, such as:

Steinmantel	Löwenstein	Ständerbühl
Jesuitenstein	Harfe	Schalksberg

Strips of the site Leiste are called Innere Leiste, Felsenleiste, and Aussere Leiste.

There are 160 villages in Franconia, the vineyards of which produce honest wine, for the honest thirst of the local people who have no wish and no chance to compete in the world's markets.

The State *Hofkellerei* is the largest owner of vineyards in Franconia: nearly 250 acres, which originally belonged to the Prince-Bishops of Würzburg, then to the Duchy of Würzburg, before being transferred to the Bavarian Crown in 1816. Here is a list of the vineyards now the property of the *Hofkellerei* or State Domain:

WÜRZBURG

Innere Leiste	Löwenstein	Stein-Schalksberg
Jesuitenstein	Neuberg	

RANDERSACKER

Hohenbuch	Marsberg	Spielberg
Lämmerberg	Pfülben	Teufelskeller

HÖRSTEIN

Abtsberg	Reuschberg	Schwalbenwinkel
Langenberg		

GROSSHEUBACH

Bischofsberg

Bürgerspital owns vineyards in Würzburg, Randersacker and Himmelstadt, and the Juliusspital in Würzburg, Randersacker, Escherndorf, Astheim, Dettelbach, Iphofen, Rödelsee and Bürgstadt.

The Franconian wines have a traditional bottle of their own, the *Bocksbeutel*, which is entirely different from all other wine bottles: it is flat-sided instead of cylindrical.

The origin of it is obscure. Possibly a glass-blower may once have turned out the strange shape, either accidentally or intentionally, or maybe the Low German *Bockesbeutel* (a bag in which prayer-books or other volumes were transported) had something to do with the original invention, and its name. It must be remembered, too, that there is a grape called *Bocksbeutel*, possibly a reference to its shape. Dr Kittel ascribes the origin of the name directly to the baglike shape (*Beutel*) of one of the internal organs of a goat's anatomy (*Bock*), which the characteristic Franconian flask resembles. This interpretation is far fetched. If we remember that Rabelais in *Gargantua and Pantagruel* speaks quite often of bottles called *bréviaires*, in other words of bottles similar to a *Bocksbeutel*, we can accept the solution of the puzzle as *Bockesbeutel*.

Franconia has a monopoly of its use, with the proviso that three co-operative societies in Baden are allowed to bottle an average of 30% of their yearly crop in *Bocksbeuteln* and, in specially full vintages, as 1959, up to 50% (*Mauerweine*).

Do not let us make the mistake of thinking that all Franconian wines are identical, or even similar. It is true that most wine merchants list just one wine from this large and important district, the *Steinwein*. But the Franconian wines bear on their label their birth certificate, just as do the wines of all other German wine districts. And if we really care, and take the trouble to make the wine journey through the many villages and vineyards, we shall find a wealth of difference in quality and character. And of course it is here that we find the *Main–riesling* and the *Perle*—two new vine crossings which will have a great influence on the viticulture of Franconia.

In our wine journey we shall travel through five distinctive districts. Beginning at

Frankfurt, our first stop will be in the district Alzenau: Hörstein, whose wines remind us of the Rheingau wines.

Moving along the U-formation in the Untermain district:

Erlenbach   Homburg
Grossheubach   Klingenberg
Grossostheim

We then turn aside to visit the Franconian valley of the Saale with:

Hammelburg   Sulztal
Langendorf   Schloss Saaleck
Ramsthal   Wirmsthal

In the triangle of the Main (*Maindreieck*) we come to the heart of Franconian viticulture:

Abtswind
Buchbrunn
Castell
Dettelbach
Eibelstadt
Erlabrunn
Escherndorf (Lump, Eulengrube, Hengstberg, Kirchberg, Fürstenberg)
Frickenhausen
Grosslangheim
Iphofen (Julius-Echter-Berg, Kronsberg, Kalb, Burgweg, Pfaffensteig)
Kitzingen
Köhler
Mainstockheim
Marktbreit
Nordheim
Obereisenheim
Randersacker (Pfülben, Hohenbuch, Teufelskeller, Spielberg, Marsberg, Sonnenstuhl, Altenberg, Häslein, Lämmerberg)

Retzbach
Rödelsee
Sommerach
Sommerhausen
Stetten
Sulzfeld
Thüngersheim (Johannisberg, Freiberg, Neuberg, Scharlach, Ravensburg)
Veitshöchheim (with its viticultural college, now also under the administration of the Hofkellerei: Fachtel, Wölflein, Neuberg)
Volkach
Wiesenbronn
Würzburg (In addition to the above-mentioned Stein and Leiste: Rossberg, Pfaffenberg, Schlossberg, Klinge, Gutental, Stephanspfad, Albertsleite and, last but not least, the Neuberg with its wines rich in bouquet and aroma.)
Würzburg Heidingsfeld

We end our journey in the Obermain district:

Mainberg   Schweinfurt

OTHER GERMAN WINES

All the better wines of Germany, the only wines for which there is a demand in the British Isles, the United States, and other countries outside Germany, are the wines of the Moselle, Saar and Ruwer, the Rheingau, Rhinehessia and the Nahe, the Rhein-Pfalz or Palatinate, and Franconia. There are, however, a considerable number of other wines made in Germany which enjoy a high degree of local popularity; these come from the vineyards of other parts of Germany, from the Middle Rhine and the Ahr Valley in the north to Lake Constance, or Bodensee, in the extreme south.

MIDDLE RHINE (*Mittelrhein*)

The Middle Rhine may be considered, in theory, the stretch of the Rhine valley from Bonn in the north to Bingen in the south, with Koblenz approximately in the centre. In practice, however, with the exception of some vineyards on the right bank of the river at Königswinter, south of Bonn, and at Linz, opposite the Ahr Valley, all the worthwhile wines of the Middle Rhine come from vineyards south of Koblenz. The best are those of Caub on the right bank of the Rhine and of Boppard, Oberwesel, Bacharach and Steeg, and Oberdiebach on the opposite bank.

The finest vineyard of BOPPARD is HAMM, which runs along the river on the lower slopes of the Altenberg. CAUB's best vineyards are known as Backofen, Blüchertal, and Pfalzgrafenstein. The principal wine-growing centres and the best-known vineyards are the following:

OBERWESEL
          Ölsberg   Rheinhell

BACHARACH
          Posten   Wolfshöhle

STEEG
          Flur   St Jost   Unkel
          Mühlberg

OBERDIEBACH
          Fürstenberg

On the right bank of the Rhine, LORCH and ASSMANNSHAUSEN, further up the river, although part of the Rheingau officially, produce wines more in keeping with the style and quality of the Middle Rhine wines. Assmannshausen is chiefly noted for its red wines; made from the *Pinot Noir* or *Spätburgunder*, they are considered to be the best red wines of Germany.

BERGSTRASSE

Bergstrasse is a stretch of land upon the right bank of the Rhine, part of which is in the northern tip of Baden, but most of which is in Hessia. It is a particularly fertile and sheltered piece of country, chiefly famous for its orchards, but it also has its vineyards, mostly in two *Kreise*:

BENSHEIM

Geiersberg	Kalkgasse	Streichling

HEPPENHEIM

Mausnest	Steinkopf	Stemmler
Schlossberger		

WÜRTTEMBERG–BADEN

For many years Württemberg and Baden were independent states, then in 1871 they became federal states of the German Empire. Until 1918 Württemberg was a kingdom and Baden a duchy. From then on they became republics within Germany, and that status continued until 1953.

In 1953 the two were amalgamated into the state of Württemberg-Baden, but from the viticultural point of view we still have to treat them as separate districts. In Württemberg-Baden are 72,100 viticultural holdings with a vineyard area of 17,654 hectares, which is approximately 6.5% of the whole agricultural area of the state. This is made up as follows:

North Württemberg	9,785
North Baden	2,025
South Baden	5,669
South Württemberg including Hohenzollern	175

The whole is distributed amongst 845 wine-growing communities. Important growers in Baden–Württemberg:

Staatliches Weinbauinstitut Freiburg i. BR.
Weingut Dr H. Mackenstein, Schlossruine, Burkheim am Kaiserstuhl
Freiherr v. Neveu'sche Gutsverwaltung, Durbach
H. Germann, Müllheim, Baden
Heiliggeist-Spitalstiftung, Freiburg im Breisgau
Weingut Bühler Söhne, Freiburg im Breisgau
Weingut Dr Heger, Ihringen/Kaiserstuhl
Weinbauversuchsgut des Landkreises Offenburg, Schloss Ortenberg, Baden
Staatsweingut Meersburg, Schloss Neuweier
Frhrl. v.u.z. Franckenstein'sches Rentamt, Offenburg, Baden

Weingut Fritz Blankenhorn, Schliengen/Markgräflerland
Gräflich von Berckheim'sche Schlosskellerei, Weinheim an der Bergstrasse
Fürstlich Löwenstein-Wertheim-Rosenberg'sches Weingut, Kreuzwertheim am Main
Württ. Hofkammer-Kellerei, Stuttgart
Von Stapf'sches Weingut, Erlenbach, Kreis Heilbronn
Weingut Graf Adelmann, Kleinbottwar (Kreis Ludwigsburg)
Fürstl. Hohenlohe-Waldenburg'sches Weingut, Waldenburg, Kreis Öhringen
Weingut H. Vetter

WÜRTTEMBERG

Generally speaking, the Neckar with its tributaries is the main centre of Württemberg viticulture. But the vineyards start only at the Upper Neckar near Rottenburg. In the valley of the Albtrauf we find a very little viticulture in towns like Reutlingen, which has the highest-situated vineyards of Württemberg—nearly 1,800 feet above the sea. But where the Neckar turns to the west, viticulture is the main occupation of the inhabitants, for here there are many places reached by the southern sun. In this middle part of the Neckar we find Stuttgart and to the east of Stuttgart is the beautiful Rems valley, with well-known sites such as Stettener Brotwasser, Schnaiter Halde. The greatest wine district is the lower valley of the Neckar, with 3,600 hectares of vineyards. Still part of this district, on the left side of the river, are the Enztal, the Zabertal and the Leintal; on the right side of the river, the Murrtal, the Bottwartal, the Schozachtal, the Weinsbergertal, the Kochertal and Jagsttal. It is in the Bottwar and Schozachtal that the *Schillerweine* are produced.

In addition to the vineyards along the Neckar, there are vineyards along the Tauber and in the Vorbachtal in the north-east of Württemberg which belong to Württemberg. Part of the vineyards of the Bodensee (Lake of Constance) district also belong to Württemberg.

It is noteworthy that in the eight wine-growing districts of Württemberg, a large part of the vineyards is devoted to the growing of red wine, which in 1953 came to 28% of the whole German harvest of red wine grapes. Besides the red and white wine there is a considerable production of rosé or *Schillerweine*, the red and the white grapes being planted in mixed lots in the vineyards and gathered and treated together. Today the state discourages the growing of mixed grapes in the same ground, and the quantity of *Schillerweine* is getting smaller every year. It can be said that many wine drinkers in Württemberg, and indeed many visitors to Württemberg, regret very much that these *Schillerweine* are becoming scarce, and the local demand is such that, good and even fine as some of them are, Württemberg wines are never available for export. But it was not ever thus, and the "Neckarine" wines were obtainable in the hanseatic cities and in Scandinavia during the late Middle Ages. Most Württemberg wines come from the very large number of very small vineyards which grace both banks of the Neckar valley. There are few, very few, large vineyards; the great majority belong to farmers, artisans

Plate 17 (*overleaf*). Deidesheim (*left*) and Wachenheim, in the Palatinate.

and even labourers and other wage-earners who have just enough spare time to devote to their few vines. Some of them make only just enough wine for their own home consumption, whilst others, those who make the better-quality wines, sell them through the local co-operative society.

The best of the Neckar wines are those of the Lower Neckar above and below Heilbronn, more particularly by Weinsberg, the seat of the Viticultural Institute. The upper valley of the Neckar, south of Stuttgart, may not bring forth quite so much good wine, but Stuttgart itself is the chief market for all the wines of Württemberg. It is also the seat of the Wine Growers' Co-operative Central Organization with its extensive cellars.

The most important wine-growing communities of Württemberg are:

Neckar Valley

Beilstein	Löwenstein mit Reisach und Rittelhof
Besighcim	Mundelsheim a. N.
Bönnigheim	Oberstenfeld m. Weingut Lichtenberg
Eberstadt	Stuttgart-Bad Cannstatt
Erlenbach	Stuttgart-Obertürkheim
Esslingen	Stuttgart-Rohracker
Fellbach	Stuttgart-Rotenberg
Flein	Stuttgart-Uhlbach
Grossbottwar	Stuttgart-Untertürkheim
Heilbronn	Stuttgart-Wangen
Hessigheim	Walheim
Kleinbottwar	Weinsberg
Lauffen a. N.	Willsbach
Lehrensteinsfeld	

Remstal

Beutelsbach	Schnait
Endersbach	Stetten
Grossheppach	Strümpfelbach
Grunbach i. R.	

Enztal

Horrheim	Rosswag

Zabergau

Brackenheim (red)	Nordheim
Cleebronn	Schwaigern (red)
Dürrenzimmern (red)	

Kochertal and Jagsttal

Criesbach	Verrenberg
Ingelfingen	

Württemberg Taubergrund

Bad Mergentheim	Weikersheim
Markelsheim	

BADEN

This is the country which faces Alsace and stretches from the Swiss frontier to the Bergstrasse and Hessia, and beyond Mannheim all along the right bank of the Rhine, with Württemberg and Bavaria north and east. There are many vineyards, more now than before the war, in all parts of Baden, and they produce a considerable quantity of red, white and rosé wines which vary greatly in style and flavour according to the district.

Over the last few years Baden wines have become better known. Better weather conditions in 1955, 1956 and 1957 helped to produce better and riper wines than in most other districts. The Baden wine growers have founded many local wine co-operatives, so that the smallholders can rely on the skill and experience of the co-operatives' managers. Some 80% of Baden wines are stored and treated in 110 co-operatives' cellars.

Here we must also refer to the Baden *Weissherbst*. Whereas in Württemberg rosé wine is produced by the pressing and fermentation of mixed red and white grapes, in Baden the blue Burgundy grape is treated like a white wine grape. The grapes are not fermented on the skins, but are treated as in white wines: very small particles of colour thus come into the wine, giving it a touch of rose.

Like the Palatinate wine districts, Baden too has its well-marked *Weinstrasse*, or Wine Road; it is a district which is well worth visiting. It leads from Baden-Baden via Neuweier, Lauf, Oberkirch, Oppenau, Hundseck and Richtental back to Baden-Baden.

The chief wine-producing districts of Baden from east to west and south to north are the following:

Bodensee: that is, those vineyards upon the north shore of Lake Constance, facing south. Most of them are in Baden, but not all, since both Württemberg and Bavaria have a foot in the lake, so to speak. The white wines made from these lake-side vineyards are known locally as *Seeweine*, and are pleasant, refreshing wines but no more; the best of them come from the vineyards of Meersburg and Hagnau and are made from Pinot gris (or Rülander) grapes.

Breisgau lies farther west, where the Rhine reaches Basle and swings sharply to the north; at this point there is a thirty-mile-long stretch of deep, dark soil (on the foothills of the fir-clad slopes of the Black Forest) in which the Gutedel (or Chasselas) grapes thrive, bearing quantities of fruit from which much plain but pleasant wine is made. This stretch of land, which is almost completely covered with vineyards and orchards from Basle to Freiburg, has the following communities:

Friesenheim	Kenzingen	Schmieheim
GLOTTERTAL	Köndringen	Wagenstadt
Herbolzheim	Malterdingen	

The next district, the *Markgrafschaft*, counts among its more important wine-producing villages:

Auggen (Kirchbuck, Schäf, Letten)	Kirchhofen
Britzingen	Laufen
Ebringen (Sommerberg, Klämmle)	Müllheim
Efringen-Kirchen (Katzenrain, Hard-berg, Weingarten)	Pfaffenweiler
	Rheinweiler
Ehrenstetten (Öhlberg, Kirchberg)	Schallstadt-Wolfenweiler
Haltingen (Lette, Stiege, Rohrbrunnen)	Schliengen
Istein	Sulzburg

Kaiserstuhl. North-west of Freiburg a jumble of volcanic rocks is known as the Kaiserstuhl, and there are many vineyards upon its lower slopes, mostly Ruländer or Pinot gris. They yield wines with more body and a higher alcoholic strength than other Baden wines. The best-known wine-producing districts of the Kaiserstuhl are the following:

Achkarren (Schlossberg, Rittersprung)	Königschaffhausen (Scherchbuck, Halve)
Bahlingen	Oberbergen (Winzburg, Limburg)
Bickensohl (Steinfelsen, Eichberg)	Oberrotweil (Henkenberg, Eichberg)
Bischoffingen (Enselberg)	Sasbach
Burkheim (Burgberg, Käsleberg, Feuer-berg)	Merdingen (Tüniberg)
	Rimsingen (Tüniberg)
Eichstetten	Tiengen (Tüniberg)
Endingen	Wasenweiler (Kreuzhalden, Steig, Eichen)
Ihringen (Winklerberg, Fohrenberg, Abtsweingarten)	

Following the Rhine downstream one comes to the region of Baden known as *Ortenau*, of which Offenburg is the principal township.

The vineyards of Ortenau are blessed with the poorest soil in Baden and they accordingly produce the best wine—wine which is mostly made from Riesling and, to a lesser extent, from Traminer grapes. The local name for Riesling is *Klingelberger* and the Traminer is called *Clevner*.

The most important wine-producing villages of Ortenau are as follows:

Altschweier	NEUWEIER	Tiergarten
AFFENTAL	Oberkirch	Varnhalt
Durbach	Rammersweier	Waldulm
Fessenbach	Steinbach	Zell
Kappelrodeck		

Affental, Eisental, Altschweier and Neuweier are known for their red wines. Affental, on account of a monastery which was situated in the valley (*thal*), was originally called Ave Thal, i.e. "Ave-Maria-Thal". In this part of the country "v" is pronounced as "f", so that people called the village Affental. But "Affe" in German means a monkey. As a result of all this manipulation of the language, and in order to distinguish their wine from other districts, the growers used, and still use, a bottle on which a monkey is embossed.

We come next to the *Kraichgau* with the following villages:

Bruchsal	Rauenberg
Dietlingen	Sulzfeld
Ellmendingen	Unteröwisheim
Landshausen	

Passing the Neckar river we reach Heidelberg and the Bergstrasse. The following are the villages of the Bergstrasse district belonging politically to Baden:

Heidelberg-Handschusheim	Sulzbach
Heidelberg-Rohrbach	Wiesloch
Schriesheim	

A further forty villages of Baden are situated in the *Taubergrund* and the *Maintal*, including Wertheim with its famous Kallmuth district which adjoins the Franconian wineland, dealt with above.

The Neckar flows through Baden to reach the Rhine at Mannheim, but practically the whole of its course is through the vineyards of Württemberg.

GERMANY'S RED WINES

The proportion of red wine produced in Germany is larger than most people imagine, as the statistics in the Appendices show. With the exception of the Moselle, Saar and Ruwer districts, red wines are grown in all districts.

In the production of red wines Germany employs many species of grapes. In the forefront, of course, stands the *Pinot Noir* (*Spätburgunder*), but in addition to this there are the *Limberger*, *Trollinger* (originating in the Tyrol), *Müller Vine* (Schwarz Riesling) and the *Samtrot*—a newly-developed grape from the child of the Schwarz Riesling. The best known red wines are:

THE AHR DISTRICT

The German red wine region *par excellence* is the Ahr Valley, which is also the most northerly wine region in the world. The wine produced there is called Ahr Burgundy.

The Ahr, a little river having its source in the Eiffel mountains, is very little known for its wines. It is better known for its waters. In the middle of this district lies the spa, Bad Neuenahr, with its world-famous "Apollinarisbrunnen", from which the world drinks. But its viticulture is as old as that of the Moselle, though the area of vineyards under cultivation has been reduced over the last few decades.

Its fame has long been based on its red wines, though the growing of red grapes was started only about 300 years ago. Formerly the red grapes were used to make a rosé wine known as *Ahrbleichert*.

For a long time when Germany did not import foreign wines on account of lack of currency, the Ahr products had almost a clear field and reigned supreme; but as soon as foreign wines came on the market again, the Ahr wines lost a lot of their popularity.

Moreover, the cultivation of red wine on the Ahr is waning for other reasons. The growers are of the opinion that the vineyards on the Ahr are "Burgundy-weary", an opinion based on the discovery that in many places new cuttings lack vigour in their development, while other species—when planted in vineyards earlier devoted to Burgundy wines—bear good fruit. Just as a farmer rotates his crops, so the vine-grower must from time to time change the species of vines in his vineyards. As a result of these considerations, the growers on the Ahr have begun to plant grapes which produce white wines. At the present time, red and white wines are being grown in about equal proportions.

Wine-growing communities:

Altenahr	Dernau (Lantershofen,
Rech	Herznersheim)
Walporzheim	Ahrweiler (Daubhaus)
(Honigberg)	Bad Neuenahr
Mayschloss	Bodendorf

THE FRANCONIAN DISTRICT

Franconia's red wines grow in the Untermain district, especially on the hot southern slope of the Spessart mountains or in the sandy soil of the Erv valley. In the 18th century this part of the country, between Hassloch and Klienberg, was the centre of a flourishing viticulture, but today for the most part we find in its place just a few trees and bushes. The terraces, however, are still there to remind us of the lost viticulture. And on the old site of the Hasslocher Stockmeister a new vineyard with blue Pinot grapes has been planted by the Viticultural College of Veitshöchheim. On the sites of some old vineyards, we find American vines which form the root base for the grafting of new vines now a necessary precaution in the fight against the *Phylloxera*, these American roots being sent from here to all German districts. In BÜRGSTADT, a site belonging to the Würzburger Juliusspital, the vineyards are planted with the early ripening Burgundy grapes. Adjoining Bürgstadt is MILTENBERG, known as the pearl of the Main; its wines are spicy and strong. Its vineyards are:

Helferich	Mainhölle	Steingrube

Last but not least we have to mention GROSSHEUBACH with its Bischofsberg and its Engelberg.

"Und nicht vergessen Sie vom Main der Klingenberger Rote" ("One must not forget the 'Red' from Klingenberg on the Main") which is considered a speciality among the German red wines.

OTHER DISTRICTS

Rhinehessia

Early and late Burgundy grapes are planted at Ingelheimer (Hundsweg, Langenberg, Hirschtal, Bein, Höllenweg, Steinacker, Sonnenberg), and the wines are round, velvety, with a good spicy flavour and bouquet.

Palatinate

One fifth of the wines produced in the Palatinate are red wines, but to a large extent come from the Portuguese grape which gives only a very light wine—mostly used *en carafe*. However, some full-bodied wines from the Pinot grape are made.

> Dürkheimer Feuerberg Forster Neuberg Kallstadt
> Herxheim (According to a document in the Speyer Museum dated 1597, the "Red Traminer" from Rhodt in the Oberhaardt was at that time considered to be the best wine "growing on the long chain of hills from Basle to Cologne")

Baden–Württemberg

Baden and Württemberg produce more red wine than white wine. The proportion of red to white is approximately 60% to 40%, and Baden and Württemberg each have a speciality produced from red grapes. Baden has its *Weissherbst* and Württemberg its *Schillerwein*.

Weissherbst is the wine produced from red grapes by vinification of the red grape in the same fashion as with white grapes: in other words, they are pressed immediately after the gathering and the must is separated from the skins and pips immediately after pressing. The result is a white wine tinged sometimes with grey or pink. This wine can be full-bodied and harmonious—even some *Spätlesen* are made—but generally speaking these wines, without the tannic acid of the red wine, are no more than ordinary table wines.

Württemberg has its *Schillerwein*, the name given to a wine pressed from a mixture of red and white grapes. The name has nothing to do with the poet Schiller, but is derived from the red-white (merging into pink) radiance or "shimmer" of the wine. (The German verb for "shimmer" is *schillern*.)

This species of wine was developed mainly during the worst crisis ever suffered by German viticulture—after the Thirty Years War. During that period the many devastated vineyards were hastily replanted with any kind of vine likely to afford a good crop, regardless of whether it was a red-wine or white-wine grape.

THE VINEYARDS OF GERMANY

Even nowadays the Swabians are very fond of their "*Schiller*", but its production has been drastically reduced. In Württemberg as elsewhere there is a very strong tendency —wholly admirable from the viticultural point of view—to keep grape-strains and their wines pure by selective planting, selective harvesting and selective wine-production. This tendency will no doubt lead to a still greater improvement in the quality of German wines.

The best-known red wines of Baden are Oberrotweiler Kirchberg and Affenthaler Klosterreberg. Brackenheim and Schwaigern are the best-known red-wine communities of Württemberg.

Rheingau

In very fine vintages the State Domain produces the so-called *Rot-Weiss* (red-white) wine, but only in the grade of *Edelbeerenauslese*. This is a wine resulting from a very special kind of Beerenauslese made from the late Burgundy grape. The grape-gatherers of Assmannshausen—in good vintages—have a sickle-shaped enamel container hanging from their punnets; into these containers they put the selected sleepy berries, some of which have already shrunk and dried out to a raisin-like consistency. Oddly enough, the chief purpose of this is not so much the production of a truly fine Beerenauslese as the protection of the bulk of the wine, since in these raisin-berries the beautiful blue dye in the grapeskin has been destroyed by a fungus (*Botrytis cinerea*), and the employment of these otherwise valuable berries in the manufacture of the red wine would be detrimental to its natural ruby-red colour. Now whereas, in preparing red wines, the grape mash is allowed to ferment in order that the grape-juice (colourless even in blue-skinned berries) may be enabled to absorb the blue dye from the skins, these sleepy raisin-berries are pressed immediately. The resulting coloured, rather sticky, grape-juice is then fermented on the lines of the normal white wine process. If these raisin-berries were to be fermented with the rest in the mash, the must and eventually the wine would take on an unpleasant mouldy taste. As it is, they produce a white wine, pressed from the noblest red-wine grapes; the juice having absorbed a certain amount of the skin-dye, the wine has a yellowish, brownish or reddish tinge according to its quality.

As mentioned previously, these wines are produced in the finest red vintages only and are really of exceptional quality—as was proved by the 1934, 1938 and the 1950 vintages.

Assmannshauser Höllenberg is the best-known red wine of the Rheingau.

The export of red wine in 1958 amounted to less than 4,000, in 1959 to less than 8,000 dozen bottles. Japan was the biggest buyer, followed by the United States.

To end this chapter we must frankly confess that we cannot feel enthusiastic about German red wines. In most vintages German vineyards produce red wines with insufficient ruby-red colour and the vintner must make use of the concession of the wine law to use 25% of foreign *Deckwein*, that is, imported dark-coloured red wine to give more colour to the native wine.

Chapter Five

THE GREAT VINTAGES

What is a good vintage? The vintner understands the term to mean either a vintage of splendid quality, very often with a smaller crop, or a specially large crop which is very rarely also of high quality—because large quantities of grapes and a high sugar content in the grapes are two factors which, as a rule, exclude one another.

The quality of a vintage depends not only on the vine, the site of the vineyard, and the method of cultivation of the vine, but also on the weather of the summer and autumn. By one cool night, or in a cool, rainy autumn, the quality can be influenced very badly. A hot and dry summer may create the possibility of a very good quality vintage but, shortly before the ripening of the grapes, cool weather can start and can prolong the ripening process, and this is worse if rain begins during that time. When the grapes burst and begin to rot before they are fully ripe, the quality of the wine remains poor. A night of frost can destroy the leaves and the grapes have no possibility of ripening. Such vintages remain bad, in spite of beautiful summer weather. On the other hand, if one has favourable weather in the autumn—September and October— and the weather is such that one can leave the grapes longer in the vineyard, one can produce a very good wine, even if the weather in the summer was not particularly favourable.

Everybody connected with viticulture knows that the quantity and quality of crops differ from year to year and that especially fine vintages combining both quantity and quality are made only at intervals of many years. It has been a constant ambition among *vignerons* to discover the root cause of this instability, but, as the wine is a child of the sun,

Plate 18. Sonnenuhr vineyard, at Wehlen the best site of the Moselle.

the climatic conditions must to a large extent be considered the cause of these periodical differences in quality. There is no special rhythm which one can lay down as the rhythm of quality vintages.

There is one school which holds to the 100 year rhythm; but facts contradict it. There is another theory that the quality of the wine depends on sunspot years, but, there again, the facts disprove the theory. Certainly, one condition required for a good vintage is suitable weather, *in the year before the vintage*: a warm sunny summer, so that the foundations for the blossoms of the next year are truly formed; a warm autumn, so that the vines can ripen; and a winter which is not too cold and which does not cause any frost damage to the vine. In the year of the vintage itself what is required is a spring without frosts; a sunny, warm summer; quick blossoming of the vine; occasional rain; and sufficient warm and dry weather in the autumn.

Our own theory is that especially fine vintages have always coincided with those years in which the blossoming of the vine was very early.

Here we must emphasize one point: as a good vintage depends upon a warm summer in the preceding vintage, it is easy to see why, very often, two or more good vintages follow each other, and why one bad vintage often follows another.

The growth of the vine, and especially the ripening of the grapes, are dependent not only upon a high degree of warmth and an extraordinary quantity of light; it is much more important for the increase in warmth and light—that is, an increase in the duration of sunshine hours above the average—to occur at the right moments; that is, during the blossoming time in order to produce the right quantity, and during the autumn to produce the right quality. Perhaps one should also add that it is especially grapes that ripen late which produce the great wines.

The true mark of a quality wine, its magnificent, fruity acidity, is formed in sufficient quantity only when, during the last autumn days, at the height of maturation, over-ripeness occurs in the shape of "noble-rottenness", the real perfection of the ripening process. To obtain a good wine in northern districts, it is necessary to postpone the harvest as long as possible, to wait with patience and courage for the full ripening of the grape—which is, after all, the finishing point for all the hard work of the year. It is actually the last two or three weeks before the picking of the grapes which decide if there will be a good quality or a lesser quality wine.

In Germany the climate is not equable, it is not the same every year. It is not sur-prising, therefore, that really great vintages are very rare. Most vintages in Germany do not produce great wines—*Spitzenweine*—but just agreeable table wines, light wines of which one can enjoy a glass or bottle, wines to which one can sit down just in order to quench one's thirst. There is a saying in Germany that great vintages are as rare as great statesmen.

If we speak of good and excellent vintages, of the very best vintages, we must also remember that they do not occur simultaneously in all German districts. This is illustrated by the following list of vintages, indicating the districts in which the vintage was good. From this list it is clear that very often just one or two districts in a vintage are blessed with fine weather and produce good wine, a good vintage, a vintage to lay down, a vintage to remember; whereas the other districts produce no more than the ordinary table wines and thirst-quenchers, of which we spoke only a few lines ago. For instance, Palatinate wines do not flourish in exceptionally dry years, when Rheingau wines of the very highest quality may be produced.

THE BEST VINTAGES (nineteenth and twentieth centuries)

1811
Quantity and quality excellent, sweet, rich. Known as the *Kometenwein*, the Comet vintage, in the annals of gastronomy; sung and praised by Goethe. In all German districts a large quantity of wine was made, and most of it of superlative excellence. The wonder year of the century.

1822
Rheingau, Rhinehessia, Palatinate, Franconia, Moselle, Nahe, Middle Rhine, Ahr, Baden, Württemberg: a very large quantity of very fine wine was made. The best wines were those of the Rheingau, which were the peers of the great 1811 Rheingauers.

1834
The same as 1822, with the exception of Nahe, Moselle, Middle Rhine, and Württemberg. An early vintage and a very good one. A good quantity and all of remarkably fine quality.

1846
The same as 1822, abnormally high degree of sugar, very sweet wines.

1857
Rheingau, Franconia, Baden and Württemberg: a great deal of wine was made, most of it of exceptionally fine quality and high alcoholic strength.

1859
Palatinate and Baden: only in these two districts was the wine equal to 1857, but in the other districts, too, good wines were made.

1862
Rheingau, Rhinehessia, Palatinate, Franconia, Moselle: a rich harvest.

1865
The finest since 1811; even better than 1822.

1868
Rheingau, Rhinehessia, Franconia, Baden: a great deal of wine and of excellent quality.

1892

Palatinate: a lot, and excellent. In other districts the quality was good.

1893

The finest since 1868—perhaps even the finest of the century. Small quantity generally; in Franconia abundant crop.

In this year, after an interval of twenty-five years, came one of the greatest vintages of the nineteenth century—a wine which, according to the judgment of experts, and as far as the memory of the then living generation went, was the best of the century. It had a wonderful ripeness; many wines were honey-sweet and of such a beautiful bouquet, spiciness and harmony that 1893 is still called the ideal of a German wine. "One had the feeling"—writes one author—"that nature had needed a long time to collect all its forces to produce such splendid wines". Prices were paid for these noble wines which, in terms of today's purchasing power of money, cannot be considered to be in reach of anyone's purse.

It was the 1893 *Steinberger Kabinett Trockenbeerenauslese* which was crowned the best of all wines of this vintage; its sister-cask was sold in 1899. Even the Neroberg in Wiesbaden produced a *Feinste Trockenbeerenauslese* (Royal Prussian Domain). Kaiser Wilhelm was handed this wine as a cup of honour in 1907 and when the wine was tasted again in 1951, on the occasion of the visit of Professor Heuss to Kloster Eberbach, it was considered still fresh and young and was admired by all who had the good fortune to taste it. Incidentally, the Steinberg produced various casks of Trockenbeerenauslese: cask 66, cask 100 and cask 118. It was the latter cask which was considered the best of this fine 1893 vintage.

The best Palatinate was *Forster Ziegler Auslese* (DM.17,300 per 1,000 litres) von Buhl.

1900

This, the first vintage of the twentieth century, was especially praised by experts in the Palatinate as one of the most beautiful vintages. When the grapes were already ripe, a very short spell of rain created ideal conditions for the development of noble-rottenness; the results were musts of high sugar content, but wines which were especially difficult to treat. Those in the hands of the right cellar-master developed into very noble growths, especially Riesling and Traminer wines.

Forster Freundstück Riesling Edelbeerenauslese.

Forster Jesuitengarten Beerenauslese (Weingut Bassermann-Jordan) 232° Öchsle.
    (This wine was given as a present to Prince Regent Luitpold of Bavaria for his
    eighty-fifth birthday in 1900 by the combined town councils of the Palatinate.)

Erbacher Marcobrunn Trockenbeerenauslese (Rheingau) State Domain.

1904

A great Rheingau vintage; good in other districts. In the Palatinate, this vintage did not reach the quality of 1900. There were many ordinary wines produced, especially as the small growers, on account of the early rottenness of the grapes, would not wait with their picking; but late-gathered grapes produced wines of great quality. The giant of this vintage is the *Rauenthaler Trockenbeerenauslese*—a wine which had the name "Hat Off Wine". When the wine was knocked down at the auction on May 26, 1906, all present stood up and called out "Hats off!" as a tribute to this great wine. Only after this vintage was Rauenthal recognized as a producer of the greatest wines of the Rheingau.

> *Steinberger Hochfeine Trockenbeerenauslese* (State Domain).
>
> *Piesporter Goldtröpfchen* (Kesselstatt). The most expensive Moselle sold before 1914.

1911

The number 11 is a good omen in viticulture, so the saying goes, and the Germans say that 1911 was a repetition of the famous 1811 vintage. The late summer was very dry, and the heavy soil of the Rheingau, where there was also a little more rain, produced much greater wines than, for instance, did the dry soil of the Palatinate.

> *Deidesheimer Grainhübel Riesling Trockenbeerenauslese* (Bassermann-Jordan), 131° Öchsle.
>
> *Deidesheimer Rennpfad Riesling Trockenbeerenauslese* (Price: DM.19,000 per 1,000 l.).
>
> *Schloss Vollrads Trockenbeerenauslese* (200° Öchsle) See tasting note in Appendix Five.
>
> *Schloss Johannisberger Edelbeerenauslese* Best cask No. 75 (May 1913, 24,011 RM.).
>
> *Rauenthaler Wieshell Cabinet Trockenbeerenauslese* (Prussian Domain).

1920

This vintage produced three different classes of wine: a very small wine, a wine of average quality, and *Hochgewächse—Spitzenweine*—as are produced by the sun only once in a century or half a century. The sugar content of the must went up to 280 degrees and the noble-rottenness in some sites was so excellent that some of the 1920 wines surpassed even the finest of the 1921's. Among the giants of this vintage we have to name the *Kiedricher Gräfenberg Trockenbeerenauslese*, best cask No. 20, Estate Bottling Dr A. Weil; a wine which Graf Zeppelin took with him on his first world journey in his airship.

> *Deidesheimer Kieselberg Riesling Beerenauslese*, 133° Öchsle (von Bassermann-Jordan).
>
> *Forster Freundstück Riesling Beerenauslese* (von Buhl), 160° Öchsle; 9.6% acidity.
>
> *Kiedricher Gräfenberg Trockenbeerenauslese*, best cask No. 20 (Dr Weil).
>
> *Rauenthaler Wissel-Blümchen Trockenbeerenauslese*, 180° Öchsle; 11.5% acidity.
> (Tasted by us in 1961, still fresh, fine with dryish finish. It showed its beauty at the ripe age of forty-one years!)

1921

The main characteristics of the celebrated "sun-vintage" are the high quality, the richness and the fullness of its wines. The 1921 wines have been judged quite differently at various times. Whereas in the beginning great enthusiasm created a great demand,

Plate 19. Sylvaner grapes.

some wines were bottled too early and were very disappointing; but those wines which were fully treated and matured in cask (especially those coming from the hill-sites of Hallgarten, Johannisberg, Schloss Vollrads and Rauenthal), produced wines of exceptionally fine quality and staying power. The giant of this vintage is the 1921 *Steinberger Kabinett Trockenbeerenauslese* of the Prussian Domain. Only if one sipped this wine, when it was six years old, at the auction on February 9, 1927, if one saw and listened to the bidding for this wine and experienced the excitement when it was knocked down at the price of 173 Marks per bottle, can one describe the beauty of this wine.

On the same day, *Serriger Vogelsang Trockenbeerenauslese* (State Domain, Trier) cost 128 DM.

Erbacher Marcobrunn Trockenbeerenauslese Cabinet (State Domain) Rhg.

Forster Jesuitengarten Trockenbeerenauslese (Bassermann-Jordan) 200° Öchsle.

Forster Freundstück Riesling Trockenbeerenauslese (von Buhl) 254° Öchsle; 13% acidity.

Berncasteler Doktor und Graben Trockenbeerenauslese (Wwe. Dr Thanisch).

1934

was that rare thing, a heavy crop vintage, with excellent ripe wines, combining body and finesse. It was a sunny year—a year of sunshine from spring to harvest-time, and many great Beerenauslese and Trockenbeerenauslese wines were produced. The Prussian Domain produced the *Steinberger Kabinett Trockenbeerenauslese*, a wine with enormous body and extract; the Schloss Vollrads, a honey-sweet Trockenbeerenauslese wine, with beautiful aroma and great finesse. These are the greatest of this vintage in the Rheingau. Schloss Vollrads produced, besides the great Trockenbeerenauslese, the finest Beerenauslese, nobly sweet, with enormous bouquet and a very delicate fruitiness. On the same level was the *Hallgartener Deutelsberg Riesling Beerenauslese*, Estate Bottling Engelmann. Here, then, are the giants of 1934:

Schloss Vollrads Trockenbeerenauslese.

Steinberger Cabinet Trockenbeerenauslese.

Deidesheimer Grainhübel Riesling Trockenbeerenauslese 194° Öchsle (Grand Prix World Exhibition, Paris, 1937) Estate Bottling Bassermann-Jordan.

Schloss Vollrads Beerenauslese.

Hallgartener Deutelsberg Riesling Beerenauslese (F. K. Engelmann).

1937

was a sunny, excellent vintage, with beautiful, ripe wines of noble character; sweetness and acidity were well balanced. The sugar content of the must went up to 258 degrees. The trade was willing to pay up to £14 per bottle in the growers' cellars for these "presents from heaven" as they called them. Rauenthal again produced the greatest giant—*Rauenthaler Hühnerberg Trockenbeerenauslese* (a *Spitzenwein*)—a wine of a quality which is difficult to describe; the body, the bouquet and the spiciness, the noble sweetness, the fruity acidity.

Forster Freundstück Riesling Trockenbeerenauslese, Est. Bottling von Buhl, 157°
   Öchsle; 10.4% acidity.

Deidesheimer Kieselberg Riesling Trockenbeerenauslese, 165° Öchsle, Bassermann-
   Jordan.

Hochheimer Kirchenstück Trockenbeerenauslese, Estate Bottling Aschrott.

Rauenthaler Hühnerberg Trockenbeerenauslese (State Domain), 265° Öchsle.

Schloss Vollrads (best cask) *Trockenbeerenauslese*, 190°.

Rüdesheimer Hinterhaus Trockenbeerenauslese, 210°.

Berncasteler Doctor und Graben Trockenbeerenauslese (Wwe. Dr Thanisch).

1949

This was also a dry year, but not as dry as 1947: the wines had a little more acidity
than the 1947 vintage, but in great harmony, and the wines of 1949 were elegant wines.
Early bottled 1949's had staying power and showed marvellous development in bottle.

Deidesheimer Kieselberg Riesling Trockenbeerenauslese (von Buhl), 204° Öchsle;
   10.4 ‰ acidity. Their 1950 *Deidesheimer Leinhöhle Riesling Trockenbeerenauslese*
   had: 245° Öchsle; 9.8 ‰ acidity.

Forster Jesuitengarten Riesling Trockenbeerenauslese (Bassermann-Jordan), 212°
   Öchsle. (Incidentally, the wine of the same description, of the 1950 vintage,
   had 233°!)

Zeltinger-Wehlener Sonnenuhr Trockenbeerenauslese (J. J. Prüm).

1953

This was a year of rain and sunshine at the right times and in the right quantities,
and even on dry ground the grapes had the chance to attain full ripeness, and even
to develop noble-rottenness. It was just this which distinguishes the 1953 wines from
so many other good vintages, that the dampness of the harvesting time produced noble-
rottenness, even in sites where one was not accustomed to meet it, and everywhere
were produced *Spitzenweine* of the first order. In the Palatinate it is considered a vintage
on the same level as 1900, 1911 and 1921—even though dry years in the Palatinate
are not usually conducive to production of the highest class wines.

Deidesheimer Leinhöhle Riesling Trockenbeerenauslese (von Buhl), 215° Öchsle;
   7.3 ‰ acidity.

Forster Jesuitengarten Riesling Trockenbeerenauslese (Bassermann-Jordan), 213°
   Öchsle.

Schloss Vollrads Trockenbeerenauslese, 180° Öchsle.

Hattenheimer Nussbrunnen Trockenbeerenauslese Kabinett (Gathered on November
   18, 1953) Freiherr Langwerth von Simmern.

1959

Here is a vintage which is in everybody's memory, which soon after the harvesting
time was pronounced "the vintage of the century". In the districts of the Rheingau
and the Moselle, with heavy soil, we find the finest of the 1959 wines, and in this

connection we must not forget the Nahe. There was no shortage of underground water for the roots of the vines to reach, so that even in the very sunny period of the summer there was no danger that the life of the vine would be affected; but even where noble-rottenness could not set in, and we do not find *Spitzenweine* in quantity, the Beerenauslese and Trockenbeerenauslese, the wines generally produced, show body and a natural sweetness, a honey sweetness, as has not been seen since 1921. To illustrate the greatness of the 1959's, here are some selections of various estates:

Kiedricher Gräfenberg Trockenbeerenauslese, 270° Öchsle; 17.2‰ acidity.

Berncasteler Doctor Riesling Trockenbeerenauslese (Dr Thanisch), 312° Öchsle!

Summing up, the great vintages of this century:

In the Palatinate we count sixteen, and of these sixteen, we can give five the attribute "excellent": 1900, 1911, 1921, 1953, 1959.

In the Rheingau, eight: 1904, 1911, 1921, 1934, 1937, 1949, 1953, 1959.

Looking at the list of the *Spitzenweine* one must ask oneself if there is any wine worth £4, £5 or £10 or even more. One is often asked this question—especially by those who never had, or never took, the opportunity to taste these wines, those who drink always the same wine from the beginning to the end of the year. Our answer is very simple: great wines are works of art, works of nature's art, and they are to be valued as such. They are available in small quantities only, and valued accordingly. They are unique in their composition and in their taste, and they have rarity value. A bottle of wine can be worth £15 or £20 or more, if there are people interested in acquiring it. And whoever has the opportunity of drinking these "kings of wine" will not repent.

Of course, one might reply: works of art keep for ever; they increase in value with age and rarity; and they are not consumed. They go from generation to generation, in the same family, and are enjoyed by generations as long as they exist. This is true, but although wines as such may live only twenty, thirty, fifty years, these wines live for ever in the memory of those who enjoyed them, and their value lies in this rarity. Only a few living people had the pleasure of tasting the 1893 *Steinberger Cabinet Trockenbeerenauslese* or a 1911 *Schloss Vollrads Trockenbeerenauslese*, and nobody can buy the memory of them.

To illustrate the differences of quality which exist even in the greatest vintages, here are some figures relating to quality and price in a few selected famous vineyards:

The *"Spitzen"* of the State Domain Trier in this century

	Sugar content (Öchsle)	Acidity (promille)	Prices per Fuder of 1,000 litres
1921			
Avelsbacher Hammerstein	268°	8.1	
Ockfener Bockstein	226°	16.6	
Serriger Vogelsang	290°	16	

1937

Avelsbacher Hammerstein	135°	8	7,000 RM.
Ockfener Bockstein	120°	8.5	7,000 RM.
Serriger Vogelsang	150°	12.2	9,000 RM.

1947

Avelsbacher Thielslei	95°	7.4	17,500 RM.
Ockfener Heppenstein	92°	8.4	17,800 RM.
Serriger Vogelsang	99°	5.8	18,000 RM.

1949

Avelsbacher Hammerstein	150°	13.1	25,000 DM.
Avelsbacher Thielslei	121°	10.1	17,500 DM. (ice wine)
Ockfener Bockstein	118°	9.6	14,500 DM.
Serriger Vogelsang	126°	9	17,000 DM.

1953

Avelsbacher Hammerstein	118°	9.9	6,000 DM.
Ockfener Heppenstein	100°	9.9	6,800 DM.
Serriger Vogelsang	104°	8.1	7,500 DM.

1959

Avelsbacher Hammerstein Trockenbeerenauslese	264°	19.8
Ockfener Bockstein Trockenbeerenauslese	136°	12.8
Serriger Vogelsang Trockenbeerenauslese	248°	18

NOTES ON SOME OTHER TWENTIETH CENTURY VINTAGES

1915

A very fine summer and an unusually early vintage. There was a great deal of wine made, all of it good and some of it of superlative quality.

1917

Much damage done by May and October frosts, but the summer was very fine. A fair amount of wine was made, from fine to great in quality.

1925

Yet another bad vintage although some of the wine made was not quite so bad as that of the three previous vintages. How, in an odd vintage, some outstanding wines can be produced is shown by the quality and price of some 1925 Palatinate wines, viz:

Forster Kirchenstück Riesling Beerenauslese (Weingut W. Spindler-Forst) at 40 DM. per bottle and

Forster Freundstück Riesling Trockenbeerenauslese (v. Buhl) at 52 DM. per bottle.

1927
The seventh successive bad vintage, the worst series of years on record. There was very little wine made and none of it was of any quality.

1929
The first good vintage since 1921. There was not a very large quantity of wine made, but all of it was very good.

1933
A better vintage than any since 1929; there was a great deal of wine made, most of it quite good.

1939
One of the worst vintages on record; hardly any wine made and none of it any good.

1943
A very good vintage as to both quality and quantity.

1945
A fine summer and autumn were responsible for some excellent wines, but the quantity produced was much smaller than it would have been had it not been for the war. Most 1945's were so luscious and attractive when quite young that they were never given the chance to show how great they would be if allowed to grow in bottle.

1947
A very fine sunny year when a great deal of wine was made, all of it good or very good. Many wines, though, lacked balancing acidity and were short-lived.

1954
A complete failure: May and October frosts, and a wet summer in between.

1957
Another poor summer, but a fine autumn saved the vintage from being a total failure; some quite good wines were made from the late-gathered grapes in the Moselle Valley.

1960
An enormous harvest, of average quality.

1961
Half the quantity of 1960, but fuller wines. Many ice wines made, even some from Lake Constance (*Seewein*).

Chapter Six

SEKT, OR
GERMAN SPARKLING WINE

"Sekt" is the generic name now adopted for all sparkling wines made in Germany. According to one opinion the name "Sekt" was given to German sparkling wines because, in England, champagne is known as Sec and Extra Sec, Dry or Extra Dry. Others, however, have another theory regarding the origin of the name.

When in 1815 the actor Ludwig Devrient came to the Berlin Court Theatre he often played Falstaff in *Henry IV*. In the scene at the Boar's Head Tavern, Falstaff orders the servitor to bring a "cup of sack". The German translation of "sack" is "Sekt". From the stage Devrient carried this nomenclature into his Berlin "pub", the wine-restaurant of Lutter and Wegner where he used to sit imbibing champagne with his friend and crony, E. T. A. Hoffmann. The waiter became accustomed to bringing Devrient his champagne whenever he called out, "Hey, villain, bring me a glass of Sekt!" Since then, the word has established itself in Germany as the correct designation for sparkling wine, although it was in fact meant not for champagne, a beverage unknown in the days of Henry IV, but for sherry.

Which of the two theories is correct does not matter very much, but it is certain that in Germany there were sparkling wines known as *Schaumweine* a very long time before the name Sekt came into use.

In Germany, as in Luxembourg, Alsace and Champagne, that is, at or near the northern limit of the area in which grapes may be expected to ripen in the open, the early frosts of the winter check the final stages of the fermentation of the new wine soon after it is made. When the sun returns, in the spring, the new wines start "working" again, sending up bubbles as they proceed with the fermentation of whatever proportion of the grape-sugar is still in the wine. This is why sparkling wines were known in Champagne, and also in Germany, long before they were imitated in Italy and elsewhere —practically in every part of the world where grapes grow and where wine is made. Wine lovers greatly appreciate what is called *Spritzig Mosel* or Saar wine, that is to say a wine which still has just a spark of liveliness; and it is certain that from early times there were wine growers and others in the Rhineland who managed to make some sparkling wines for their own consumption and for the entertainment of their friends.

Probably the taste of the Rhinelanders for sparkling wine and the desire to produce some of their own date back to the twenty years from 1795 to 1814, during which the French were in practically continuous occupation of the Rhineland from Strasbourg to Koblenz. The manufacture of sparkling wines in Germany was first established at Esslingen in 1826, and soon after in Grüneberg in Silesia. Esslingen is the centre of the Neckar viticulture: 4% Sylvaner, 6% Riesling, 88% Trollinger and 2% others.

The sparkling-wine manufacturers use wines from all the Württemberg districts, and of course imported wines as well. In 1960 the output reached 69 million bottles. (In the same year, Germany imported 18 million bottles of Champagne and other sparkling wines, and exported 1,014,375 bottles, in addition to the 976,888 bottles sold to the allied armies in Germany.)

The sparkling-wine firms started in those districts where the wine was nearly undrinkable unless it was improved or sweetened, for here they had plenty of the necessary raw material. By 1850 there were forty-three firms producing sparkling wines in Germany, with a yearly production of 1,275,000 bottles—or just over a million litres. By 1885 the numbers had increased to 150 manufacturers, with a yearly turnover of 6,000,000 bottles; by 1903, 225 firms with a turnover of 11,000,000 bottles. In 1953, though, according to Dr Günther-Herzog, (*Die Deutschen Sektkellereien—Ihre Entwicklung und Ihre Bedeutung für den Deutschen Weinbau*), there were only 63 manufacturers with a turnover of 9,692,905 bottles, which represented only two thirds of the 1936 turnover. Since then, however, the German tax on sparkling wine has been reduced, with the result that both the turnover and the number of manufacturers have increased. In the first year of this tax reduction, 1953, the turnover went up to 15,156,530 bottles and has increased steadily ever since.

There are no still wines in the world possessing a greater measure of individuality than the great wines of the Rhineland: as we have seen, they are sold not only with the name of the vineyard and the date of the vintage of their birth, but also with the name of the grapes from which they were made and with the indication of how and when the grapes were picked—Spätlese, Auslese, Trockenbeerenauslese, etc.—and even with the number of the particular cask in which they were reared before being bottled. But there is nothing like this individuality when it comes to the sparkling wines of Germany. There is seldom an indication of the vineyards they come from, still less of the year in which they were made. Their anonymity enables the firms who specialize in the trade to buy wine where and when it suits them, and also to blend wines in any way they consider best to ensure a continuity of the standard and quality of the different brands under which they market their wines. Until 1914 the German sparkling-wine manufacturers used to buy large quantities of wines at vintage time from growers and shippers of Champagne who were only too pleased to sell at very reasonable prices wines of the second and third pressings of their grapes. Although such wines had not the breeding or finesse of the *cuvée*, or first-pressing wines, they were very welcome in Germany for blending with German and other wines intended to be made into sparkling wines.

After 1918, the Germans no longer had the means, even if they had had the wish, to buy wine in France. But today again, especially during the last few years when there has been a shortage of German wines, large quantities of foreign still wines were imported for the sole purpose of manufacturing Sekt.

There is no secret about the manner in which still wines can be made sparkling, in Germany or anywhere else. There are three ways of doing it, which may be called good, better and best. The best method is called the *Flaschengärung* or *méthode champenoise*, the way in which champagne is made. It means bottling the wine with just the right proportion of sugar in it to ensure that, after fermentation has run its course within the securely stoppered bottle, it will have produced the right proportions of carbonic acid gas to make the wine sparkling: too much sugar would mean too much gas and a burst bottle; too little means a few half-hearted bubbles only. The drawback is that where wine does ferment in bottle and produce its own carbonic acid gas, it also throws off bits and pieces of sediment which would completely spoil the look of the wine in the glass, to say nothing of its taste: it cannot be allowed to remain in the wine. Getting this sediment to slide slowly down the bottle until it is packed against the inner face of the cork is not only a slow process, but also one which requires a skilled hand. Then comes the *dégorgement*: moving the cork out of the bottle without losing any of the wine or letting the gas escape, and yet getting rid of all the sediment in the neck of the bottle. This also demands skilled and costly handling. After this, the wine in the bottle is both brilliant and sparkling: it is sweetened more or less, or not at all, according to the taste of the different markets where it will be offered for sale. It is finally stoppered with a fine and expensive cork, which is securely wired to the ring on the neck of the bottle. This *méthode champenoise* is admittedly the best, but, like all that is best, it is also the most costly.

The next best way of making sparkling wines—which is the way many sparkling wines are made in Germany—is the *vase clos* or "tank" method, which may be described as "machine-made" as opposed to "hand-made". In this method, the wine is fermented not in individual bottles but in securely closed tanks, and when the fermentation is over and the wine saturated with its own carbonic acid gas, it is filtered into bottles and sweetened more or less; it is finally securely corked in the same way as before.

The third method, which may be good enough when cheapness is the first consideration, is to pump just the right amount of carbonic acid gas into a bottle of still—and

Plate 20.   Bad Kreuznach, in the Nahe district.
Plate 21.   The Kafels vineyard at Norheim, in the Nahe district.

always sweet—wine, to make it effervescent, just like "fizzy" lemonade. If this method has been used, it has to be stated on the label: the term used is *Kohlensäurezusatz*.

Since 1919 it has been illegal in Germany to use the name "Champagne" in connection with any German sparkling wine (or "Cognac" in connection with brandy). The one and only provision of the Peace Treaty which concerned wine was very simple, but so fair that it was neither amended nor scrapped (as were most, if not all, the other provisions of the same Peace Treaty): it stipulated that the territorial names of wines, (not of French wines alone but, of course, of German and other wines as well), would be protected by German law to the same extent and in the same manner as they were protected by French law. By the Treaty of March 8, 1960, between France and Western Germany, both countries agreed to apply and observe each other's wine laws.

"Sekt" has now been universally accepted as the name belonging to the sparkling wines of Germany and to them alone, but all the more important firms who make and market German sparkling wines have succeeded in getting their own names and brands recognised and demanded without "Sekt", "*Schaumwein*", or any other tag added to it. *Söhnlein Rheingold*, for instance, is perfectly well known by all who, in Germany, have the means or the chance to drink sparkling wine; to call the wine *Söhnlein Rheingold Sekt* would be superfluous; even *Söhnlein Champagne*, if it were legal, would be unwise since it would inevitably suggest a comparison, as dangerous as it is unnecessary, between two different wines, one German and the other French. The name of the firm responsible for the quality and style of the wine in the bottle with just one identification name added to it, a name as easy to remember as possible, is all that is really necessary. This is why the more popular sparkling wines of Germany are those known by the name of the manufacturers, of which in 1961 there were 119.

There are, however, a comparatively small number of sparkling wines which are sold under the name of their native village or vineyard, such as Sparkling Bernkasteler, Sparkling Schloss Johannisberger, Sparkling Scharzberger, Sparkling Steinberger, and so on. According to German law, when a sparkling wine is sold under a specified territorial appellation, not less than two thirds of the wine in the bottle must come from vineyards named on the label: it is possible that the other third allowed might be so good as to improve the blend (everything is possible), but it is more likely to be wine appreciably cheaper than the rest, so that the wine can be offered for sale at competitive prices.

There is in Germany another sparkling wine besides Sekt, or *Schaumweine*, or sparkling wine proper. It is a semi-sparkling wine known as *Perlwein*, similar to the French *Vinperlé*. It is made in tanks, for initial cheapness, and this is sufficient to save *Perlwein* from the luxury tax levied upon Sekt: hence its popular appeal. Incidentally, *Perlwein* must not be made up to mislead the public. It is therefore bottled in ordinary hock bottles and closed with crown corks—not with champagne corks and wire.

There is no possible doubt about the immediate popularity that German sparkling wines have enjoyed overseas from a very early date. Even as long ago as 1834 the wine list of the United States Hotel in Philadelphia listed sparkling hock at 3 dollars per bottle, whereas sparkling burgundy was listed at 2 dollars and 50 cents, and champagne, whether French or American, did not cost more than 2 dollars per bottle!

Since then, the sparkling wine industry of Germany has moved to the Rhineland, chiefly to Wiesbaden, Frankfurt-on-Main, Koblenz, Mainz, Hochheim-on-Main and Wachenheim (Palatinate). Sparkling wines are made in a number of other places, but Hessen has 47.4% and the State Rheinland-Pfalz 42.6% share in the country's total production of Sekt.

Chapter Seven

GERMAN BRANDY

The German Wine Law contains, in paragraph 18 under the heading *Weinbrand-Weinbrandverschnitt-Cognac*, the following definition:—"*Trinkbranntwein*: Wine whose alcohol has been won exclusively from wine, and which has been distilled according to the method of Cognac, can be called *Weinbrand* (Brandy)."

The word *Weinbrand* means nothing else but "burnt wine". *Weinbrand* for German grape brandy is synonymous with the word *Branntwein*. The alcohol contained in wine is known as the *Weingeist*, whereas the alcohol resulting from the fermentation of other fruits is called alcohol or spirit.

Aristotle knew that there were combustible materials in wine, but he did not understand how to separate the alcohol from the watery substances of the wine. Distillation of brandy was discovered in Europe in the eleventh or twelfth century. We know too that the Chinese had discovered the secrets of distillation by the thirteenth century at the latest. Li-Chi-Tschin, in his encyclopedia of the sixteenth century, reports that the Chinese knew about distillation of Araki (or, in Chinese, *Alaki*) from rice-wine in 1260–1360, in the time of the Mongolian dynasty.

Brandy was much enjoyed by sick people, but by others too; one of the characteristics of brandy praised in literature is that it strengthens the memory and gladdens the heart. The classical country for this distillation is, of course, France.

The great wine district of Charente is famous, not for the vinification of table wines, but for distillation. In the centre of this district is Cognac, which produces the most noble brandy of all. St-Emilion, Colombard and other white grapes are cultivated there; the soil and climate are excellent for their growth and ripening.

Almost as famous is the district of Armagnac, part of the Gascogne in the South of France. Other districts are not so important, but the wines from Beziers, Cette, Marseilles, Montpelier and Narbonne are used for distillation. According to French law, however, the wines coming from those districts cannot be used for the distillation of Cognac because, according to both French and German law, "Cognac" is a pure geographical denomination and must not be used for wines of any other district. Brandies from other districts are sold as "alcool de vin".

The beginning of German wine distillation, the manufacture of *Weinbrand*, was caused by the bad economic conditions in which some Rhenish wine-growers found themselves in the middle of the nineteenth century when many of the small and mediocre wines were not saleable at all. The first German to use the Cognac method for distilling these low-quality wines was an apothecary, P. Dahlem of Trier, and he was quite successful with his products. He showed them at various exhibitions, including Paris 1866 and Metz 1868, and he won prizes. It is unnecessary to say that his factory had to overcome many difficulties, especially as the Germans continued to prefer imported brandy. When the state introduced protective measures on imported brandies, this helped the new industry to establish itself, and German brandy was even exported to England and the United States.

Although Germany is quite famous for distilleries, let it be said immediately that it does not produce any wines which could be useful for distillation—or, rather, that although Germany produces wines which could be used for distillation, and might produce some good brandies, generally speaking for economic reasons this is not done. The German distilleries, if they use German wine at all, tend to use those wines which have been confiscated by the government as being concoctions that are not allowed to be sold as wine. If, for instance, the grower adds too much sugar to the wine in a bad vintage, this wine must not be sold; it is confiscated and sold to distilleries for the preparation of brandy. The same thing happens if the sulphur content is too high, or if he offers or sells his wine under a misleading denomination.

The wines which are used for distillation in Germany come from all over the world. Quite a good proportion still comes from the Charente—from the original Cognac district—but it is usually mixed with wine from other parts of the world—Italy, Greece, Spain, Bulgaria, Hungary, Yugoslavia, or from any wine-producing country which has wines for distillation to offer. The reason for this is, of course, quite clear: German wines are too expensive, even more expensive than the Charente wines which are grown for brandy in the district in which Cognac is made.

This method alone allows German distilleries to compete with French Cognac—at least in Germany, for the German distiller buys wine which may be useful for his brandies wherever he finds it. In Germany, as in all countries, fiscal laws have a great influence on the brandy trade for good or evil.

The German distiller imports the wines at exactly the strength he needs, and in order to achieve this the foreign wines are imported not as natural wines but as fortified wines.

Plate 22.   Edelfäule—noble-rotten grapes for
making *Trockenbeerenauslesen.*

This is done by adding brandy distilled in the district of the imported wine. In Germany the duty is levied per 100 Kg. of a basic wine up to 23 % alcoholic strength, so by importing the wines in this state not only duty but freight is saved.

To give an idea of German brandy distillation, here are recent total import figures, expressed in terms of hectolitres, of basic wine for conversion into brandy:

1936	191,150
1938	270,588
1949	631,179

These figures are still increasing.

From five litres of the imported 23 % wine, one litre of distillate is produced. As a rule, the German distiller has agreements with his suppliers that the wines he imports should be prepared in the same way as the wines he imports from the Charente. This ensures that the basic wines are at least similar in their method of vinification, although, on account of the different soil and climate, they can never be considered identical in quality with the wines of the Charente.

After the ending of fermentation the wines do not undergo a racking from the lees, but are distilled together with the lees after the principle secondary fermentation is over. In a normal wine the yeast content is approximately 5 promille, and wines are imported into Germany from the various countries of origin after the first fermentation, still mixed with the yeast produced by the fermentation.

The first *Branntwein* was made in the same way as it is made today—by distillation, that is, by steaming and condensation. Nothing has changed in this method in all the centuries. More often than not, corn, potatoes and other cereals, rather than wine, were used for the basic product. For a long time *Branntwein* distillation was lost altogether—after all, spirit made from potatoes and cereals was much cheaper than brandy made from wine, especially from German wine, which contains very little alcohol; but the brandy of today is different from the brandy made centuries ago.

Cognac distillers learnt to use a second distillation after the first (the *brouilles*). In this way they gained the heart of the brandy. It is also true that newly distilled brandy gains in quality by storage in special oak casks made from trees in the French Limousin and Angoumois district.

Here is a short description of the way brandy is distilled in Cognac.

Water boils and evaporates after reaching 212° Fahrenheit, whereas alcohol and aromatic substances are converted into steam at 172° or 174°. The object, therefore, is to raise the temperature of the wine just high enough to evaporate only the valuable ingredients, thus separating them from the water content. This operation is called "burning" or "distilling" the wine, and it is performed in "stills"—enormous copper boilers which have been used, almost in their present form, since the earliest days of brandy making, except that they are no longer heated with wood or coal, but with steam.

The heated alcoholic and aromatic substances, which evaporate during the distillation process, are again condensed to liquid by cooling. As a result of this first distillation, also called "crude burning", they become a liquid with about 40% alcohol content. For further enrichment and purification, and to reach an alcohol content of about 70%, which is essential for continued development, a second distillation, or "fine-burning", is performed. During the cooling process, following this second distillation, the condensed alcoholic vapours are carefully separated into three parts. The middle-flow, the "heart", is regarded as fine-brandy—a clear, water-like fluid which is then stored in huge receptacles made of glass-lined concrete.

In theory this procedure may seem rather simple, but in practice it is complicated. Adjustment of temperatures during the two distillation processes, obtaining the right degree of heat at the moment most advantageous to the accumulation of the aromatic substances, as well as the timely separation of the initial-, middle- and after-flow by means of sampling odour and flavour, are achievements of the highest order.

After a short time the wine-distillate is transferred from the concrete receptacles to the so-called *barriques*—hogsheads—in which it must be stored for a long period. The *barriques* are made of the rare and costly wood of the Limousin oak tree. In them the brandy loses its harshness; air infiltrates through the pores in the wood, causing some of the alcohol to oxydize, and by this process products are formed which give the brandy its much renowned softness. At the same time, the so-called esters develop. But the wood of the Limousin oak tree contributes still more; nature has endowed it with delicate ingredients such as resin and tanning matter which, together with pigments, are gradually extracted during the long storage process and give some colour to the once colourless liquid.

Each barrel of brandy has its individuality. The influence of the wood on maturity, softness, aroma and colouring varies as much as the wines out of which the brandy has been distilled. To balance these differences to some extent, the wine-distillate is from time to time blended in large vats and then transferred back to the *barriques*. This process is repeated several times until full maturity of the wine-distillate has been reached, but it is not yet the final product. Not until the brandy has reached the "blending room" does the last and decisive procedure take place. There, finally, the selected brandies are mixed in large vats, and bottled.

German brandy is made in exactly the same way and the qualities obtainable vary enormously; none are equal to the finest Cognac, although some good German brandies can be bought.

Germany has also found export outlets for her brandies. In 1957, 73,000 litres were exported to the United States, Belgium and Switzerland, which were the leading customers. In subsequent years, the figure has increased.

Chapter Eight

CASKS, GLASSES AND BOTTLES

CASKS

Oak was unchallenged for many centuries as the best home a German wine could possibly wish for, and the coopers of the Rhineland were unexcelled for the size as well as the artistic decorations of their vats and casks. White wines were kept in enormous tuns, none more famous than the Great Tun of Heidelberg, 31 feet by 21 feet, holding 150 Fuders, or 600 hogsheads, of wine: it was built in 1663 to replace an earlier one holding 132 Fuders.

The pride of Bremen has long been the *Rosenwein*, the wine kept in a great tun known as the *Rosentun* on account of a bronze bas-relief of roses at its head. This great tun was originally laid down in 1624 and filled with twelve vats of the finest wine of that vintage, six from Johannisberg and six from Hochheim. In the next cellar there are twelve other great butts, each one of them named after one of the twelve Apostles, and filled only a few years after the *Rosentun*. There are yet other casks, mere hogsheads, in another nearby cellar—they might be called the "Disciples"—filled with younger wines. As and when any of the *Rosenwein* is drawn off to gladden the heart of V.I.P.'s and alleviate their infirmities, a like quantity is drawn from one of the "Apostles" to keep "*Rosen*" full to the bung, and the same quantity of a younger vintage is drawn from one of the "Disciples" to fill up the "Apostle". Whether the Jerez vintners copied Bremen or not is immaterial, but the "Solera" system of Bremen is older than that of Jerez.

Many German towns, large and small, were proud of the capacity and carvings of the great tuns in their municipal cellars, even more than of the wine which they held—inevitably blends of wines of a number of successive vintages. Tübingen, Grüningen and Königstein, for instance, could never compete with Bremen in size or wealth, but they all boasted a larger municipal great tun than that of Bremen.

Great tuns were never removed from their original cellars, less cumbrous containers being used to deliver wine sold within the land or shipped overseas. German wines were sold retail mostly by the Stübchen in Germany, and in England by the gallon, which was the measure nearest to the Stübchen: Rhenish was usually sold wholesale in Germany by the aum (aam, ohm, awne or ahm), known in England as a "piece" or a "butt", of about 40 gallons; and occasionally by the *fat* or *vat* (called a tun in England), and holding about five aums. It is, however, quite impossible ever to be certain of the actual contents of old German wine measures and containers: so many of them had the same name but not at all the same size. Here is a list of some of those still used today, giving the capacity of each in litres.

Rheingau

| Stück | 1,200 | Logel | 50 | Mass | 2 |
| Halbstück | 600 | Eicher | 10–12 | Schoppen | $\frac{1}{2}$ |

Rhinehessia

| Stück | 1,200 | Ohm | 150 | Schoppen | $\frac{1}{2}$ |
| Halbstück | 600 | | | | |

Bavaria (Donau)

| Eimer | 60 | Mass | 1 | Schoppen | $\frac{1}{4}$ |

Bavaria (Lake of Constance)

| Fuder | 1,220 | 15 Bayr. Mass | 16 | 1 Butte | 50 |
| Eimer | 68 | | | | |

Palatinate

Stück	1,200	Ohm	150	Eicher (Stütz)	10
Fuder	1,000	Logel	40	Schoppen	$\frac{1}{2}$
Halbstück	600				

Franconia

Stück	1,200	Ohm	150	Eicher	10
(formerly	1,124)	Eimer	75	Schoppen	$\frac{1}{4}$
Fuder	900	Butte	40	Mass	1–1.17
Halbstück	600	Beerbutte	180		
(formerly	562)				

Plate 23. Castle Ehrenfels, in the Rheingau, between Rüdesheim and Assmannshausen.

Plate 24. Nierstein vineyards on the Rhinefront, in Rhinehessia, between Nierstein and Nackenheim.

Moselle, Saar and Ruwer

Fuder	960	Ohm	160	Kessel (Eicher type)	6–7
Zulast	480	Bürde (Hotte type)	40	Schoppen	½

Baden

Fuder	1,500	Ohm	150	Mass	1½

Nahe

Stück	1,200	Eimer	160	Viertel	8
Fuder	1,000	Schoppen	½	Remies'chen	¼
Halbstück	600	Mass	1		

Württemberg

Eimer	300	Schoppen rund	½	Eiche (of wine casks)	
Imi	18¾	Stütze	10–15	approx.	150
Mass	1.875				

JARS OR JUGS

Oak was not the only home given to German wines in olden days. They were also kept and sent to distant markets in capacious pot-bellied stoneware jars or jugs which were first made in the early years of the sixteenth century in the Rhineland, and copied in England during the second half of the seventeenth century. The very large number of these jugs which still exist today is sufficient proof in the first place that they must have been made in very considerable quantities, and in the second that there was quite a brisk demand for German wine in the Netherlands, the Baltic ports, and in England where such "Greybeards", as they are commonly known, are by no means rare even today. Their name was due to the bearded head or mask stamped in relief upon their short necks. There are also either floral or armorial decorations which occasionally occur on the brown or grey salt glaze of their rotund bodies.

In England, the more popular (and quite unjustified) name for the Greybeard jugs has been "Bellarmine", upon the assumption that the bearded mask on the neck was the caricature of the Jesuit Cardinal Bellarmine, a widely known writer and Catholic theologian who was highly unpopular in Protestant countries. Strange to say, as late as 1849 one William Chaffers read a paper before the British Archaeological Association in which he claimed that he was justified in "christening anew" the Greybeards with the name of Cardinal Bellarmine, which had been one of the names given to them during the previous two hundred years. That Chaffers was entirely wrong is beyond argument, since it is known that Greybeards were made in the Rhineland before Bellarmine was born in 1542, and one of them may be seen in the Tower of London dated 1560, when the future cardinal was but eighteen, presumably beardless, and certainly quite unknown.

Ben Jonson, who had a lot to say about Greybeards, does not mention Bellarmine's name or any other. Cartwright, however, gives the jugs two different names in his play *The Ordinary* in 1634: "Like a larger jug, which some men call a Bellarmine, but we a conscience." In the same play, however, the author refers to the same greybeard jug mentioning that the mask is said to represent Eglon, King of Moab, "a very fat man" (*Judges III*, 17). Dr Plot in his *Natural History of Oxfordshire* (1676) says that greybeard jugs were called "D'Alva Bottles" on the assumption that the head was the caricature of the Duke of Alva, Spanish Governor of the Netherlands.

Evelyn, in *Numismata* (1697), also mentions the Duke of Alva "of whom there are a thousand pictures not on medals only but on every Jugg-Pot . . ."

Why the pottery workers of the Rhine should have ever bothered to stamp upon the neck of their stoneware jugs the head of a Jesuit Cardinal (before he was even born), or of a Spanish Governor of the Low Countries (who meant nothing to them), or of a King of Moab out of Holy Writ (of which they had never heard), does not appear to make sense. Nor did any of those people whose names have been given to the Greybeards ever have any connection whatever with wine or vineyards. Our own suggestion is that the bearded head on the Greybeards was, as near as they could make it, the representation of Father Rhine, an invariably bearded figure in all the old statues and portraits. It seems to us only natural that potters who worked exclusively for Rhine vintners would have chosen the head of Father Rhine for jugs used solely for Rhine wines to be sent to distant markets. It was as good as a pictorial "made in Germany" device, or rather "made on the Rhine".

Besides the bearded head of Father Rhine upon the neck, the smooth and spacious rotundity of the Greybeards gave artists a chance to display their skill in stamping floral and foliate decorations, or else some heraldic or armorial design, chiefly the arms of the German and Dutch towns where the demand for Rhine wine was greatest. Of all the heraldic designs upon Rhineland Greybeards, the arms of Queen Elizabeth puzzled antiquarians quite a lot, until the mould of those English Arms was found on a kiln site, at Rären, in the Rhineland, where evidently Greybeards were made to the order of merchants trading in Rhine wine in England.

All Greybeards to be found on the Continent were most likely made in Germany or the Low Countries, but in England it is not at all easy to tell Rhineland-made from English-made Greybeards. Charles I granted a patent, in 1626, to Thomas Rons and Abraham Cullen, whose first kiln was probably in the City of London: their Greybeards are difficult to tell from the Rhineland models unless, as often happens, arms, crests, or initials give some indication of the tavern or cookshop owners to whom the Greybeards were originally sold. *The Times* of Saturday, July 19, 1958, published an article "Antiques and Pictures" which gave interesting information about Greybeards, some of which has been incorporated in this chapter.

WINE GLASSES

Venice and Murano hold a very important place in the history of modern glass on two major counts, the first being the artistic merit of the glasses due to their creative genius, and the second, perhaps the more important of the two, being the lead which their craftsmen gave to the glassmakers of France, England, Germany and the Netherlands. Their influence, however, was less noticeable in Germany than anywhere else and the *Römer*, the most typical Rhineland glass, may claim a closer association with the early Romans than with the Venetians. Its very name is said by some to be due to the tradition of its early Roman ancestry.

What is perhaps the most remarkable feature of the *Römer* is that in a world of ever-shifting fashions the popularity of this glass has not been affected by changing habits and taste. Unlike those beautiful English eighteenth-century ale, wine and cordial glasses, which are now in museums and the cabinets of private collectors, the *Römer* is still in common use after some three hundred years. There cannot be more positive evidence that the *Römer*, besides the appeal of its pleasing appearance, which is merely a matter of taste, is also admirably suited for the purpose for which it was originally made, that of drinking and enjoying wine—a matter of taste also, no doubt, but less liable to changes of mood.

The Romans imported wine, when they occupied the Rhineland, and taught the natives how to grow grapes in the open and how to make wine; they also taught them how to make vessels of glass, and, like viticulture, glass-making has flourished in Western Germany ever since. Proofs of the fame which the Rhineland glass-makers enjoyed abroad are not lacking; there is, for instance, the recorded despatch to Jarrow, in Northumbria, by Cuthbert, Bishop of Mainz, of a glass-maker from his diocese in response to an appeal from Benedict, Bishop of Wearmouth. Albert Hartshorne, in his monumental work on English and other glasses (*Old English Glasses*, London, 1897), remarks that the glass drinking vessels found in the tombs of Merovingian and Frankish tombs on the Continent were made from late Roman models with small bases or feet and devices so distinctive and so constant as to point to a common source of supply, presumably Cologne or Trier, and within the sixth and seventh centuries.

According to Francis Buckley (*European Glass*, London, 1926), glass-making was carried on in the Rhineland continuously from the days of the Roman occupation to our own. There are still in existence glasses of the Merovingian and Carolingian periods which prove that the custom of drinking wine from glass vessels was widespread in the Rhineland long after the Romans had left. Those early German glasses were small, rather thick and ornamented with "stringing", and with applied little lumps or bosses, technically known as "prunts" and called *Nuppen* by the Germans. These *Nuppen* or "prunts", which were in all probability inspired by the projecting bosses of earlier Roman drinking cups, are the most distinctive form of ornamentation of the Rhineland wine glasses, the most typical of which was the *Römer*, a tall, cylindral green glass, without a lid, studded all along its sides with *Nuppen*, its green colourings being classified as moss green, apple green, yellow green, olive green and sea green: it had a glass ring at the base, but no foot. Presently this ring or base was replaced by a narrow spun foot whilst the top or mouth of the glass was widened to a bowl and eventually the height of the foot was raised until the beautiful seventeenth-century *Römer* reached its most perfect proportions with the bowl about 4 inches, the stem 3 inches and the foot 1 inch high. During the seventeenth and eighteenth centuries the bowl, which is, of course, the most important part of the glass, remained practically the same, but the foot rose steadily, always at the expense of the stem until at the end of the eighteenth century the stem had practically disappeared and there was only room between foot and bowl for an almost invariably quilled neckband and three or four stamped *Nuppen* or "prunts" set horizontally. As the foot rose it also broadened out, giving to the glass perfect stability on table or shelf. *Römer* have been for the past three hundred years the most typically German as well as the most suitable glasses for the service and enjoyment of wine; their bowl is now often made white, which does not add to their visual attractiveness but enables the drinker to appraise and enjoy the beautiful colour of the wine in the glass.

The nineteenth-century hock glass, which may be called the rival of the *Römer*, is not lacking in grace and artistic charm, but it does not "sit" as the *Römer* does on the table nor does it fit so well in the hand. It has a flat foot and a long rod of a stem at the end of which the bowl opens out like a flower on its stem: there is, of course, no room for any *Nuppen* or other ornamentations. Sometimes the stem and bowl are both of cut glass, white or coloured, and there is no denying that the finest of these modern hock glasses can add to the beauty of a well-laid dinner table; they are always taller than all other wine glasses, which is an added attraction, but they are distinctly top-heavy, whereas one can grasp and hold a *Römer* of wine with much greater assurance and tisasfaction.

"All the ancient varieties of the Rhine-land glasses have been reproduced at Ehrenfeld, near Cologne, not with the natural artistic irregularities inseparable from the old examples, but with the frigid accuracy associated with modern science. Fanciful names such as 'Dagobert-Römer', 'Wieland-Humpen', 'Weinbecher-Clodwig', 'Gambrinus-Pokal', etc. have been given to these productions, apparently for identification for purposes of trade." (Albert Hartshorne, *op. cit.*)

Römers and hock glasses are Rhineland glasses for Rhenish and Moselle wines, but there are other German wine glasses, chiefly from Silesia and Bavaria, which ought not to be overlooked. The mountains which divide Bavaria in the south and Silesia in the north from Bohemia were covered with dense forests which provided glass-makers with an almost inexhaustible source of fuel, whilst suitable quartz, sand and other minerals were available in many locations. Hence the importance of the glass-making industry, more particularly in the valleys and on the north and south slopes of the Riesengebirge ranges. Herr v. Czihak (in *Schlesische Gläser*, Breslau, 1891) has shown that there was

The first four glasses are *Römer* of traditional designs favoured in different districts: (*left to right*) Baden and Franconia, Rheingau, Moselle, Nahe. Below these, the slender glass on the left is a "Treveris" Moselle glass from Trier (Treves), followed by two modern glasses in general use for hocks and Moselles and a modern Sekt glass.

one glass-works in Silesia in the fourteenth century and at least three in the fifteenth and sixteenth, which were increased to seven in the seventeenth century. At the present day there are fifty-six glass-works in six principal centres, a wonderful testimony to the merits of the local materials. Most of the forests, unfortunately, have literally gone up in smoke, but there is coal in plenty.

The glass-makers of Silesia became famous chiefly for cut glass and for coloured, engraved and enamelled glasses, as did the glass-makers of Bohemia. Ruby glass was brought to perfection about 1679 by Johann Kunckel, a distinguished Silesian chemist, while in the service of Frederick William, Elector of Brandenburg, at his glass-works on the Isle of Peacocks at Potsdam. In Bavaria, glass-makers appear to have devoted more attention to the making of mirrors than of drinking glasses.

By far the most spectacular, as well as the most distinctive, drinking glasses from Silesia, Bavaria and Saxony were large, tall, cylindrical glasses, plain or decorated, with or without a lid, which are usually known as *Humpen* or "brimmers". They are chiefly used on ceremonial occasions, for pledging honoured guests; in France such glasses are called *verres de parade*. Small and plain glasses must have been made for daily use which met the fate of all domestic glasses and crockery, but some of the great *Humpen* survived, owing to the greater care taken of them as valuable specimens of the glass-maker's art. Some of these *Humpen* are beautifully decorated, the most striking of them all being the *Reichs* or *Adlesgläser* (empire or eagle glasses). They vary very little in shape, being usually plain cylinders with low bases and rims ornamented with gildings of various colours. On one side of the glass the Imperial double-eagle is enamelled with its wings spread, each head crowned and nimbed; or else the imperial orb of sovereignty in place of the eagle. Round the rim of the glass is usually inscribed, with certain variations, "Das heilige Römische Reich mit sampt seinen Gliedern" ("the Holy Roman Empire, with all its subjects"). The date is generally at the back of the glass, the earliest recorded being 1547; but they continued to be made until about 1725, together with other large enamelled glasses.

The *Kurfursten* and the *Apostel Humpen* are also highly decorative and very large glasses, the first displaying the Emperor surrounded by the seven Electors mounted on white horses; the second with caricatures rather than portraits of the Apostles, each one with his own emblem.

The *Pass-glas* is a cylindrical glass from 8 to 9 inches high tapering from $3\frac{3}{4}$ to $2\frac{1}{2}$ inches in diameter at the top to 3 or $1\frac{3}{4}$ inches immediately above the base. It is decorated by a stringing which sometimes encircles the glass spirally and in other specimens forms a number of rings more or less equidistant from each other, the intervening space being occasionally marked with numerals.

BOTTLES

Wine tastes much better out of a glass than when drunk from a cup, even a cup made of solid gold or silver, let alone pewter or pottery, which is why there were wine glasses long before wine bottles were made of glass. It was only about two hundred years ago that wine bottles were first used, as we use them today, as a home for wine to await our pleasure. Earlier glass wine bottles were merely decanters, containers which were filled in the cellar below, then brought to the table to be passed from hand to hand among the guests, or for their glasses to be filled and refilled by serving men. Old wine, in the past, was aged in wood. Bottle ageing became a possibility only in comparatively modern times, that is to say after the cork bark first came to be used for making stoppers some three hundred years ago, and especially after the invention, fifty or sixty years later, of the corkscrew, which allowed a cork to be driven hard into the neck of the bottle with the certainty of getting it out again when the wine was wanted. It was then, and then only, that cylindrical wine bottles were made which could be binned away horizontally without any fear of the wine oozing out when left alone for months or years to mellow and mature slowly. During the many centuries when there were wines but no corkscrews, bottles were mostly made of leather, wood, pewter or pottery, which were not so easily cracked or smashed as when made of glass. Sir Kenelm Digby has been credited with the introduction of the first wine bottles made of glass to England, in 1632, only nine years after the grant by James I to Sir Robert Mansell of letters patent to make objects of glass. Be that as it may, there is no lack of evidence to show that glass wine-bottles, at first with a long funnel-like neck and a fat globular body, were replaced fairly quickly during the latter part of the seventeenth century by the Fulham stoneware jugs, made in imitation of the Rhineland Greybeards, and the Lambeth Delft bottles, those charming and much smaller jugs of glazed pottery. Many of those Delft bottles are dated, very few of them after 1653, the latest date of all being 1672; it is most likely that by then they had been replaced by wine bottles made of dark green glass, used exclusively as decanters.

But not all wine bottles were made in pre-corkscrew days to stand squarely, or rather roundly, upon the table after having been filled from the cask. People did not spend the whole of their lives by their own fireside. Many travelled a great deal on foot or on horseback, on business or pleasure, and also from shrine to shrine, on pilgrimage. Princes and bishops travelled in great style, with armed escorts and loaded wagons, but everybody else travelled with very little baggage: it was so much safer. There was one piece of personal equipment, however, which was carried by all; it was a *costrel* or pilgrim's bottle. Circular or pear-shaped, it was flat, with a small spout and a couple of rings or lugs for a rope which was flung over the shoulder and held the *costrel* at one's side, or *costó*. These pilgrim's bottles were made in all kinds of materials before being made of glass, but in size they hardly varied at all, holding just about a quart of wine, a moderate quantity which appears to have been accepted as a fair draught for a thirsty man for the best part of two thousand years. There is, indeed, very little difference in size and shape between the wine flasks of Egypt's twenty-sixth Dynasty (656–525 B.C.) and the pilgrim's bottles of the Middle Ages.

We have so far failed to find out how and why the old *costrel* or pilgrim's bottle happened to be chosen, as it obviously was, as the pattern of the *Bocksbeutel*, the glass wine bottle used to this day for the white wines of Franconia, and for a few wines of a small district of Baden (*Mauer Weine*). The present hock and Moselle bottles, the first made of red-brown glass and the other of blue-green glass, are quite modern, not much more than a hundred years old. At the beginning of the last century, bottles of various shapes—but never *Bocksbeuteln*—were used for bottling hocks and Moselles; many of them were very similar to the present day burgundy bottle, which gradually became slimmer as well as taller.

Whatever their style and size, all German bottles are exceedingly well dressed. There are no wine labels comparable in artistic merit to some of the finest German wine labels. But even more valuable is the completeness of the information they give—the names of village and vineyard where the wine comes from; the date of the vintage of its birth; the name of the grape from which it was made and when it was picked; the name and titles, if any, of the owner of the vineyard or of the merchant who bottled the wine. No other country's wines carry such a concise yet complete birth certificate, usually displayed with both skill and taste.

Plate 25. Old casks in the cellars at Östrich-Winkel,
in the Rheingau.
Plate 26. New enamelled metal casks in the same cellars.

Appendix One

WINE-PRODUCING
COMMUNITIES

Community	District	Area (hectares)	Wine produced red	white
Abenheim	Rhinehessia	73.3	R	W
Abstatt	Württemberg	71	R	W
Abtswind	Franconia	42.8		W
Achkarren	Baden	76	R	W
Affaltrach	Württemberg	33	R	W
Affental	Baden	60	R	
Ahrweiler	Ahr	230	R	W
Albersweiler	Palatinate	144	R	W
Albig	Rhinehessia	110	R	W
Albisheim	Palatinate	24	R	W
Albsheim	Palatinate	29	R	W
Alf	Moselle	69		W
Alken	Moselle	33		W
Allensbach	Lake Constance	5.6		W
Allmersbach	Württemberg	100	R	W
Alsenz	Palatinate	43	R	W
Alsenz/Nahe	Nahe	70		W

Community	District	Area (hectares)	Wine produced red	white
Alsheim	Rhinehessia	306	R	W
Altdorf	Palatinate	43	R	W
Altenahr	Ahr	70	R	W
Altenbamberg	Palatinate	36		W
Altenburg	Weissenfels	6.5	R	W
Altschweier	Baden	23	R	W
Alzey	Rhinehessia	105	R	W
Andel	Moselle	13		W
Appenheim	Rhinehessia	58	R	W
Appenhofen	Palatinate	54	R	W
Archshofen	Württemberg	7	R	W
Armsheim	Rhinehessia	85	R	W
Arnstein	Lower Franconia	1.17	R	W
Arzheim	Palatinate	152	R	W
Asperg	Württemberg	25	R	W
Aspisheim	Rhinehessia	152		W
Asselheim	Palatinate	85	R	W
Assmannshausen	Rheingau	75	R	W
Astheim	Franken	15.8		W
Au	Baden	4.5		W
Auen	Nahe	17		W
Auenstein	Württemberg	90	R	W
Auggen	Baden	140		W
Aulhausen	Rheingau	10		W
Avelsbach	Moselle	200		W
Ayl	Saar	61		W
Bacharach	Middle Rhine	89		W
Bachem	Ahr	40	R	W
Bachenau	Württemberg	4.5	R	W
Bad Dürkheim	Palatinate	800	R	W
Badenheim	Rhinehessia	34.7	R	W
Badenweiler	Baden	12		W

Community	District	Area (hectares)	Wine produced red	white
Bad Kösen	Saale	6.5	R	W
Bad Kreuznach	Nahe	373		W
Bad Krozingen	Baden	13		W
Bad Mergentheim	Württemberg	3		W
Bad Münster am Stein	Nahe	18		W
Bad Neuenahr	Ahr	29	R	W
Bad Salzig	Middle Rhine	2		W
Bad Wimpfen	Baden	1.6	R	W
Bahlingen	Baden	135		W
Ballrechten	Baden	75		W
Bamlach	Baden	20		W
Battenberg	Palatinate	25	R	W
Bausendorf	Moselle	9		W
Bayerfeld–Steckweiler	Nahe	35		W
Bechenheim	Rhinehessia	6		W
Becherbach	Palatinate	5.5		W
Bechtheim	Rhinehessia	192.5	R	W
Bechtolsheim	Rhinehessia	44.8	R	W
Beckstein	Franconia	31		W
Beilstein/ Untermosel	Moselle	16		W
Beilstein/ Württemberg	Württemberg	102	R	W
Bekond	Moselle	39		W
Bellheim	Palatinate	12	R	W
Bellingen	Baden	32		W
Benningen	Württemberg	16	R	
Bensheim	Rhinehessia	70		W
Berghaupten	Baden	3.5	R	W
Berghausen	Palatinate	12		W
Bergzabern	Palatinate	75	R	W
Berlichingen	Württemberg	5		W

Community	District	Area (hectares)	Wine produced red	white
Bermatingen	Bodensee	7		W
Bermersheim	Rhinehessia	23	R	W
Bermersheim/Worms	Rhinehessia	31.7	R	W
Bernkastel–Kues	Moselle	180		W
Besigheim	Württemberg	92	R	W
Beuren	Württemberg	15		W
Beutelsbach	Württemberg	85	R	W
Bickensohl	Baden	45	R	W
Biebelhausen	Saar	10		W
Biebelnheim	Rhinehessia	40.3	R	W
Biebelsheim	Rhinehessia	42.6	R	W
Bieringen	Württemberg	12	R	W
Bietigheim	Württemberg	27	R	W
Billigheim	Palatinate	30	R	W
Bingen	Rhinehessia	247.2	R	W
Bingen–Büdesheim	Nahe	114	R	W
Bingen Kempten	Rhinehessia	70	R	W
Bingerbrück	Nahe	33		W
Binsfeld	Franconia	2		W
Birkweiler	Palatinate	145	R	W
Bischheim	Palatinate	6		W
Bischoffingen	Baden	75	R	W
Bissersheim	Palatinate	78	R	W
Blansingen	Baden	24		W
Bobenheim	Palatinate	66	R	W
Böbingen	Palatinate	18		W
Böchingen	Palatinate	107	R	W
Bockenau	Nahe	35		W
Bodendorf	Ahr	5	R	W
Bodenheim	Rhinehessia	275	R	W
Bohlingen	Lake Constance	5.1		W
Bolanden	Palatinate	6		W

Plate 27. Kaub, in the Middle Rhine district.
Plate 28. The Lorelei Rock.

Community	District	Area (hectares)	Wine produced red	white
Bollschweil	Baden	15		W
Bombach	Baden	10	R	W
Bönnigheim	Württemberg	200	R	W
Boos	Nahe	13.5		W
Boppard	Middle Rhine	106.5		W
Bornheim	Palatinate	16.7	R	W
Bornheim	Rhinehessia	48		W
Bornich	Middle Rhine	55		W
Bosenheim	Rhinehessia	62	R	W
Bottenau	Baden	25	R	W
Böttigheim	Franconia	3.6	R	W
Bötzingen	Baden	77.1	R	W
Brackenheim	Württemberg	60.6	R	W
Braubach	Middle Rhine	28.2		W
Brauneberg	Middle Rhine	54		W
Braunweiler	Nahe	45		W
Breisach	Baden	14.5	R	W
Breitscheid	Middle Rhine	20		W
Bremm	Moselle	105		W
Bretzenheim	Nahe	105	R	W
Breunigsweiler	Württemberg	8.5	R	W
Brey	Middle Rhine	6		W
Briedel	Moselle	115		W
Briedern	Moselle	55		W
Britzingen	Baden	65		W
Brodenbach	Moselle	13		W
Bruchsal	Baden	58	R	W
Bruttig	Moselle	86		W
Bubenheim	Rhinehessia	2	R	W
Buchbrunn	Franconia	20		W
Buchholz	Baden	11	R	W
Budenheim	Rhinehessia	2		W

Community	District	Area (hectares)	Wine produced red	white
Bühl–Kappelwindeck	Baden	15	R	W
Bühlertal	Baden	34.5	R	W
Buggingen	Baden	50		W
Bullay	Moselle	39		W
Bullenheim	Franconia	26.5		W
Burg	Moselle	80		W
Bürg	Württemberg	1.7	R	W
Burgen/Bernkastel	Moselle	45		W
Burgen/St Goar	Moselle	26		W
Burgscheidungen	Saale	3	R	W
Burgsponheim	Nahe	32		W
Burkheim	Baden	55	R	W
Burrweiler	Palatinate	200	R	W
Callbach	Palatinate	20		W
Carden	Moselle	16.5		W
Casbach	Middle Rhine	4	R	W
Castell	Franconia	17.1	R	W
Castel–Staadt	Saar	10		W
Cleebronn	Württemberg	130	R	W
Cleversulzbach	Württemberg	78	R	W
Cochem	Moselle	90		W
Colgenstein–Heidesheim	Palatinate	12	R	W
Cölln	Nahe	8		W
Creglingen	Württemberg	5	R	W
Criesbach	Württemberg Kocher–Jagsttal	30	R	W
Dackenheim	Palatinate	81	R	W
Dahenfeld	Württemberg	23	R	W
Daimbach	Franconia	3		W
Dalberg	Nahe	21		W
Dalheim	Rhinehessia	112	R	W

Community	District	Area (hectares)	Wine produced red	white
Dalsheim	Rhinehessia	180	R	W
Dammheim	Palatinate	39	R	W
Damscheid	Middle Rhine	22		W
Dattenberg	Middle Rhine	16	R	W
Dattingen	Baden	28		W
Dautenheim	Rhinehessia	25.5	R	W
Deidesheim	Palatinate	400	R	W
Dellhofen	Middle Rhine	23		W
Derdingen	Franconia	77	R	W
Dernau	Ahr	150	R	W
Dertingen	Franconia	32		W
Desloch	Nahe	10		W
Dettelbach	Franconia	16.62		W
Dettingen	Württemberg	7		W
Detzem	Moselle	65		W
Deubach	Württemberg	52		W
Dexheim	Rhinehessia	77.7	R	W
Dhron	Moselle	80		W
Diebach	Franconia	5		W
Dieblich	Moselle	11		W
Diedesfeld	Palatinate	330	R	W
Diedesheim	Neckar	4.2	R	W
Diefenbach	Württemberg	23	R	W
Dielkirchen	Nahe	56.7		W
Dienheim	Rhinehessia	3	R	W
Dierbach	Palatinate	14	R	W
Diersburg	Baden	24	R	W
Diesbar	Saxony	3.6		W
Dietersheim	Rhinehessia	10	R	W
Dietlingen	Baden	90	R	W
Dilmar	Moselle	3.83		W
Dingolshausen	Franconia	6.5		W

Community	District	Area (hectares)	Wine produced red	white
Dintesheim	Rhinehessia	5		W
Dirmstein	Palatinate	200	R	W
Dittelsheim	Rhinehessia	149	R	W
Dittwar	Franconia	5		W
Dolgesheim	Rhinehessia	41.9	R	W
Dörnbach	Nahe	3	R	W
Dorn–Dürkheim	Rhinehessia	66.6	R	W
Dörrenbach	Palatinate	110	R	W
Dörscheid	Middle Rhine	17	R	W
Dorsheim	Nahe	75	R	W
Dörzbach	Württemberg	12	R	W
Dossenheim	Baden	22	R	W
Dottingen	Baden	25		W
Dromersheim	Rhinehessia	140	R	W
Duchroth	Palatinate	112		W
Dudenhofen	Palatinate	105		W
Durbach	Baden	170	R	W
Dürrenzimmern	Württemberg	70	R	W
Duttweiler	Palatinate	101	R	W
Ebelsbach	Franconia	1.7		W
Ebernburg	Nahe	65	R	W
Ebersheim	Rhinehessia	72	R	W
Eberstadt	Württemberg	113	R	W
Ebringen	Baden	110		W
Eckelsheim	Rhinehessia	62		W
Eckenroth	Nahe	10		W
Edenkoben	Palatinate	450		W
Edesheim	Palatinate	315	R	W
Ediger	Moselle	108		W
Efringen–Kirchen	Baden	40		W
Ehrenbreitstein	Middle Rhine	15		W
Ehrenstetten	Baden	70	R	W

Community	District	Area (hectares)	Wine produced red	white
Eibelstadt	Franconia	41.5	R	W
Eibensbach	Württemberg	18	R	W
Eichelberg	Baden	20		W
Eichelberg	Württemburg	39	R	W
Eichenbühl	Franconia	1.9	R	W
Eichstetten	Baden	100	R	W
Eimeldingen	Baden	15.8		W
Eimsheim	Rhinehessia	51.2	R	W
Einselthum	Palatinate	32.50	R	W
Eisental	Baden	70	R	W
Eisingen	Baden	34	R	W
Eitelsbach	Saar–Ruwer	22		W
Elfershausen	Franconia	20		W
Ellenz–Poltersdorf	Moselle	110		W
Eller	Moselle	65		W
Ellerstadt	Palatinate	130	R	W
Ellhofen	Württemberg	25	R	W
Ellmendingen	Baden	90		W
Elpersheim	Württemberg	12	R	W
Elsenz	Baden	11		W
Elsheim	Rhinehessia	102.8	R	W
Eltville	Rheingau	165.5		W
Endersbach	Remsthal, Württemberg	49	R	W
Endingen	Baden	178	R	W
Engehöll	Middle Rhine	100		W
Engelstadt	Rhinehessia	49	R	W
Engental	Franconia	6		W
Enkirch	Moselle	184		W
Ensch	Saar–Ruwer	50		W
Ensheim	Rhinehessia	100	R	W
Enzberg	Württemberg	6.8	R	W

Community	District	Area (hectares)	Wine produced red	white
Eppelsheim	Rhinehessia	18	R	W
Erbach	Rheingau	160		W
Erbes–Büdesheim	Rhinehessia	23.8		W
Erden	Moselle	65		W
Erlabrunn	Franconia	36.9		W
Erlenbach	Franconia (Marktheidenfeld)	18.8		W
Erlenbach	Franconia (Obernburg)	3.4	R	W
Erlenbach	Württemberg	215	R	W
Erligheim	Württemberg	42	R	
Ernsbach	Württemberg	8	R	W
Ernst	Moselle	130		W
Erpel	Middle Rhine	5.5	R	W
Erpolzheim	Palatinate	96	R	W
Ersingen	Baden	50.5		W
Eschbach	Baden	17		W
Eschbach	Palatinate	100		W
Eschelbach	Württemberg	34	R	W
Eschenau	Württemberg	47	R	W
Escherndorf	Franconia	78.1		W
Esselborn	Rhinehessia	1.8		W
Essenheim	Rhinehessia	74	R	W
Essingen	Palatinate	138	R	W
Esslingen	Württemberg	100	R	W
Ettenheim	Baden	20	R	W
Eussenheim	Franconia	6		W
Fachbach	Middle Rhine	9		W
Fahr	Franconia	25.4		W
Fankel	Moselle	52		W
Fastrau	Saar–Ruwer	26		W
Feil–Bingert	Nahe	73		W

Community	District	Area (hectares)	Wine produced red	white
Feldberg	Baden	22		W
Fell	Saar–Ruwer	55		W
Fellbach	Württemberg	178	R	W
Fellerich	Saar	22		W
Fessenbach	Baden	26	R	W
Feuerthal	Franconia	5		W
Filzen	Moselle	56		W
Filzen	Saar	25		W
Fischingen	Baden	46		W
Flein	Württemberg	150	R	W
Flemlingen	Palatinate	107		W
Flomborn	Rhinehessia	25	R	W
Flonheim	Rhinehessia	122	R	W
Flörsheim	Rheingau	3		W
Föhrental	Baden	3.8	R	W
Forchtenberg	Württemberg	20	R	W
Forst	Palatinate	206	R	W
Framersheim	Rhinehessia	17	R	W
Frankfurt-am-Main–Seckbach	Rheingau	1.5		W
Frankweiler	Palatinate	147	R	W
Franzenheim	Saar	13		W
Frauenzimmern	Württemberg	21.6	R	W
Freckenfeld	Palatinate	10.5	R	W
Freiburg/Breisgau	Baden	84	R	W
Freilaubersheim	Rhinehessia	40		W
Freimersheim	Palatinate	40	R	W
Freinsheim	Palatinate	245	R	W
Freisbach	Palatinate	4.7		W
Frettenheim	Rhinehessia	17	R	W
Freudenstein	Württemberg	25	R	W
Freyburg	Saale	30	R	W

Community	District	Area (hectares)	Wine produced red	white
Frickenhausen	Franconia	49.8	R	W
Friedelsheim	Palatinate	150	R	W
Friesenheim	Baden	3.4		W
Friesenheim	Rhinehessia	33.4	R	W
Fuchsstadt	Franconia	4		W
Fürfeld	Rhinehessia	30		W
Fussgönheim	Palatinate	14.5	R	W
Gabsheim	Rhinehessia	26	R	W
Gaienhofen	Lake Constance	3	R	W
Gau-Algesheim	Rhinehessia	150	R	W
Gau-Bickelheim	Rhinehessia	100	R	W
Gau-Bischofsheim	Rhinehessia	60	R	W
Gau-Grehweiler	Palatinate	4.6		W
Gau-Heppenheim	Rhinehessia	48		W
Gaulsheim	Rhinehessia	4	R	W
Gau-Odernheim	Rhinehessia	110	R	W
Gau-Weinheim	Rhinehessia	65	R	W
Geddelsbach	Württemberg	30	R	W
Geinsheim	Palatinate	32.5	R	W
Geisenheim	Rheingau	81.3		W
Gellmersbach	Württemberg	40	R	W
Gemmrigheim	Württemberg	41	R	W
Gengenbach	Baden	7	R	W
Genheim	Nahe	16		W
Gensingen	Rhinehessia	41.4	R	W
Gerbach	Palatinate	6	R	W
Gerbrunn	Franconia	6		W
Gerlachsheim	Franconia	9		W
Gerlingen	Württemberg	10	R	
Gerolsheim	Palatinate	53	R	W
Gerolzhofen	Franconia	1.11		W
Gimbsheim	Rhinehessia	32.8	R	W

Community	District	Area (hectares)	Wine produced red	white
Gimmeldingen	Palatinate	160	R	W
Gleisweiler	Palatinate	84	R	W
Gleiszellen–Gleishorbach	Palatinate	58	R	W
Gochsen	Württemberg	3.8	R	W
Göcklingen	Palatinate	150	R	W
Godramstein	Palatinate	220	R	W
Golgenstein–Heidesheim	Palatinate	7.8	R	W
Golk	Saxony	3.7	R	W
Gönnheim	Palatinate	112	R	W
Goseck	Saale	2		W
Gossmannsdorf	Franconia	11	R	W
Gottenheim	Baden	29	R	W
Graach	Moselle	134		W
Gräfenhausen	Palatinate	14.5	R	W
Gräfenhausen	Württemberg	14.5	R	
Grantschen	Württemberg	50	R	W
Grenzach	Baden	17.5	R	W
Grewenich	Moselle	4		W
Grolsheim	Rhinehessia	40	R	W
Gronau	Hessische Bergstrasse	4.9		W
Gronau	Württemberg	10	R	W
Grossbockenheim	Palatinate	135	R	W
Grossbottwar	Württemberg	130	R	W
Grossfischlingen	Palatinate	36	R	W
Grossgartach	Württemberg	59	R	W
Grossheppach	Württemberg	61	R	W
Grossheubach	Franconia	29.9	R	W
Grosskarlbach	Palatinate	112	R	W
Grosslangheim	Franconia	35.4		W

Community	District	Area (hectares)	Wine produced red	white
Grossniedesheim	Palatinate	25	R	W
Grossostheim	Franconia	16	R	W
Gross-Sachsen	Badische Bergstrasse	6	R	W
Gross-Umstadt	Hessische Bergstrasse	20		W
Grosswallstadt	Franconia	5	R	W
Gross-Winternheim	Rhinehessia	95.3	R	W
Grunbach	Württemberg	53	R	W
Grunnern	Baden	26		W
Grünstadt	Palatinate	36	R	W
Güglingen	Württemberg	40.50	R	W
Güls	Moselle	24		W
Gumbsheim	Rhinehessia	50	R	W
Gündelbach	Württemberg	35	R	W
Gundelfingen	Baden	3.6		W
Gundelsheim	Württemberg	42	R	W
Gundersheim	Rhinehessia	112	R	W
Gundheim	Rhinehessia	75	R	W
Guntersblum	Rhinehessia	250	R	W
Güntersleben	Franconia	5.4	R	W
Gutenberg	Nahe	110		W
Haagen	Baden	2.8		W
Haardt	Palatinate	150	R	W
Haberschlacht	Württemberg	38	R	W
Hackenheim	Rhinehessia	91.9	R	W
Häfnerhaslach	Württemberg	17	R	W
Hagnau	Lake Constance	48	R	W
Hahnheim	Rhinehessia	65	R	W
Hainfeld	Palatinate	203	R	W
Hallgarten	Rheingau	250		W
Haltingen	Baden	26		W

Community	District	Area (hectares)	Wine produced red	white
Hambach	Hessische Bergstrasse	16		W
Hambach	Palatinate	356	R	W
Hammelburg	Franconia	43.2		W
Hammerstein	Middle Rhine	42	R	W
Hangen–Weisheim	Rhinehessia	25	R	W
Hanweiler	Württemberg	15	R	W
Hargesheim	Nahe	43		W
Harsberg	Württemberg	42	R	W
Harxhcim	Palatinatc	37	R	W
Harxheim	Rhinehessia	60	R	W
Haslach	Baden	8.3		W
Hattenheim	Rheingau	200	R	W
Hatzenport	Moselle	46		W
Hechtsheim	Rhinehessia	23	R	W
Hecklingen	Baden	30		W
Heddesheim	Nahe	224	R	W
Heidelberg/ Handschusheim	Baden	9.8	R	W
Heidelberg/ Rohrbach	Baden	39	R	W
Heidelsheim	Baden	15	R	W
Heidesheim	Rhinehessia	16.4	R	W
Heilbronn	Württemberg	441	R	W
Heiligenstein	Palatinate	18.6		W
Heiligenzell	Baden	3	R	W
Heimbach	Baden	7		W
Heimersheim	Ahr	70	R	W
Heimersheim	Rhinehessia	55.5	R	W
Heinsheim	Baden	6		W
Helfant	Moselle	20		W

Community	District	Area (hectares)	Wine produced red	white
Hemsbach	Badische Bergstrasse	16	R	W
Heppenheim	Hessische Bergstrasse	48	R	W
Heppenheim	Rhinehessia	37.5	R	W
Herbolzheim	Baden	40	R	W
Hergenfeld	Nahe	20		W
Hergolshausen	Franconia	3		W
Herten	Baden	5.2	R	W
Hertingen	Baden	14		W
Hertmannsweiler	Württemberg	4.5	R	W
Herxheim am Berg	Palatinate	156		W
Hessheim	Palatinate	9		W
Hessigheim	Württemberg	112	R	W
Hessloch	Rhinehessia	109.6	R	W
Hetzerath	Moselle	6		W
Heuchelheim/ Bergzabern	Palatinate	78	R	W
Heuchelheim/ Frankenthal	Palatinate	23	R	W
Heuholz	Württemberg	42	R	W
Heuweiler	Baden	4	R	W
Hillesheim	Rhinehessia	68	R	W
Hilsbach	Baden	14	R	W
Himmelstadt	Franconia	12		W
Hirzenach	Middle Rhine	18		W
Höchberg	Franconia	1.2	R	W
Hochheim	Rheingau	205	R	W
Hochstätten	Nahe	40		W
Hockweiler	Moselle	4		W
Hof unter Lembach	Württemberg	30	R	W
Hoheim	Franconia	2		W

Community	District	Area (hectares)	Wine produced red	white
Hohen–Sülzen	Rhinehessia	80	R	W
Hohenfeld	Franconia	4.4		W
Hohenhaslach	Württemberg	130	R	
Hohenstein	Württemberg	25	R	W
Homburg	Franconia	17.7		W
Honnef	Middle Rhine	8.9	R	W
Hönningen	Middle Rhine	14	R	W
Höpfigheim	Württemberg	35	R	W
Horkheim	Württemberg	17	R	W
Horn	Lake Constance	3.9	R	W
Horrheim	Württemberg	100	R	W
Horrweiler	Rhinehessia	80.8	R	W
Hörstein	Franconia	25	R	W
Hösslinsülz	Württemberg	40	R	W
Hüffelsheim	Nahe	27		W
Hügelheim	Baden	34		W
Hugsweier	Baden	8.5	R	W
Hüllenberg	Middle Rhine	9		W
Humprechtsau	Franconia	3		W
Hupperath	Moselle	4.5		W
Hüttenheim	Franconia	22.3		W
Ibersheim	Rhinehessia	17		W
Ickelheim	Franconia	3.5		W
Iffigheim	Franconia	1		W
Igel	Moselle	9		W
Ihringen	Baden	300		W
Ilbesheim	Palatinate	177	R	W
Illingen	Württemberg	20	R	W
Ilsfeld	Württemberg	30.5	R	W
Immenstaad	Baden	4.5		W
Impfingen	Franconia	1.25		W
Impflingen	Palatinate	48	R	W

Community	District	Area (hectares)	Wine produced red	white
Ingelfingen	Württemberg	50	R	W
Ingelheim	Rhinehessia	365	R	W
Ingenheim	Palatinate	48.1	R	W
Ingolstadt	Franconia	3.6		W
Insheim	Palatinate	29	R	W
Iphofen	Franconia	124		W
Ippesheim	Franconia	21.5		W
Ippesheim	Rhinehessia	16.5	R	W
Irsch/Saarburg	Moselle	66		W
Irsch/Trier	Moselle	12		W
Istein	Baden	22		W
Jagsthausen	Württemberg	7.5	R	W
Jechtingen	Baden	35	R	W
Jeckenbach	Nahe	4.5		W
Johannisberg	Rheingau	132.5	R	W
Jugenheim	Rhinehessia	118	R	W
Kaimt	Moselle	42		W
Kalkofen	Nahe	6		W
Kallstadt	Palatinate	320	R	W
Kamp	Middle Rhine	25	R	W
Kanzem	Moselle	60		W
Kappelrodeck	Baden	65	R	W
Kappishäusern	Württemberg	5		W
Kapsweyer	Palatinate	9	R	W
Karlstadt	Franconia	15.1		W
Karweiler	Ahr	12	R	W
Kasbach	Middle Rhine	11	R	W
Kasel	Moselle	71		W
Kattenes	Moselle	11		W
Katzenbach	Palatinate	14		W
Kaub	Middle Rhine	95		W
Kenn	Moselle	23		W

Community	District	Area (hectares)	Wine produced red	white
Kenzingen	Baden	25	R	W
Kerzenheim	Palatinate	2		W
Kesselfeld	Württemberg	10	R	W
Kesten	Moselle	60		W
Kestert	Middle Rhine	13		W
Kettenheim	Rhinehessia	19		W
Kiechlinsbergen	Baden	40	R	W
Kiedrich	Rheingau	113	R	W
Kindenheim	Palatinate	100	R	W
Kinheim	Moselle	102		W
Kippenhausen	Lake Constance	3.5		W
Kippenheim	Baden	30	R	W
Kippenheimweiler	Baden	3		W
Kirchberg a.d. Murr	Württemberg	4.5	R	W
Kirchheim a.d. Eck	Palatinate	105	R	W
Kirchheim a.d. Neckar	Württemberg	60	R	W
Kirchheimbolanden	Palatinate	17	R	W
Kirchhofen	Baden	100		W
Kirrweiler	Palatinate	400	R	W
Kirschroth	Nahe	24		W
Kitzingen	Franconia	23		W
Klein–Umstadt	Hessische Bergstrasse	6.7		W
Kleinbockenheim	Palatinate	125	R	W
Kleinbottwar	Württemberg	37	R	W
Kleingartach	Württemberg	54	R	W
Kleinheppach	Württemberg	38	R	W
Kleinkarlbach	Palatinate	100	R	W
Kleinkems	Baden	11		W
Kleinniedesheim	Palatinate	28	R	W
Kleinochsenfurt	Franconia	9.3		W
Kleinwallstadt	Franconia	7		W

Community	District	Area (hectares)	Wine produced red	white
Klein–Winternheim	Rhinehessia	11.2	R	W
Klepsau	Baden	7.8		W
Klingen	Palatinate	46	R	W
Klingenberg am Main	Franconia	15.3	R	W
Klingenberg	Württemberg	8.5	R	W
Klingenmünster	Palatinate	79	R	W
Klotten	Moselle	85		W
Klüsserath	Moselle	160		W
Knittelsheim	Palatinate	8	R	W
Knittlingen	Württemberg	40	R	W
Knöringen	Palatinate	78		W
Kobern	Moselle	40		W
Koblenz	Middle Rhine	29		W
Kocherstetten	Württemberg	1.1		W
Kohlberg	Württemberg	5.6		W
Köhler	Franconia	19.9		W
Köllig	Moselle	24		W
Kommlingen	Moselle	40		W
Köndringen	Baden	25		W
Könen	Moselle	20		W
Köngernheim	Rhinehessia	29.3		W
Königheim	Franconia	14		W
Königsbach	Palatinate	135	R	W
Königschaffhausen	Baden	45	R	W
Königshofen	Baden	21	R	W
Königshofen	Franconia	12		W
Königswinter	Middle Rhine	20	R	W
Konstanz	Lake Constance	9.2	R	W
Konz–Karthaus	Moselle	65		W
Korb–Steinreinach	Württemberg	90	R	W
Kövenich	Moselle	21		W

Plate 29. Still life with Schönberger Sekt, in honour of the doyen of the German Sekt industry, Eugen Schönberger.

Community	District	Area (hectares)	Wine produced red	white
Köwerich	Moselle	26		W
Krassolzheim	Franconia	4		W
Krautsostheim	Franconia	2		W
Krebsweiler	Nahe	4		W
Kressbronn	Lake Constance	11	R	W
Krettnach	Moselle	63		W
Kreuzberg	Ahr	6	R	W
Kreuzweiler	Moselle	5.6		W
Kreuzwertheim	Franconia	1.5		W
Kriegsheim	Rhinehessia	38.4	R	W
Kröv	Moselle	200		W
Krutweiler	Moselle	9		W
Künzelsau	Württemberg	3		W
Lachen–Speyerdorf	Palatinate	80	R	W
Lahr	Baden	20	R	W
Laibach	Württemberg	1		W
Lambsheim	Palatinate	31	R	W
Landau	Palatinate	36	R	W
Landshausen	Baden	11		W
Langenbeutingen	Württemberg	10.5	R	W
Langenbrücken	Baden	21		W
Langenlonsheim	Nahe	250		W
Langscheid	Middle Rhine	11		W
Langsur	Moselle	14		W
Laubenheim	Nahe	130	R	W
Laubenheim	Rhinehessia	150	R	W
Lauda	Franconia	9.5	R	W
Laudenbach	Badische Bergstrasse	13	R	W
Laudenbach	Franconia	2.64	R	W
Laudenbach	Württemberg	43	R	W
Lauf	Baden	3.5		W

Community	District	Area (hectares)	Wine produced red	white
Laufen	Baden	75		W
Lauffen	Württemberg	226	R	W
Laumersheim	Palatinate	70	R	W
Lautenbach	Baden	11	R	W
Lauterecken	Palatinate	10	R	W
Lay	Moselle	21		W
Lehmen	Moselle	33		W
Lehrensteinsfeld	Württemberg	102	R	W
Leimen	Badische Bergstrasse	35.7	R	W
Leinsweiler	Palatinate	82	R	W
Leiselheim	Baden	20		W
Leistadt	Palatinate	190	R	W
Leiwen	Moselle	226		W
Lengfurt	Franconia	7	R	W
Leonbronn	Württemberg	4.5	R	W
Lettweiler	Palatinate	29		W
Leutershausen	Badische Bergstrasse	12	R	W
Leutesdorf	Middle Rhine	115	R	W
Liel	Baden	43		W
Lienzingen	Württemberg	7.5	R	W
Liersberg	Moselle	17		W
Lieser	Moselle	110		W
Lindelbach	Franconia	1.7		W
Linz	Middle Rhine	6	R	W
Lipburg	Baden	5		W
Lippoldsweiler	Württemberg	3	R	W
Löchgau	Württemberg	35	R	W
Löf	Moselle	12		W
Löffelstelzen	Württemberg	7	R	W
Lohnweiler	Palatinate	4		W

Community	District	Area (hectares)	Wine produced red	white
Longen	Moselle	7		W
Longuich	Moselle	44		W
Longuich–Kirch	Moselle	28.7		W
Lonsheim	Rhinehessia	48.3	R	W
Lorch	Rheingau	235	R	W
Lorchhausen	Rheingau	68	R	W
Lörrach	Baden	12		W
Lörzweiler	Rhinehessia	81	R	W
Lösnich	Moselle	36		W
Löwenstein mit Reizach und Rittelhof	Württemberg	130	R	W
Ludwigsberg	Württemberg	17	R	W
Ludwigshöhe	Rhinehessia	51.3		W
Lützelsachsen	Badische Bergstrasse	4	R	W
Machtilshausen	Franconia	12		W
Mahlberg	Baden	14	R	W
Maienfels	Württemberg	15	R	W
Maikammer	Palatinate	645	R	W
Mailheim	Franconia	7	R	W
Mainberg	Franconia	15.9		W
Mainstockheim	Franconia	36.3		W
Mainz	Rhinehessia	1.4		W
Mainz–Kostheim	Rheingau	89	R	W
Mainz–Weisenau	Rhinehessia	6.8	R	W
Malsch	Badische Bergstrasse	50	R	W
Malschenberg	Baden	33	R	W
Malterdingen	Baden	50		W
Mandel	Nahe	100		W
Mannweiler	Nahe	15.3		W

Community	District	Area (hectares)	Wine produced red	white
Manubach	Middle Rhine	65		W
Mappach	Baden	7		W
Marbach	Franconia	6		W
Marbach	Württemberg	10	R	W
Maring–Noviand	Moselle	113		W
Markdorf	Lake Constance	5.7	R	W
Markelsheim	Württemberg	85		W
Markgröningen	Württemberg	46	R	W
Markt–Einersheim	Franconia	16.5		W
Marktbreit	Franconia	19.3		W
Marktsteft	Franconia	4.6	R	W
Martinstein	Nahe	4		W
Martinsthal	Rheingau	53		W
Massenheim	Rheingau	7.4		W
Mauchen	Baden	34	R	W
Mauchenheim	Palatinate	30	R	W
Maulbronn	Württemberg	22.2	R	W
Mayschoss	Ahr	116	R	W
Mechtersheim	Palatinate	16.8	R	W
Meckenheim	Palatinate	90	R	W
Medard	Nahe	5	R	W
Meddersheim	Nahe	70		W
Meersburg	Lake Constance	46	R	W
Mehring	Moselle	114		W
Meimsheim	Württemberg	36	R	W
Meisenheim	Nahe	34		W
Meissen	Saxony	27	R	W
Merbitz	Saxony	1	R	W
Merdingen	Baden	80	R	W
Merl	Moselle	135		W
Mertesdorf	Moselle	53		W
Mertesheim	Palatinate	10	R	W

Community	District	Area (hectares)	Wine produced red	white
Merxheim	Nahe	35		W
Merzhausen	Baden	5.5		W
Merzweiler	Nahe	1.5		W
Mesenich	Moselle	61		W
Mesenich/ Untermosel	Moselle	19		W
Mettenheim	Rhinehessia	122.6	R	W
Metzdorf	Moselle	8		W
Metzingen	Württemberg	30	R	W
Michelbach	Franconia	15		W
Michelbach	Württemberg	9	R	W
Michelfeld	Baden	7.4	R	W
Miltenberg	Franconia	3.6		W
Minheim	Moselle	71		W
Mittelheim	Rheingau	120		W
Möckmühl	Württemberg	11.6	R	W
Möglingen	Württemberg	2.5	R	W
Mölsheim	Rhinehessia	64	R	W
Mommenheim	Rhinehessia	92.2	R	W
Monsheim	Rhinehessia	46.5	R	W
Monzernheim	Rhinehessia	84	R	W
Monzingen	Nahe	125		W
Morsbach	Württemberg	1.4		W
Morschheim	Palatinate	7		W
Mörsfeld	Palatinate	5		W
Mörstadt	Rhinehessia	18.2	R	W
Mörzheim	Palatinate	117	R	W
Moselkern	Moselle	42		W
Müden	Moselle	66		W
Mühlacker	Württemberg	4	R	W
Mühlbach	Baden	20	R	W
Mühlhausen	Baden	38	R	W

Community	District	Area (hectares)	Wine produced red	white
Mühlheim an der Eis	Palatinate	38	R	W
Mülheim	Moselle	52		W
Müllheim	Baden	125		W
Münchweier	Baden	8		W
Mundelsheim	Württemberg	135	R	W
Mundingen	Baden	6.3	R	W
Münster	Württemberg	8.5	R	W
Münsterappel	Palatinate	14		W
Münster bei Bingerbrück	Nahe	210	R	W
Münster–Sarmsheim	Nahe	210	R	W
Munzingen	Baden	96	R	W
Murr	Württemberg	12	R	W
Mussbach	Palatinate	382	R	W
Nack	Rhinehessia	8		W
Nackenheim	Rhinehessia	70	R	W
Nassau	Lahn	20	R	W
Neckarmühlbach	Badisches Neckargebiet	4.3	R	W
Neckarsulm	Württemberg	131	R	W
Neckarweihingen	Württemberg	11	R	W
Neckarzimmern	Badisches Neckargebiet	9	R	W
Neef	Moselle	90		W
Nehren	Moselle	7.5		W
Neipperg	Württemberg	72	R	W
Nennig	Moselle	36		W
Nenzenheim	Franconia	13		W
Nerzweiler	Palatinate	2	R	W
Nesselried	Baden	16	R	W
Neu–Bamberg	Rhinehessia	28		W

Community	District	Area (hectares)	Wine produced red	white
Neuershausen	Baden	4.4	R	W
Neuffen	Württemberg	27		W
Neuhausen	Württemberg	36	R	W
Neuleiningen	Palatinate	47	R	W
Neumagen	Moselle	105		W
Neusatz	Baden	7	R	W
Neuses	Franconia	28.6	R	W
Neusetz	Franconia	4.5		W
Neustadt an der Weinstrasse	Palatinate	207	R	W
Neustadt	Württemberg	16	R	W
Neuweier	Baden	140	R	W
Niebelsbach	Württemberg	8.5	R	
Niederberg	Middle Rhine	15		W
Niederbrechen	Lahn	1.1	R	W
Niederburg	Middle Rhine	24.1		W
Niederdollendorf	Middle Rhine	10	R	W
Niedereisenbach	Nahe	8.1		W
Niederemmel	Moselle	105	R	W
Niederfell	Moselle	20		W
Nieder-Flörsheim	Rhinehessia	145	R	W
Niederhausen	Nahe	118	R	W
Niederhausen	Palatinate	23		W
Niederheimbach	Middle Rhine	30		W
Nieder-Hilbersheim	Rhinehessia	32.6	R	W
Niederhochstadt	Palatinate	68	R	W
Niederhofen	Württemberg	3.5	R	W
Niederhorbach	Palatinate	45	R	W
Niederkirchen	Palatinate	160	R	W
Niederlustadt	Palatinate	4.5		W
Niedermennig	Moselle	45		W

Community	District	Area (hectares)	Wine produced red	white
Niedermoschel	Palatinate	26		W
Niedernhall	Württemberg	24	R	W
Nieder-Olm	Rhinehessia	37.8	R	W
Niederrimbach	Württemberg	3.5	R	W
Niederrimsingen	Baden	16	R	W
Nieder-Saulheim	Rhinehessia	160	R	W
Niederschopfheim	Baden	19.4		W
Niederstetten	Württemberg	50	R	W
Niederwalluf	Rheingau	35	R	W
Nieder-Wiesen	Rhinehessia	1	R	W
Niefernheim	Palatinate	38.5	R	W
Nierstein	Rhinehessia	600		W
Nittel	Moselle	170		W
Nochern	Middle Rhine	22		W
Nonnenhorn	Lake Constance	6.8		W
Nordhausen	Württemberg	324	R	W
Nordheim	Franconia	129		W
Nordheim	Württemberg	150	R	W
Nordweil	Baden	30	R	W
Norheim	Nahe	56		W
Nussbaum	Nahe	13.5		W
Nussdorf	Palatinate	208	R	W
Oberachern	Baden	10	R	W
Oberbillig	Moselle	66		W
Oberderdingen	Württemberg	90	R	W
Oberdiebach mit Winzberg und Rheindiebach	Middle Rhine	110	R	W
Oberdollendorf	Middle Rhine	12.5	R	W
Oberdürrbach	Franconia	1.1	R	W
Obereggenen	Baden	176		W
Obereisenheim	Franconia	30.9		W

Community	District	Area (hectares)	Wine produced red	white
Oberemmel	Moselle	120		W
Oberfell	Moselle	30		W
Ober-Flörsheim	Rhinehessia	27.6	R	W
Oberglottertal	Baden	2	R	W
Obergriesheim	Württemberg	4	R	W
Obergrombach	Baden	30	R	W
Oberhausen	Palatinate	23.5	R	W
Oberheimbach	Middle Rhine	95	R	W
Oberhochstadt	Palatinate	35	R	W
Oberkirch	Baden	36	R	W
Oberlahnstein	Middle Rhine	25		W
Oberlauda	Franconia	4.8		W
Oberleinach	Franconia	18.5		W
Oberlustadt	Palatinate	13	R	W
Obermoschel	Palatinate	37		W
Obernbreit	Franconia	4		W
Oberndorf	Palatinate	22		W
Obernhof	Lahn	10	R	W
Ober-Olm	Rhinehessia	30	R	W
Oberrotterbach	Palatinate	56		W
Oberrotweil	Baden	100	R	W
Obersasbach	Baden	6	R	W
Ober-Saulheim	Rhinehessia	45.7	R	W
Oberschopfheim	Baden	42		W
Oberschüpf	Franconia	5.7	R	W
Oberschwarzach	Franconia	10		W
Oberspay	Middle Rhine	100		W
Oberstenfeld mit Weingut Lichtenberg	Württemberg	100	R	W
Oberstetten	Württemberg	12	R	W
Oberstreit	Nahe	7		W

Community	District	Area (hectares)	Wine produced red	white
Obersülzen	Palatinate	17	R	W
Obervolkach	Franconia	12.3		W
Oberwalluf	Rheingau	15	R	W
Oberweier	Baden	7	R	W
Oberweiler im Tal	Palatinate	2	R	W
Oberwesel	Middle Rhine	110	R	W
Obrigheim	Palatinate	31	R	W
Ochsenbach	Württemberg	38	R	W
Ochsenfurt	Franconia	1.8		W
Ockenfels	Middle Rhine	4	R	W
Ockenheim	Rhinehessia	150	R	W
Ockfen	Moselle	90		W
Odenbach	Palatinate	6	R	W
Odernheim	Nahe	70		W
Ödheim	Württemberg	43	R	W
Offenau	Württemberg	4	R	W
Offenbach/Glan	Nahe	30		W
Offenbach am Queich	Palatinate	17	R	W
Offenheim	Rhinehessia	19.6	R	W
Offstein	Rhinehessia	26.2	R	W
Ohlsbach	Baden	7	R	W
Öhningen	Lake Constance	7	R	W
Ölbronn	Württemberg	10	R	W
Olnhausen	Württemberg	2.5	R	W
Onsdorf	Moselle	18		W
Oppenheim	Rhinehessia	282.2		W
Ortenberg	Baden	70	R	W
Osann	Moselle	100		W
Osthofen	Rhinehessia	208	R	W
Östrich	Rheingau	271	R	W
Östringen	Baden	40	R	W

Community	District	Area (hectares)	Wine produced red	white
Ötisheim	Württemberg	32	R	W
Ötlingen	Baden	14		W
Ottersheim	Palatinate	17	R	W
Owen	Württemberg	4.5		W
Palzem	Moselle	31		W
Partenheim	Rhinehessia	81	R	W
Patersberg	Middle Rhine	12	R	W
Pellingen	Moselle	25		W
Perl	Moselle	16		W
Perl–Oberhof Sehndorf	Moselle	53		W
Perscheid	Middle Rhine	23		W
Pfaffenhausen	Franconia	2		W
Pfaffenhofen	Württemberg	53	R	W
Pfaffen–Schwabenheim	Rhinehessia	72.7	R	W
Pfaffenweiler	Baden	87		W
Pfeddersheim	Rhinehessia	60	R	W
Pfedelbach	Württemberg	11.30	R	W
Pferdsfeld	Nahe	2		W
Pfullingen	Württemberg	1.2	R	W
Piesport	Moselle	62		W
Planig	Rhinehessia	75	R	W
Platten	Moselle	23		W
Pleidesheim	Württemberg	4	R	W
Pleisweiler–Oberhofen	Palatinate	71	R	W
Pleitersheim	Rhinehessia	15		W
Pluwig	Moselle	3.5		W
Pölich	Moselle	54		W
Pommern	Moselle	75		W
Poppenweiler	Württemberg	85	R	W

Community	District	Area (hectares)	Wine produced red	white
Prappach	Franconia	3		W
Proschwitz	Saxony	5	R	W
Pünderich	Moselle	84		W
Radebeul	Saxony	9.5		W
Ralingen	Moselle	6		W
Rammersweier	Baden	24	R	W
Ramsthal	Franconia	24		W
Ramsweiler	Palatinate	2.5	R	W
Randersacker	Franconia	158.7	R	W
Ranschbach	Palatinate	97	R	W
Rappach	Württemberg	11.5	R	W
Rauenberg	Baden	120	R	W
Rauenthal	Rheingau	86		W
Raumbach	Nahe	30		W
Rech	Ahr	68	R	W
Rechtenbach	Palatinate	70	R	W
Rehborn	Palatinate	26		W
Rehlingen	Moselle	38		W
Reichenau	Lake Constance	10	R	W
Reichenbach	Baden	7	R	W
Reichholzheim	Franconia	4		W
Reil	Moselle	170		W
Remagen	Middle Rhine	3	R	W
Remlingen	Franconia	2.2		W
Repperndorf	Franconia	10		W
Rettigheim	Badische Bergstrasse	12.5		W
Retzbach	Franconia	7.5		W
Retzstadt	Franconia	23.3	R	W
Reusch	Franconia	2		W
Reutlingen	Württemberg	10	R	W
Rheinbreitbach	Middle Rhine	1.8	R	W

Community	District	Area (hectares)	Wine produced red	white
Rheinbrohl	Middle Rhine	33	R	W
Rhens	Middle Rhine	24		W
Rhodt unter Rietburg	Palatinate	270	R	W
Riedlingen	Baden	6.5		W
Rielingshausen	Württemberg	10	R	W
Riet	Württemberg	5	R	W
Rietenau	Württemberg	5	R	W
Ringelbach	Baden	7.5	R	W
Riol	Moselle	16		W
Rivenich	Moselle	40		W
Riveris	Moselle	6		W
Rockenhausen	Palatinate	28		W
Rödelsee	Franconia	47.5		W
Röllfeld	Franconia	1.9	R	W
Rommelshausen	Württemberg	12	R	W
Rommersheim	Rhinehessia	24.5	R	W
Roschbach	Palatinate	97.5		W
Rosswag	Württemberg	35	R	W
Rotenberg	Baden	22	R	W
Röttingen	Franconia	10		W
Roxheim	Nahe	84		W
Rück	Franconia	5		W
Rüdesheim–Eibingen	Rheingau	89		W
Rüdesheim/Nahe	Nahe	25		W
Rüdesheim/Rheingau	Rheingau	271		W
Rüdisbronn	Franconia	3.2		W
Rümmelsheim	Nahe	95	R	W
Ruppertsberg	Palatinate	174		W
Ruwer	Moselle	18		W
Saarburg mit Beurig und Niederleuken	Moselle	92		W

Community	District	Area (hectares)	Wine produced red	white
Sachsenflur	Franconia	3.2		W
St Goar	Middle Rhine	12		W
St Goarhausen	Middle Rhine	24.4		W
St Johann	Rhinehessia	85	R	W
St Katharinen	Nahe	17		W
St Martin	Palatinate	292	R	W
Sasbach	Baden	19	R	W
Sasbachwalden	Baden	17.8	R	W
Sausenheim	Palatinate	132	R	W
Schallbach	Baden	3.1		W
Schallstadt	Baden	42		W
Schelingen	Baden	6.5	R	W
Scheppach	Württemberg	10	R	W
Scherzingen	Baden	24		W
Schimsheim	Rhinehessia	31	R	W
Schlatt	Baden	5		W
Schleich	Moselle	18		W
Schliengen	Baden	50		W
Schloss Böckelheim	Nahe	60		W
Schloss Saaleck	Franconia	25		W
Schluchten	Württemberg	16.5	R	W
Schmidhausen	Württemberg	30	R	W
Schmieheim	Baden	5.3	R	W
Schmittweiler	Palatinate	4		W
Schnait	Württemberg	130	R	W
Schoden	Moselle	50		W
Schöneberg	Nahe	20		W
Schonungen	Franconia	4.8		W
Schorndorf	Württemberg	8	R	W
Schornsheim	Rhinehessia	44.4		W
Schozach	Württemberg	23	R	W
Schriesheim	Badische Bergstrasse	7		W

Community	District	Area (hectares)	Wine produced red	white
Schuttern	Baden	3		W
Schützingen	Württemberg	16.8	R	W
Schwabbach	Württemberg	18		W
Schwabenheim	Rhinehessia	125	R	W
Schwabsburg	Rhinehessia	98	R	W
Schwaigern	Württemberg	90	R	W
Schwegenheim	Palatinate	15	R	W
Schweich	Moselle	65		W
Schweigen	Palatinate	28	R	W
Schweigern	Franconia	28		W
Schweighofen	Palatinate	8		W
Schweinfurt	Franconia	8.5	R	W
Schweppenheim	Nahe	57		W
Seefelden	Baden	45		W
Segnitz	Franconia	16		W
Sehndorf	Moselle	2.5		W
Seinsheim	Franconia	23		W
Selzen	Rhinehessia	105.2		W
Senheim	Moselle	75		W
Serrig	Moselle	100		W
Sexau	Baden	5	R	W
Sickershausen	Franconia	8		W
Siebeldingen	Palatinate	145	R	W
Siebeneich	Württemberg	20	R	W
Siefersheim	Rhinehessia	50	R	W
Siglingen	Württemberg	18	R	W
Simmern	Nahe	1.5		W
Sinzheim	Baden	65	R	W
Sitters	Palatinate	3		W
Sobernheim	Nahe	25		W
Sölden	Baden	5.5		W
Söllingen	Baden	4		W

Community	District	Area (hectares)	Wine produced red	white
Sommerach	Franconia	69.6		W
Sommerau	Moselle	5		W
Sommerhausen	Franconia	18.9		W
Sommerloch	Nahe	40		W
Sörgenloch	Rhinehessia	15	R	W
Sörnewitz	Saxony	30	R	W
Spielberg	Württemberg	13	R	W
Spiesheim	Rhinehessia	90	R	W
Sponheim	Nahe	40		W
Sprendlingen	Rhinehessia	150	R	W
Stadecken	Rhinehessia	75	R	W
Stadelhofen	Baden	7	R	W
Stammheim	Franconia	15.5		W
Staudernheim	Nahe	12		W
Staufen	Baden	45	R	W
Steeg	Middle Rhine	85	R	W
Stein am Kocher	Badisches Neckargebiet	7		W
Steinbach	Baden	65	R	W
Steinbach	Württemberg	4	R	W
Stein–Bockenheim	Rhinehessia	23.8		W
Steinheim a. d. Murr	Württemberg	14	R	W
Steinweiler	Palatinate	16.5	R	W
Sternenfels	Württemberg	25	R	W
Stetten	Franconia	21		W
Stetten	Württemberg	90	R	W
Stockheim	Württemberg	57	R	W
Stromberg	Nahe	3		W
Strümpfelbach	Württemberg	70	R	W
Stuttgart	Württemberg	332.5	R	W
Sulz	Baden	10.5	R	W
Sülzbach	Württemberg	23.5	R	W

Community	District	Area (hectares)	Wine produced red	white
Sulzburg	Baden	3		W
Sulzfeld	Baden	40	R	W
Sulzfeld	Franconia	65		W
Sulzheim	Rhinehessia	62	R	W
Sulztal	Franconia	9.1	R	W
Tairnbach	Badische Bergstrasse	12	R	W
Talheim	Württemberg	80	R	W
Tamm	Württemberg	15	R	W
Tannenkirch	Baden	20		W
Tarforst	Moselle	15		W
Tauberbischofsheim	Franconia	5.6		W
Tauberrettersheim	Franconia	15.2		W
Tauberzell	Franconia	2.3		W
Tawern	Moselle	13		W
Temmels	Moselle	46		W
Theilheim	Franconia	2		W
Thörnich	Moselle	35		W
Thüngen	Franconia	1.3		W
Thüngersheim	Franconia	97.4	R	W
Tiefenbach	Baden	48	R	W
Tiefenthal	Rhinehessia	6	R	W
Tiengen	Baden	15		W
Tiergarten	Baden	30	R	W
Traben–Trarbach	Moselle	180		W
Traisen	Nahe	34		W
Trechtingshausen	Middle Rhine	38		W
Treis	Moselle	83		W
Trier	Moselle	130		W
Trimberg	Franconia	10		W
Trittenheim	Moselle	137		W
Tübingen	Württemberg	3	R	W

Community	District	Area (hectares)	Wine produced red	white
Tutschfelden	Baden	35		W
Überlingen	Lake Constance	6	R	W
Ubstadt	Baden	19		W
Udenheim	Rhinehessia	90		W
Uffhofen	Rhinehessia	53	R	W
Ulm	Baden	10	R	W
Ülversheim	Rhinehessia	98.5		W
Undenheim	Rhinehessia	30		W
Ungstein	Palatinate	269	R	W
Unkel	Middle Rhine	26	R	W
Unkenbach	Palatinate	13.5		W
Unterdürrbach	Franconia	10.9	R	W
Untereisenheim	Franconia	27.2		W
Untereisesheim	Württemberg	2.7	R	W
Unterglottertal	Baden	13	R	W
Untergriesheim	Württemberg	1.5	R	W
Untergrombach	Baden	18	R	W
Unterheimbach	Württemberg	35	R	W
Unterjesingen	Württemberg	20	R	W
Unterleinach	Franconia	19		W
Unteröwisheim	Baden	25	R	W
Unterriexingen	Württemberg	10	R	W
Untersteinbach	Württemberg	4	R	W
Ürzig	Moselle	50		W
Vaihingen/Enz	Württemberg	13	R	W
Vallendar	Middle Rhine	8		W
Valwig	Moselle	77		W
Varnhalt	Baden	70		W
Veitshöchheim	Franconia	46.1	R	W
Veldenz	Moselle	42		W
Vendersheim	Rhinehessia	58	R	W
Venningen	Palatinate	100	R	W

Community	District	Area (hectares)	Wine produced red	white
Verrenberg	Württemberg	25.4	R	W
Vögisheim	Baden	26		W
Volkach	Franconia	34.6		W
Vollmersweiler	Palatinate	6		W
Volxheim	Rhinehessia	90	R	W
Vorbachzimmern	Württemberg	41	R	W
Wachenheim	Palatinate	350	R	W
Wachenheim	Rhinehessia	60	R	W
Wackernheim	Rhinehessia	16	R	W
Wagenstadt	Baden	34	R	W
Wahlheim	Rhinehessia	19.3		W
Waldböckelheim	Nahe	91		W
Waldenburg	Württemberg	8.5	R	W
Waldhilbersheim	Nahe	102.5	R	W
Waldlaubersheim	Nahe	47		W
Waldrach	Moselle	74		W
Waldulm	Baden	45	R	W
Wallburg	Baden	2.2	R	W
Wallertheim	Rhinehessia	88	R	W
Wallhausen	Nahe	250		W
Walporzheim	Ahr	85	R	W
Walsheim	Palatinate	146	R	W
Waltershofen	Baden	11.5		W
Wasenweiler	Baden	60	R	W
Wasserliesch–Reinig	Moselle	22		W
Wawern	Moselle	29		W
Wehlen	Moselle	104		W
Wehr	Moselle	18		W
Weigenheim	Franconia	9		W
Weikersheim	Württemberg	18	R	W
Weil am Rhein	Baden	28	R	W

Community	District	Area (hectares)	Wine produced red	white
Weiler	Lake Constance	2.7	R	W
Weiler bei Bingerbrück	Nahe	26	R	W
Weiler bei Monzingen	Nahe	62		W
Weiler a.d. Zaber	Württemberg	14	R	W
Weilheim a.d. Teck	Württemberg	5.5		W
Weinähr	Lahn	10.5	R	W
Weingarten	Palatinate	20	R	W
Weinheim	Badische Bergstrasse	10.3	R	W
Weinheim	Rhinehessia	100		W
Weinolsheim	Rhinehessia	65	R	W
Weinsberg	Württemberg	158	R	W
Weinsheim	Nahe	50		W
Weisenheim am Berg	Palatinate	183	R	W
Weisenheim am Sand	Palatinate	313	R	W
Weissbach	Württemberg	9		W
Welgesheim	Rhinehessia	50	R	W
Wellen	Moselle	22		W
Wellmich	Middle Rhine	17		W
Welmlingen	Baden	12		W
Wendelsheim	Württemberg	4	R	W
Werbach	Baden	15		W
Werlau	Middle Rhine	20		W
Westheim	Franconia	5		W
Westheim	Palatinate	2		W
Westhofen	Rhinehessia	300	R	W
Westum	Ahr	10.2	R	W
Wettelbrunnen	Baden	20		W
Weyher	Palatinate	137	R	W
Wicker	Rheingau	27		W

Community	District	Area (hectares)	Wine produced red	white
Widdern	Württemberg	40	R	W
Wiesbaden	Rheingau	4.5		W
Wiesbaden/Dotzheim	Rheingau	2		W
Wiesbaden/Frauenstein	Rheingau	35	R	W
Wiesbaden/Schierstein	Rheingau	20		W
Wiesenbronn	Franconia	42.6		W
Wiesloch	Badische Bergstrasse	105.5	R	W
Wies Oppenheim	Rhinehessia	19	R	W
Willsbach	Württemberg	74	R	W
Wiltingen	Moselle	168		W
Wincheringen	Moselle	87		W
Windesheim	Nahe	139	R	W
Windischenbach	Württemberg	21	R	W
Winkel	Rheingau	217	R	W
Winnenden	Württemberg	26	R	W
Winningen	Moselle	212		W
Winterbach	Württemberg	1.1	R	W
Winterborn	Palatinate	7.5	R	W
Winterhausen	Franconia	14		W
Wintersheim	Rhinehessia	6.8	R	W
Wintersweiler	Baden	17		W
Wintrich	Moselle	100		W
Winzenheim	Nahe	45	R	W
Wipfeld	Franconia	18		W
Wirmsthal	Franconia	10		W
Wittlich	Moselle	50		W
Wolf	Moselle	43		W
Wolfenweiler	Baden	70		W
Wolfsheim	Rhinehessia	70	R	W
Wolfstein	Palatinate	5.2	R	W
Wollbach	Baden	13		W

Community	District	Area (hectares)	Wine produced red	white
Wollmesheim	Palatinate	95	R	W
Wöllstein	Rhinehessia	80.9	R	W
Wonsheim	Rhinehessia	30.5	R	W
Worms	Rhinehessia	26	R	W
Worms–Herrnsheim	Rhinehessia	39	R	W
Worms–Horchheim	Rhinehessia	21	R	W
Worms–Leiselheim	Rhinehessia	24	R	W
Worms–Weinsheim	Rhinehessia	5.8	R	W
Wörrstadt	Rhinehessia	75	R	W
Wöschbach	Baden	3		W
Würzburg	Franconia	300	R	W
Zaberfeld	Württemberg	21	R	W
Zaisersweiher	Württemberg	15	R	W
Zeil	Franconia	4		W
Zell	Franconia	10		W
Zell	Moselle	212		W
Zell	Palatinate	69	R	W
Zell–Weierbach	Baden	70	R	W
Zeltingen–Rachtig	Moselle	224		W
Zeutern	Baden	25		W
Ziegelanger	Franconia	9.5		W
Zornheim	Rhinehessia	125	R	W
Zotzenheim	Rhinehessia	44.7	R	W
Zunsweier	Baden	27.6	R	W
Zwingenberg	Hessische Bergstrasse	10.1	R	W

PRODUCTION OF WINE
1938-62

Year	Area under viticulture (hectares)	Crop	
		hectolitres per hectare	total (hectolitres)
1938	73,000	33.4	2,438,000
1949	51,487	26.5	1,363,000
1951	52,521	59.3	3,112,000
1952	53,359	50.8	2,713,000
1953	54,486	45.1	2,456,000
1954	58,142	52.6	3,098,000
1955	59,961	40.1	2,405,000
1956	59,695	15.6	929,000
1957	58,743	38.5	2,264,000
1958	59,136	81.1	4,796,000
1959	60,995	70.5	4,302,000
1960	64,180	115.8	7,433,000
1961	66,265	53.9	3,574,000
1962	67,137	59.5	3,993,000

PRODUCTION OF WINE
VINTAGE 1962

| FEDERAL STATE | Area | Production | | |
Wine District	(hectares)	hectolitres per hectare	total (hectolitres)	white wine (hectolitres)	red wine (hectolitres)
NORTH-RHINE					
WESTPHALIA	35	21.8	762	675	87
Middle Rhine	35	21.8	762	675	87
HESSIA	2,830	41.6	117,611	116,227	1,384
RB Darmstadt (Bergstr.)	212	35.3	7,475	7,391	84
RB Wiesbaden (Rheingau)	2,618	42.1	110,136	108,836	1,300
RHEINLAND-PFALZ	46,687	62.2	2,902,362	2,523,746	378,616
RHEINLAND-NASSAU	14,154	63.9	905,064	890,044	15,020
Middle Rhine	1,204	41.8	50,336	49,610	726
Nahe (RB Koblenz)	3,124	46.9	146,571	145,343	1,228
Upper Moselle	728	105.7	76,950	76,950	—
Saar	1,062	60.2	63,932	63,932	—
Ruwer	324	67.8	21,967	21,967	—
Middle Moselle	4,499	78.0	350,922	350,922	—
Lower Moselle	2,624	66.2	173,709	173,709	—
Ahr	565	35.0	19,787	6,753	13,034
Lahn	24	37.1	890	858	32
RHINEHESSIA	15,837	47.0	744,791	667,241	77,550

PALATINATE	16,696	75.0	1,252,507	966,461	286,046
Middle Haardt	5,203	78.6	409,112	262,752	146,360
Upper Haardt	8,729	77.9	680,099	604,886	75,213
Lower Haardt with Zellertal	2,041	68.9	140,527	76,184	64,343
Nahe (RB Palatinate)	723	31.5	22,769	22,639	130
BADEN-WÜRTTEMBERG	15,084	56.2	848,455	554,979	171,210
North Württemberg	6,692	38.0	254,332	86,523	92,087
North Baden	1,802	46.8	84,307	54,042	12,228
South Baden	6,507	78.0	507,241	413,197	66,435
South Württemberg– Hohenzollern	83	31.0	2,575	1,217	460
BAVARIA	2,444	21.7	53,029	52,197	832
Franconia and other districts	2,444	21.7	53,029	52,197	832
SAARLAND	57	100.0	5,700	5,682	18
TOTAL	67,137	58.5	3,927,919	3,253,506	552,147

RB = *Regierungsbezirk*, a territorial division roughly equivalent to a county.

Reprinted from Statistisches Bundesamt Wiesbaden, Fachserie B Weinmosternte 1962.

EXPORT OF GERMAN WINES

figures in hectolitres

	1954	1955	1956	1957	1958	1959	1960	1961	1962
Aden	—	—	—	—	—	—	—	85	97
Argentina	—	—	—	—	—	—	161	241	167
Australia	103	107	67	118	187	165	277	355	382
Austria	290	259	450	599	—	—	6,726	269	270
Bahrain and Qatar	—	—	—	—	—	—	—	83	63
Belgium and Luxembourg	3,899	3,850	4,250	3,766	4,458	6,224	5,938	7,583	6,140
Bolivia	—	—	—	—	—	—	—	49	34
Brazil	454	46	137	304	—	—	—	234	153
British Guiana	—	—	—	—	—	—	—	16	—
British Honduras	—	—	—	—	—	—	179	175	201
British West Indies	87	143	147	179	222	170	182	135	201
Canada	693	870	1,634	1,632	1,774	2,388	2,881	2,975	3,450
Canary Islands	—	—	—	—	—	—	7	15	—
Ceylon	—	—	—	—	—	—	—	21	—
Chile	—	—	—	—	—	—	—	11	—
Colombia	203	100	148	127	—	—	91	141	59
Costa Rica	—	—	—	—	—	—	—	40	—
Cyprus	—	—	—	—	—	—	—	26	—

	1954	1955	1956	1957	1958	1959	1960	1961	1962
Czechoslovakia	488	—	544	1,049	982	1,750	1,285	1,789	2,916
Denmark	1,841	1,607	2,509	2,431	3,266	4,928	6,859	7,870	7,194
Dominican Republic	—	—	—	—	—	—	622	24	—
Dutch Antilles	—	—	—	—	—	—	—	43	—
Ecuador	—	—	—	—	—	—	—	56	62
Egypt	—	—	—	—	—	—	—	29	—
Ethiopia	—	—	—	—	—	—	1,105	17	49
Finland	418	653	1,085	935	820	824	1,208	1,184	2,412
France	1,655	1,483	1,529	1,132	688	360	437	514	342
Ghana	—	—	—	—	—	—	112	160	49
Greece	32	47	50	35	—	—	—	54	58
Guatemala	—	—	—	—	—	—	—	59	—
Honduras	—	—	—	—	—	—	—	16	—
Hong Kong	—	—	—	—	—	—	193	245	258
Iceland	—	—	—	—	—	—	—	58	53
India	—	—	—	—	—	—	63	57	44
Indonesia	—	—	—	—	—	—	—	24	—
Iran	—	—	—	—	—	—	52	—	—
Iraq	—	—	—	—	—	—	54	69	166
Ireland	223	204	339	290	565	692	764	922	911
Italy	171	147	154	195	186	215	422	774	947
Kenya and Uganda	106	138	151	178	172	297	335	285	354
Kuwait	—	—	—	—	—	—	73	54	72
Lebanon	—	—	—	—	—	—	88	62	—
Liberia	—	—	—	—	—	—	47	73	83
Libya	—	—	—	—	—	—	52	57	—
Malta and Gibraltar	—	—	—	—	—	—	71	89	83
Mexico	150	55	372	226	—	—	71	61	355
Morocco	—	—	—	—	—	—	—	20	—
Netherlands	4,179	4,631	5,478	4,538	4,839	8,351	8,214	10,124	8,735
New Guinea	—	—	—	—	—	—	22	3	—
New Zealand	96	180	187	169	72	176	318	309	407
Nigeria	—	—	—	—	—	—	252	191	234
Norway	146	908	575	656	178	774	1,309	1,502	1,108
Pakistan	—	—	—	—	—	—	—	54	53
Panama	—	—	—	—	—	—	—	52	—
Paraguay	—	—	—	—	—	—	1,102	22	—
Peru	42	89	108	152	—	—	—	138	178
Philippine Islands	—	—	—	—	—	—	45	75	51

	1954	1955	1956	1957	1958	1959	1960	1961	1962
Poland	—	—	—	—	—	—	—	16	—
Portugal	—	—	—	—	—	—	82	60	63
Puerto Rico	—	—	—	—	—	—	61	66	—
Rhodesia and Nyasaland	—	—	—	—	—	—	—	184	159
Saar	8,787	11,593	12,800	10,047	—	—	—	—	—
Sierra Leone	—	—	—	—	—	—	536	54	40
Singapore	—	—	—	—	—	—	—	170	114
South Africa	307	511	363	244	335	301	368	238	229
South Vietnam	—	—	—	—	—	—	—	12	—
Spain	—	—	—	—	—	—	94	122	95
Sudan	—	—	—	—	—	—	—	19	—
Sweden	4,152	4,932	5,059	5,350	5,449	6,562	6,558	8,506	9,463
Switzerland	3,529	2,098	2,519	2,579	2,185	2,679	3,357	4,155	4,461
Tanganyika	—	—	—	—	—	—	—	39	—
Thailand	—	—	—	—	—	—	—	46	33
Turkey	—	—	—	—	—	—	—	113	72
United Kingdom	16,984	19,966	21,477	22,636	25,682	30,594	43,321	45,306	38,691
United States	15,081	16,789	21,484	23,390	24,704	32,170	32,416	44,002	39,325
Uruguay	—	—	—	—	—	—	—	86	77
Venezuela	357	412	559	593	592	587	—	158	304
Zanzibar and Pemba	—	—	—	—	—	—	—	17	—
TOTAL	64,473	71,818	84,175	83,550	77,356	100,207	128,410	142,958	131,737

THREE TASTINGS OF GREAT GERMAN WINES

To round off our journey through the German wine districts and through the ages, we present a picture of some tastings of these wines, to show in some instances the great possible differences between wines of the same district; in others—when we describe wines of the same estate—the effect of age on the wine. We arranged these tastings, where we could, in congenial surroundings, tasting the wines with friends and then sitting down to a meal which was partnered by one of the wines. We must add that, in all cases, the Beeren- and Trockenbeerenauslese wines were tasted after the meal—before the coffee—to partner the dessert. They were memorable meals. Our notes intend to show the age a fine German wine can reach and the pleasure it can give.

SCHLOSS VOLLRADS TASTING NOTES

Directors' Club, London, April 26, 1961. GUEST OF HONOUR: Count Matuschka-Greiffenclau.

1911 *Trockenbeerenauslese* (*Original sweetness* 200° *Öchsle; bottled April* 24, 1918)
Wonderfully well preserved after 50 years. One of the greatest wines of the vintage. The noble ripeness has aged into spiciness, and behind it there is a firm ripeness of bouquet.

The original sweetness has disappeared, leaving a full, dry, noble flavour, and only at the very end does it slightly show its age; without this, one would imagine it to be decades younger. The sample shows that here is an aristocrat!

1915 *Trockenbeerenauslese* (148° *Öchsle; bottled December* 19, 1922)
This wine, which had a quarter less richness than the 1911, has aged much more to
a golden ochre colour and is now rather dry and past its prime, probably owing to
a war-time or post-war cork.

1920 *Trockenbeerenauslese* (225° *Öchsle; bottled March* 5, 1949)
A golden brown colour. Recalls the "old brown hocks" which were so esteemed in
England in the 18th century and before. Although it has some of the characteristics
of a fine old Madeira, due to its ageing, it has nobility and finesse and a full, fruity
flavour with some sugar left, but all in a well-balanced harmony.

1921 *Trockenbeerenauslese* (190° *Öchsle; bottled May* 2, 1927)
The attractive, deep, full golden colour of the wine is matched by the ripe spiciness
of bouquet. The flavour is full and ripe with medium sweetness. Although it shows
some age, it does not look as old as the 1920 vintage; though less rich than the 1920,
it is finer and more elegant.

1933 *Trockenbeerenauslese* (156° *Öchsle; bottled September* 1, 1936)
The medium to light golden yellow colour makes the wine look younger than it is,
as it has the slight *spritz* still apparent in the wine. The fresh bouquet has overtones
reminiscent of lime tree flowers in the sunshine, while the flavour with its elegant
fruity acidity will go on developing for a number of years yet. The wine is still very
young and fresh and has no sign of age.

1934 *Trockenbeerenauslese* (160° *Öchsle; bottled June* 2, 1937)
The medium yellow colour of a wine approaching its prime is matched by the ripe,
spicy, and very fruity bouquet, while the medium rich nobility of the flavour rounds
it into a harmonious whole. A young vigorous youth, fuller in body than the 1933,
still being sweet with fine aroma and great finesse. One of the greatest of a fine vintage.

1937 *Trockenbeerenauslese* (170° *Öchsle; bottled April* 1, 1940)
The medium to light golden yellow colour indicates a wine which is still maturing.
The bouquet is somewhat reminiscent of the 1933 vintage, but much more spicy and
noble. The flavour, which is very ripe and fruity with a taste of ripe grapes, is backed
by a firmness towards the finish—which might round off as the wine gets older. A
great and noble beauty! It may live for ever.

1947 *Trockenbeerenauslese* (176° *Öchsle; bottled May* 20, 1950)
A medium, deep golden colour which makes the wine appear older than its three
predecessors, and although the bouquet seems fully developed, or perhaps over-
developed, and the flavour with its medium sweetness and medium ripeness is well
developed, there is still a firmness towards the end; but it has less life and future than
the 1933, the 1934 or the 1937. It will be senile soon.

1953 *Trockenbeerenauslese* (180° Öchsle; *bottled February* 3, 1956)
The medium light yellow colour indicates that the wine is approaching its first youthful prime, where the ripe, round, flavoury bouquet and taste make a harmonious symposium which hints at further beauties still to develop in years to come. I would like to see it in 1975.

1959 *Beerenauslese* (*bottled April* 1960)
The light, yellow colour and the freshness of the bouquet evoke a picture of springtime, where the charm of the bouquet with its reminiscence of lime tree flowers matches the elegant freshness of the flavour. A very elegant baby, of great promise!

POSTSCRIPT
Two 1959 *Trockenbeerenauslesen* (170° and 200°) were bottled in May 1961. They combine the qualities of the 1953 and the 1937 vintages. May our children and grand-children enjoy many pleasures, and may these wines complement those pleasures.

TASTING OF NAHE WINES

Roman Wall House, London, January 8, 1962. GUEST OF HONOUR: Mr Cyril Ray.

Kreuznacher Hinkelstein Riesling Spätlese 1959 (*Estate bottling Anheuser*)
This is still a yellow, very little developed, Nahe wine, showing a typical Moselle-type bouquet of Riesling character. It is very flavoury and elegant, with medium body; very harmonious with a flavour which lingers—a wine that will live for another 6–8 years to reach its best.

Kreuznacher Gutental Riesling Spätlese 1959 (*Estate bottling Finkenauer*)
Fuller than the Hinkelstein, it has a very fine slight vanilla bouquet, fruity acidity and fine elegance. The thirst quenching fruity acidity is emphasized finally, and this will keep this wine for quite another decade.

Kreuznacher Narrenkappe Riesling Feinste Auslese 1959 (*Estate bottling Anheuser*)
Richer, and shows a pale golden colour; a typical fruity Nahe bouquet, with a slight vanilla flavour. It has some carbonic acid in solution, in other words, it is *spritzig*, and this, together with its fine acidity and its firmness, give it good staying power, much finer than many Moselles of the 1959 vintage of the same description.

Kreuznacher Mönchberg Riesling Edelbeerenauslese 1959 (*Estate bottling Anheuser*)
A wine of pale golden yellow colour, which in its bouquet shows on the one side pourri noble-rottenness combined with the soil character of the *Mönchberg*. It is a round, ripe and very fruity wine, and, as an *Edelbeerenauslese*, medium-full to full, still green in its finish, needs many years to mature, to reach its best; a wine to sip after dinner as a natural liqueur.

Kreuznacher Gutental Mollenbrunnen Riesling Trockenbeerenauslese 1959
This exceptionally fine Trockenbeerenauslese of the 1959 vintage has a fine, fruity acidity, well balanced, which will give this rich wine a very long life. The light golden colour shows that it is in its very early stages of development and needs 8–10 years at least to mature. Fine vanilla flavour, combined with the *pourriture noble*, gives this wine outstanding bouquet and finesse, while it is very clean and not cloying. It is a wine that can only be called great, one of the giants of the 1959 vintage.

Kreuznacher Brückes Riesling Trockenbeerenauslese 1959 (*Estate bottling Anheuser*)
A wine with very full, very ripe, very sweet, very rich and "grapy" flavour, which can be compared with a 1921 wine whose description will follow; it gives us the feeling that this wine will live as long and perhaps longer, and will always be considered one of the best produced in 1959 in the Nahe. Our judgment has been confirmed by the fact that this wine was awarded in 1961 the great Rhenish Wine Prize, and also the Great Prize of the Chamber of Agriculture in Frankfurt.

Winzenheimer Berg Roseneck Riesling Edelbeerenauslese 1937
This wine, 24 years old, was long past its best, and the lack of *pourriture noble* means that it cannot be considered a great wine.

Schloss Böckelheimer Königsfels Riesling Trockenbeerenauslese 1921 (*Estate bottling Anheuser*)
Here is a wine over 40 years old; its colour is now deep golden, perhaps very slightly brownish, but its spiciness, its fruitiness, its very full ripeness, and its full rich body, with a fine acidity finish, has preserved it, and it still stands out as a giant, with many more years of life to come.

Kreuznacher Brückes Riesling Trockenbeerenauslese 1949
This wine has a very deep ochreous golden colour, more brown than the 1921, and gives the impression of being older than the 1921 wine. One feels that this wine has been fine, even great, but matured much too quickly, and should have been drunk when it was ten years old, perhaps twelve years old. It might have been in cask a little too long. This wine proves that it is not always wise to wait until in one's opinion a wine reaches its very best. This class of wine should be tasted first when five or six years old, so that one can then judge when its peak will come. One should never say, just because a wine is a Trockenbeerenauslese, that it needs 8, 10, 12 and more years to develop. There are exceptions, and it is a great pity when a wine lover and proprietor of a fine wine misses a wine's best and mature time for consumption.

WINE TASTING

Grosvenor House, London, January 17–18, 1962. GUEST OF HONOUR: Prof. Dr. Breider.

1959 Würzburger Jesuitenstein Scheu-Riesling
Bouquet like a rose and peach garden: wine which stays with you. Will reach its best in 1967–68; staying power till 1972.

1959 Hörsteiner Reuschberg–Abtsberg Riesling Spätlese
The peachy flavour of this wine reminds one of a fine Rheingau wine of the Marcobrunn or Rauenthal vineyards. Elegant, fine, noble, with a touch of sweetness—should be at its best in 1968 and last until 1975.

1959 Randersackerer Spielberg Riesling Spätlese
Agreeable, spicy bouquet; fine, fruity acidity; *pourriture noble*. Will reach its best in 1968–70, with long staying power.

1959 Thüngersheimer Neuberg Scheurebe Spätlese
Very rich, pleasing, noble bouquet of elegant character, and fine, fruity acidity. This wine will reach its best in 1965–66, but has staying power for another 10 years.

1959 Würzburger Innere Leiste Mainriesling
Rich peach-apricot bouquet, good body, juicy with enormous character and a fine pleasing acidity. Will reach its best between 1967 and 1970, with staying power for another decade or two.

1959 Hörsteiner Abtsberg Mainriesling Spätlese
A fine, soft bouquet, reminding one of peaches and ripe apricots. Elegant in body with much vivacity. Will reach its best in 1967–70, with staying power for another decade or two.

1959 Veitshöchheimer Wölflein Perle Beerenauslese
A fine, spicy bouquet; round, good body with noble sweetness. Will reach its best in 1970–72, with more decades to come.

1959 Würzburger Stein Sylvaner Trockenbeerenauslese
A full, rich dessert wine, noble in character, with honey flavour. Will be at its best between 1975 and 1980, with staying power until 2,000.

1959 Hörsteiner Abtsberg–Reuschberg Riesling Trockenbeerenauslese
Noble Riesling bouquet combined with fruity body make a harmonious balance. This noble, exceptional wine from two vineyards of the village Hörstein will improve for 10–15 years, with staying power for a period that cannot yet be determined.

EXCERPTS FROM
GERMAN WINE LAW

The protection of the wine-consuming public by law is of very recent date. The first wine-law in Germany was dated April 20, 1892; before that, there was only a general clause in the criminal code prohibiting the sale of falsified beverages or beverages which had gone bad.

The Wine Law of 1892 was followed by a new law of 1901, which again was altered by the Wine Law of 1909 and the Wine Law of 1930. The last is still valid, though with many additions and alterations as a result of the seven by-laws decreed between 1932 and 1958. The purpose of the Wine Law is to protect the consumer, so that he is not offered any wine which could be damaging to his health, nor any imitations and falsified wines, nor wines under misleading names.

How necessary the Wine Laws were is shown by Husenbeth in his *Wine-Cellar* (1834), where he speaks about blending of wines of various districts: "This abuse has of late years also been practised by the Rhenish travellers who, instead of importing real Hock and Moselle wine, have imposed the cheaper Palatinate wines at high prices, and with high-sounding names, as the best Hocks and Moselles, while they are known to have sold the same wines by their own Palatine names to others at very low prices." Furthermore, as long as it was not laid down how much a wine could be sweetened in bad vintages, unscrupulous wine-growers and wine-merchants added a lot of sugar-water to their wines.

Here are some excerpts from German Wine Law.

1. The addition of *sugar* to German wines is regulated by the Wine Law of 1930.

Article III states:

> Sugar (or sugar dissolved in pure water) may be added to grape-must or wines (in the case of red wine also to grape-mash) derived from home-grown grapes, provided that this is done for the purpose of supplementing a natural lack of sugar or alcohol, or counteracting a natural excess of acid, to an extent sufficient to produce in the said wines a composition equal to that of wines derived in a good year from grapes of the same kind and origin without extraneous additions.
>
> Such addition may however in no case make up more than one fourth of the whole quantity of the liquid.

2. *Labelling.* Article V of the By-law lays down this interpretation of paragraph 5 of the Wine Law:

> It is considered as misleading if fancy names are used in immediate connection with names of communes, or if they are otherwise apt to be taken as names of communes or sites, even if made with the special addition *Handelsmarke* (trade mark) and therefore a punishable offence. (Wines misleadingly labelled may be confiscated.)

3. *Blending.* German white wines can be blended regardless of quality, district of origin, or age. A Baden wine may be blended with a Rheingau, a 1961 vintage with a 1949, a Riesling with a Sylvaner, as long as all wines of the blend are of German origin. (A German white must *not* be blended with a foreign wine.)

In most countries blends bear the name of the vineyard which has contributed more than 50 % to the blend. The German conditions for naming blends are much more difficult.

In principle, a mixture of several products may only be named after the component which forms two thirds of its volume, and determines its character, and the name of a vineyard may be used only if the component after which the mixture is called is unsweetened. Descriptions such as *Wachstum*, *Gewächs*, etc., are prohibited in naming blends. Therefore, if two Niersteiner wines with vineyard names are blended, and one part is not at least two thirds of the blend, the wine can be sold only as an ordinary Niersteiner. If the blend is two-thirds Riesling and one-third Sylvaner, it is allowed to be called Riesling.

In regulating the nomenclature of blended wines, the law confines itself to the case of blends "between products of different origin" (meaning different geographical origin), and makes no mention of the blending of different *vintages*. Writers on the subject are agreed, however, that such blends should be subjected by analogy to the same rules. This means that a blend of several different vintages may be named after one of them only if that vintage forms at least two thirds of the blend's total volume and determines its character. If no single vintage forms two thirds of any given blend, the latter may be marketed only as non-vintage wine.

4. The Wine Law limits the processes that may be applied to wine to a selected range; everything that is not specifically and expressly allowed by law is prohibited, and wines treated not in accordance with the statute are liable to confiscation. The treatment may be necessary for the genuine development of the wine, it may be necessary as cure, etc. The following are permitted:

a) *Sulphurization* (*See* page 33).

b) *Carbon dioxide* is sometimes added to wine that has grown rather stale and flat, in order to "freshen" it. There are no quantitative restrictions on the addition of this gas.

c) A maximum of ten grammes of *tannic acid* per 100 litres may be added to wine. This combines with the albuminous matters in the wine and tends to make it more durable. It also promotes the precipitation of substances inclined to cause turbidity.

d) *White clay* (kaolin) may be added in some circumstances, chiefly in the case of viscous wines.

e) Another permissible addition is purified *charcoal* prepared from wood or bones. It is used to remove certain defects, counteract some diseases, and also to improve the wine's appearance.

f) Wine-drinkers are becoming increasingly inclined to prefer young, fresh wines and to demand their complete limpidity—they expect them to be "star-bright". Wines can be clarified either by "fining" or by filtering.

The ancient method of *clarifying* wine by the use of isinglass (obtained from sturgeon or shad) is still very much to the fore. Other materials used for clarification are gelatine, agar-agar (also known as Bengal or Japan isinglass), white of egg, and white clay.

g) When wine is to be sent in barrels to tropical countries, it is permissible to fortify it by the addition of grape brandy or of high-grade pure alcohol (90 per cent alcohol content or more), up to a maximum of one per cent of the volume of the wine.

h) *Filtering* (*See* pages 33–36).

VINIFICATION OF
ICE WINES

The juice of a grape with 75° Öchsle will freeze at −3° to −4° centigrade. The freezing process in the grape is as follows.

First of all, pure water contained in the grape is formed into ice crystals, with the result that the concentration of the extracts and the sugar, but also those of the fruit, and acidities, are made stronger. The result is that the Öchsle degree of the resulting must increases. It is noteworthy that the formation and concentration of the tartaric acid does not increase in the same proportion as the sugar concentration, because, as a result of the frost, the tartaric acid is precipitated in ice crystals, and therefore the tartaric acid content decreases. The greater the degree of frost, the more ice crystals are formed and the more concentrated the extract becomes. This process can go so far that, at the end, even the extract which remains can freeze. In other words, the frost can be so strong that, instead of a must rich in extract, it can turn the other way, and a too thin must can result.

One should try to make ice wine only at 5° centigrade of frost, because when the grapes are gathered and brought into the pressing house the temperature of the must may increase sufficiently to prevent the making of ice wine altogether. In 1961 the temperature was −6.6° to −9° centigrade when the grapes were gathered. The resulting grape juice had a sugar content of approximately 25° Öchsle higher than the original. In 1962 the frost was so strong that some of the Öchsle degrees were doubled, so that the 1962 Spätlese ice wines have actually the fullness of Feine Auslese and Beerenauslese wines. It is interesting in this connection that, during the ice wine days in November

1962, the frost was strong during the night but very sunny weather prevailed during the day-time; if the grapes were not gathered before 10 o'clock in the morning, the temperature rose so much that it was impossible to make an ice wine, as the grapes started thawing long before they reached the pressing house.

It is, of course, difficult to bring must at this temperature to fermentation, and in 1962 it was necessary to use cultivated yeast, which was added to 5 % of the ice wines, which had been brought to a moderate temperature, in order to start the fermentation, which usually lasted no less than fifty days.

The average original acid content of those observed was 15.8 promille, which, during fermentation, decreased to 13 promille, as tartaric acid was precipitated in cold casks.

Famous Ice Wines

1949 Wehlener Sonnenuhr Feinste Auslese "Eiswein"

1949 Avelsbacher Thielslei "Eiswein"

1950 Schloss Johannisberger Spätlese "Eiswein"

1961 Kreuznacher Krötenpfuhl Riesling Feinste Spätlese "Eiswein"

1961 Kreuznacher St Martin Riesling Feinste Spätlese "Eiswein"

1961 Winkeler Hasensprung Riesling Auslese "Eiswein"

1961 Serriger Saarsteiner Schlossberg Riesling Spätlese "Eiswein"

1961 Trierer Kreuzberg Riesling "Eiswein" Spätlese

1961 Serriger Schloss Saarfels Vogelsang Riesling Cabinet "Eiswein"

1961 Ürziger Würzgarten Riesling Spätlese "Eiswein"

1961 Deutschherrenköpfchen Riesling "Eiswein" Spätlese

1961 Scharzhofberger Riesling Feine Auslese "Eiswein"

1961 Berncasteler Badstube Spätlese "Eiswein" Kabinett

1961 Scharzhofberger Riesling Feinste Auslese "Eiswein"

1961 Eitelsbacher Karthäuserhofberg Riesling Feinste Auslese "Eiswein"

1961 Berncasteler Badstube und Pfalzgraben Spätlese "Eiswein" Kabinett

1961 Wehlener Sonnenuhr "Eiswein" Auslese

1961 Wehlener-Zeltinger Sonnenuhr "Eiswein" Auslese

1961 Scharzberger Riesling "Eiswein" Spätlese

1961 Serriger Vogelsang Riesling "Eiswein"

1961 Oberemmeler Scharzberg "Eiswein" Edelwein

1962 Kreuznacher Narrenkappe Riesling Feinste Spätlese "Nikolaus-Eiswein"

1962 Kaseler Nies'chen Feinste Spätlese "Eiswein"

1962 Niersteiner Kehr Sylvester-Eiswein

1962 Kreuznacher Narrenkappe Riesling Hochfeine Spätlese "Eiswein" Edelgewächs

1962 Bodenheimer St Alban Riesling "Eiswein"

1962 Niersteiner Glöck Riesling St Barbara "Eiswein"

GLOSSARY OF
GERMAN WORDS AND PHRASES

Abfüllung Bottling

Apfelsäure Malic acid

aus dem Weingute From the estate or vineyard

aus der Schatzkammer From the treasure chamber

Auslese See pages 38–39

Beerenauslese See pages 39–40

Beerwein Wine made from grapes which have been removed from their stalks before pressing

Besitz (alleiniger Besitz) Sole proprietor

Bestes Fass (Fuder) Best cask

Brennwein Wine for distillation (to produce brandy)

Cabinet See pages 40–41

Creszenz (also *Kreszenz*) Growth

Deutsch German

Domäne Domain; as a rule, used for state-owned vineyards.

durchgegoren A fully fermented wine; as a rule, without a residue of unfermented sugar; a wine for diabetics.

echt Genuine

Edelauslese Selected noble grapes

Edelbeerenauslese A Beerenauslese made from noble-rotten grapes that are not dehydrated; i.e. the wine is not quite a Trockenbeerenauslese

Edelgewächs Noble growth (may be used to describe only a Beeren- or Trockenbeerenauslese)

Edelwein Noble growth

Eigengewächs, Eigenes Wachstum Own growth ("from my own vineyard")

Eiswein See pages 41–42

entkeimt (EK) Sterilized

Erben Heirs, estate of

Fass No. ... Cask No. ...

Federweisser See page 43

Feine (Feinste) Fine, Finest. (A grower producing more than one cask of the same wine will, in order to distinguish between them, describe them according to quality.)

Flaschenschild Label

Freiherr Baron

Fuder No. . . . Cask (of 1,000 l.) No. . . .

Fürst Prince

Gebrüder Brothers

Gemarkung Vineyards of a community

Geschwister Brother(s) and sister(s)

Gewächs Growth

gezuckert Sweetened

Glühwein Mulled wine; a hot wine (red or white) spiced with cinnamon or clove and sweetened

Goldbeerenauslese An Auslese made from fully ripe golden grapes (*Goldbeeren*)

Graf Count

Hauptniederlassung Head Office

Hausmarke Special *cuvée*

Haustrunk House drink (the wine the grower makes from the grapecake for his own use and that of his workers)

Hochgewächs Superb growth

Hofkellerei The cellars belonging to a royal court

Jahrgang Vintage, year

Jungferwein *See* page 43

Kabinett *See* pages 40–41

Kellerabfüllung, *Kellerabzug* Bottled in the cellar of the grower, proprietor

Kellerei Large, extended cellars

Kellereiabzug Bottled by the wine merchant (in contrast to the grower)

Kelter Grape-press

Kommerzienrat Commercial Councillor

Konsumwein *Vin ordinaire*

Korkbrand Branded cork

Kreis District

Kreszenz (also *Creszenz*) Growth

Lage Site

Land Federal State

Landwein Ordinary wine of the district

Landwirtschaftskammer Chamber of Agriculture

Lehr & Versuchsanstalt Viticultural College and Research Institute

Maiwein *See* page 43

Natur, Naturwein Natural wine

Öchsle This term indicates the number of grammes by which one litre of must is heavier than one litre of water, the sugar content representing about 25 per cent of this calibration. Thus, with a reading of 100° Öchsle, 100 litres will contain about 25 kilogrammes of sugar.

Offener Wein Wine by the glass

Original Abfüllung (*Orig.-Abfg.*) Original bottling

Originalabzug Original bottling

Originalwein Original wine

Perlwein Bubbly wine — a wine containing up to 1½ atmospheres of carbonic acid

Pfarrgut The parson's vineyard (belonging to the church and given on lease to the parson as part of his endowment)

rein Pure

Rentamt Collection Office

Rotwein Red wine

Schaumwein Sekt — sparkling wine

Schillerwein *See* page 88

Schloss Castle

Schlossabzug Bottled at the castle

Schneewein Snow wine; a term used to describe an ice wine made from grapes gathered when snow covered the vineyards

Schorle-Morle A mixture of wine and up to 50 % effervescent mineral water

Schutzmarke Trade mark

Seewein Wine from the Lake Constance district

Sekt Sparkling wine

Sektkellerei Sparkling wine manufacturer

Sonderfüllung Special *cuvée* — special bottling

Spätlese *See* page 38

Spital Hospital

Spitzengewächs The very best growth (may be used to describe only a Beeren- or Trockenbeerenauslese)

Spitzenwein The very best wine (may be used to describe only a Beeren- or Trockenbeerenauslese)

Spritzig Effervescent. (Many wines, especially some Moselles, retain some carbonic acid in solution. This prolongs the life of the wine, keeping it fresh, and should not be mistaken for fermentation.)

Staatsweingut State vineyard/Domain

Steinwein "Stone wine" — wine from the Stein site in Würzburg. The term is frequently used for all Franconian wines, but these may actually be labelled "Steinwein" only when they come from the Stein vineyard.

Stiftung A fund established for special purposes.

Traube Grape

Traubensaft Grape juice

Traubensorte Kind of grape

Trester Grape-cake

Trockenbeerenauslese *See* pages 39–40

Ungezuckerter Wein Unsweetened wine

Verband Deutscher Naturwein Versteigerer Association of growers who sell natural wine by auction

Verbessert Improved, sweetened

Verwaltung (*Gutsverwaltung*) Administration

Wachstum Growth

Wappen Crest, coat of arms

Weinbau Viticulture

Weinbaudomäne Viticultural farm

Weinbaugebiet Viticultural district

Weinberg Vineyard

Weingesetz Wine law

Weingrosshandlung Wholesale wine trade

Weingut Estate or vineyard

Weingutsbesitzer Proprietor of vineyard

Weinhandlung Wine trade

Weinkellerei(*n*) Large cellars. Very often used on the label instead of "wine merchant" or "wholesale wine merchant".

Weinstein Tartaric acid

Weisswein White wine

Winzergenossenschaft Wine growers' co-operative

Winzerwein Wine growers' association

Wwe (*Witwe*) Widow

BIBLIOGRAPHY

Bassermann-Jordan, F. *Die Geschichte des Weinbaus*, Frankfurt, 1923
Deichmann, D., and Wolff, W. *Weinchronik*, Berlin, 1950
Goldschmidt, E. *Deutschlands Weinbauorte und Weinbergslagen*, Mainz, 1920
Goldschmidt, E. *Weingesetz*, Mainz, 1933
Hallgarten, S. F. *Rhineland-Wineland*, London, 1955
Heuss, R. *Weinbau und Weingärtnerstand in Heilbronn*, Neustadt, 1950
Hieronimi, H. *Weingesetz*, Munich, 1953
Kittel-Breider, H. *Das Buch vom Frankenwein*, Würzburg, 1958
Klenk, E. *Die Weinbeurteilung*, Stuttgart, 1950
Müller, K. *Geschichte des Badischen Weinbaus*, Lahr, 1935
Müller, K. *Rhein–Main*, Frankfurt, 1940
Popp, Franz *Das Moselland und sein Wein*, Bernkastel, 1948
Redding, Cyrus *History and Description of Modern Wines*, London, 1851
Rudd, Hugh R. *Hocks and Moselles*, London, 1953
Scheu, G. *Mein Winzerbuch*, Neustadt, 1950
Schoonmaker, F. *Wines of Germany*, New York, 1956, and London, 1957
Simon, André L. *The History of the Wine Trade in England*, London, 1906
Troost, Gerhard *Die Technologie des Weines*, Stuttgart, 1953
Vogt, E. *Weinbau*, Freiburg, 1952
Vogt, E. *Der Wein*, Freiburg, 1952
Zitzen, E. G. *Der Wein in der Wort- und Wirtschaftsgeschichte*, Bonn, 1952

PERIODICALS

Deutsche Weinzeitung, Mainz, fortnightly
Der Weinbau, Mainz, monthly
Weinblatt, Neustadt, weekly

INDEX

Erratum

page 56: "Deinhard, the third part-owners, sell theirs as *Doktor und Badstube*" should read "Deinhard, the third part-owners, sell part of theirs as *Doktor und Badstube*"

NOTE

Names of wine-growing communities and
districts are in white on the maps; other
place names are in black.

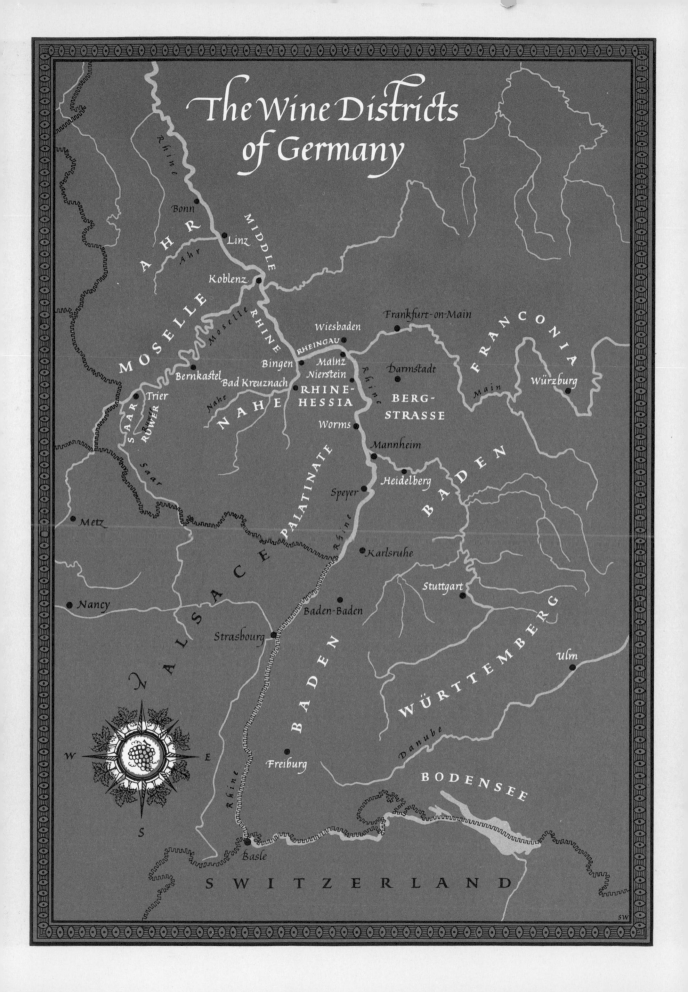

COLOGNE

Rhine

Agger

Sieg

Siegburg

BONN

Mehlen

Ober-Kasel

Königswinter

Honnef

Erpel

Linz

Singen

MIDDLE RHINE

WESTERWALD

Wied

Remagen

Bad Neuenahr

Heimersheim

Niederbreisig

Honningen

Rheinbrohl

Leutesdorf

Brohl

Andernach

AHR

Mayschloss

Altenahr

Ahrweiler

Dernau

Rech

Ahr

Neuwied

Bendorf

Rhine

KOBLENZ

EIFEL

Ehrenbreitstein

Pfaffendorf

Bad Ems

Nassau

Lahn

Limburg

Oberlahnstein

Braubach

Osterspai

Kamp

LAHN

Güls

Winningen

Capellen

Kobern

Gondorf

Lehmen

Diebich

Oberfell

Niederfell

Alken

Rhens

Löf

Boppard

Rhine

Mosel

Burg Eltz

SW

Rhine

Nahe

Assmannshausen

BINGEN

Lorch

Kaub

Bacharach
Steeg
Niederheimbach

Bad Kreuznach

St Goarshausen

St Goar
Oberwesel

Glan

KAISERSLAUTERN

HUNSRÜCK

Treis
Valwig
Bruttig
Eller
Beilstein
Cond
Ernst
Senheim
Sehl
Bremm
Nehren
Cochem
Neef
E
Eller
Merl
Zell
Pünderich
Reil
L
Burg
Enkirch
Kinhrin Kröv
Traben
Trarbach
Ürzig
Erden
Graach
BERNKASTEL
Zeltingen
Lieser
Platten
Wehlen
Kues
S
Osann
Braumeberg
Veldenz
Monzel
Wintrich
Burgen
O
Piesport
Neumagen
Trittenheim

Nahe

M
Klüsserath
Ensch
Longuich
Pölich
Detzem
Eitelsbach
Kasel
Ruwer
Kell
W
Grün-
haus
Waldrach
RUWER
Pfalzel
Sommerau

TRIER
Liersberg
Konz
Filzen
Wiltingen
Oberemmel
Ockfen

Hamm
Kanzem
Irsch
SAAR-
Ayl
Serrig
BURG

Wasserliesch

SAAR

Saar

Bingen

R H

Rhine

Lorchhausen

Lorch

Hallgarte...
Ost...
Schloss Vollrads
Mittelheim
Johannisberg
Winkel
Schloss Johannisberg
Geisenheim
Rüdesheim

Assmannshausen

Bingerbrück

BINGEN
Büdesheim
Gau-
Alges...

Weiler
Münster-
Sarmsheim

Sponsheim
Grolsheim

Waldlaubersheim

N A H E

Windesheim
Laubenheim
Langenlonsheim
Heddesheim
Gensingen

Gutenberg
Bretzenheim
Ippesheim

Roxheim
Winzenheim
Planig

Sponheim
Mandel
Bosenheim

Weinsheim

Rüdesheim
Waldböckelheim
Niederhausen
Hüffelsheim
BAD KREUZNACH
Gau-
bickelhe...

Martinstein
Schloss
Böckelheim
Norheim
Hackenheim

Monzingen
Nussbaum
Boos
BAD MÜNSTER

Merxheim
SOBERNHEIM
Duchroth
Nahe
Ebernburg
Altenbamberg

Meddersheim
Bingert

Kirschroth
Stauden-
heim
Odernheim
Fürfeld

Rehborn
Hochstätten

Raumbach

Meisenheim
Obermoschel

Nahe

Alsenz

Glan

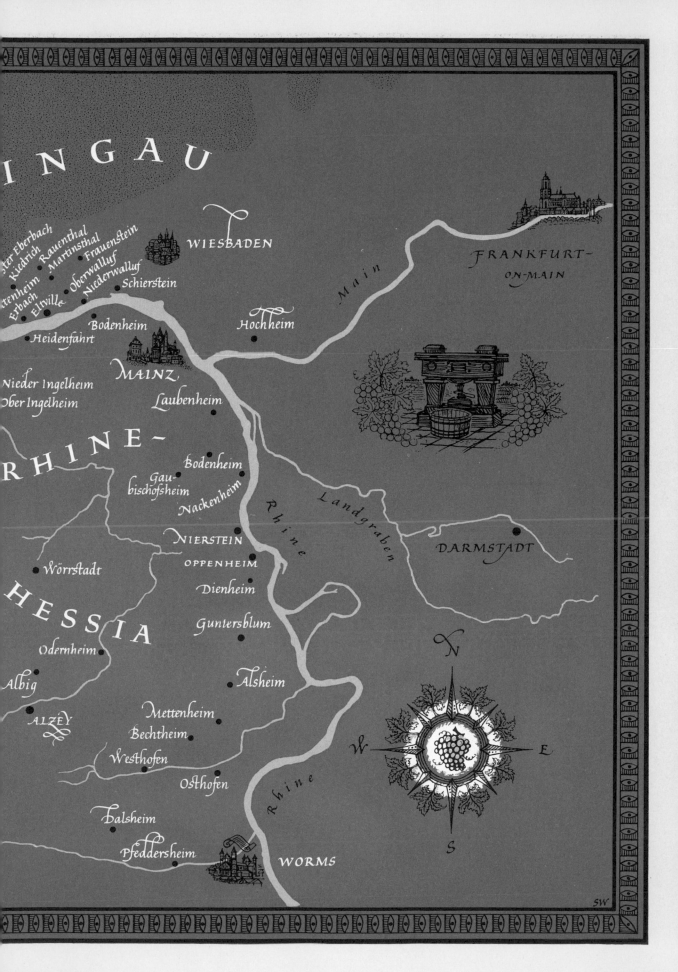

INGAU

ster Eberbach
Kiedrich   Rauenthal
tenheim   Martinsthal   Frauenstein
erbach   Oberwalluf
Eltville   Niederwalluf   Schierstein

WIESBADEN

FRANKFURT-
ON-MAIN

Main

Bodenheim
Heidenfahrt
Hochheim

Nieder Ingelheim
Ober Ingelheim

MAINZ

Laubenheim

RHINE-

Bodenheim
Gau-
bischofsheim
Nackenheim

Rhine

Landgraben

DARMSTADT

NIERSTEIN
OPPENHEIM
Dienheim

Wörrstadt

HESSIA

Guntersblum

Odernheim

Albig

Alsheim

ALZEY

Mettenheim
Bechtheim
Westhofen

Osthofen

Rhine

N

Balsheim
Pfeddersheim

WORMS

Rhine

W   E

S

SW

FRANCONIA

Schweinfurt · Mainberg
Haßfurt
Obereisenheim
Eschendorf · Volkach
Nordheim · Dettelbach
Buchbrunn · Castell
Kitzingen · Iphofen
Sulzfeld
Marktbreit
Frickenhausen
Ochsenfurt

Main

Schwein

WÜRZ-
BURG · Randers-
acker

Stetten
Retzbach · Thüngersheim
Veitshöchheim

Karlstadt
Saale · Bad Kissingen

Hammelburg

Gemünden

Lohr
Mühl-
bach
Erlabrunn

Homburg
Heidingsfeld
Brombach

Elbelstadt
Winterhausen
Sommerhausen

Tauberbischofsheim

TAUBERGRUND

Tauber

Lauda

Mergentheim

Uffenheim

Rothenburg

KOCHER & JAGSTTAL

Griesbach
Ingelfingen · Künzelsau
Niedernhall · Verrenberg

Eschelbach
Harsberg

Jagst

Neuenstadt · Weinsberg
NECKARTAL · HEILBRONN
LOWER · Sontheim
Schwaigern · Flein
Haber- · Neipperg · Lauffen
schlacht · Brockenheim · Zu
Gundels- · Auenstein
heim · Cleebronn

Mespelbrunn

Mark-
heidenfeld
Prozelten Lengfurt

Kreuz-
wertheim
Bürgstadt
Miltenberg

Wasserlos
Hörstein

Grossostheim
Klein-
Wallstadt

Klingenberg
Heubach

BERGSTRASSE

Eberbach

Schriesheim

Neckar

Wiesloch

KRAICHGAU
Sulzfeld

Bruchsal

The Heidelberg Tun

FRANKFURT

Main

DARMSTADT

Bensheim

Weinsheim

HEIDELBERG

WIESBADEN

MAINZ

Rhine

WORMS

MANNHEIM

Neustadt

KARLSRUHE

Bingen

Bad
Kreuznach

Alzey

KAISERS-
LAUTERN

Landau

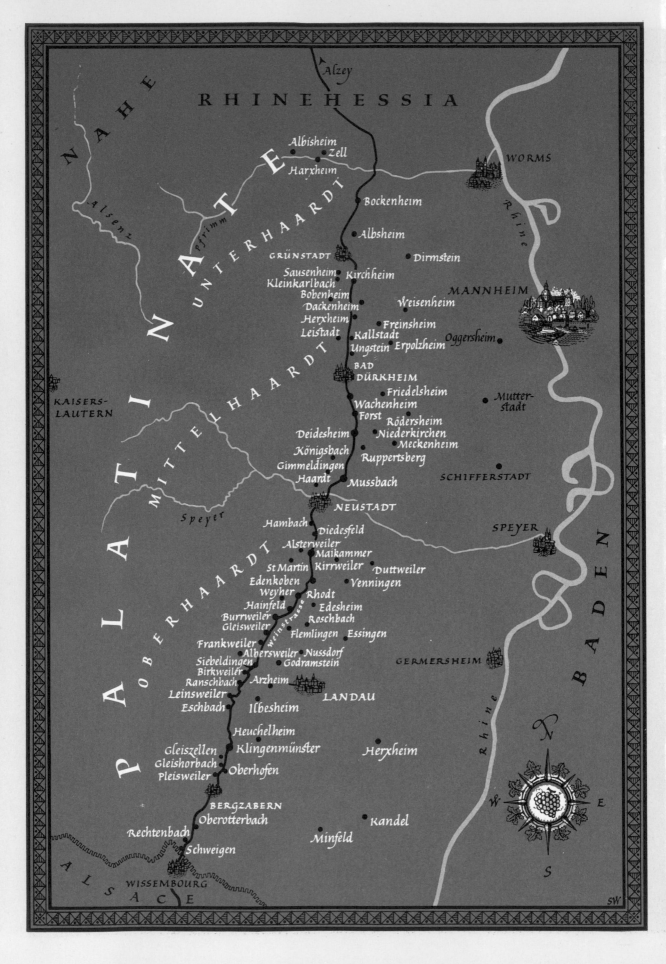